DALMATIANS TODAY

Patches Silverstone

Howell Book House

HOWELL
BOOK
HOUSE

New York

HOWELL BOOK HOUSE
A Simon & Schuster / Macmillan Company
1633 Broadway
New York, NY 10019

MACMILLAN is a registered trademark of Macmillan, Inc.

Library of Congress Cataloging-in-Publication data
available on request.

ISBN 0–87605–136–0

Manufactured in Singapore

10 9 8 7 6 5 4 3 2 1

CONTENTS

**For Harold and Dene Silverstone,
with my love.**

ACKNOWLEDGEMENTS

For the last ten months I have plagued the life out of Dalmatian lovers world-wide, and I should like to find room to mention some of those who have been so generous with their support and kindness. In particular, I thank Mary-Pat Butterfield who, I estimate, typed more than three-quarters of a million words while I endeavoured to find the right way of expressing eighty thousand.

Mrs Joan Agate-Hilton; Shirley and Peter Aldenhoven; Mrs Dorothy Allen; Mrs Lily Barmettle-Emch (Switzerland); Mrs Diana Beale; Mrs Val Beggs (New Zealand); Mr V. Belles (Spain); Mr and Mrs Kenneth Berg (USA); Mrs C. Blinko (Canada); Mrs Penny Bolton; Mr Keith Butt, MA VetMB Cantab MRCVS; Mrs Sally Clegg (France); Mrs Celia Cox, B Vet Med Cert VR FRCVS (Hearing Assessment Clinic); Mrs Monica Davidson; Mme Liliane de Ridder-Onghena (Belgium); Dr David Doane (USA); Mrs Gwen Eady; Mrs Julia Freeman; BSc Hons (Animal Health Trust); Mrs Susan Gatheral-Graham; Mrs M. N. van Gelderen-Parker (Holland); Miss Karen Goff; Miss Oonagh Gore; Mrs Carrie Graham-Weall; Mrs Kirsti Greibrokk (Norway); Mrs Ann-Marie Hammarlund (Sweden); Colonel David Hancock, MBE FIMgt FTS MILAM; Mrs Janet Harding; Mrs Barbara Kacens (Luxembourg); Mrs Pat Kindersley; Mrs Regina Kossiki (Germany); Dr. R Last; Mr James Lennox; Mrs Paddy Lockett (New Zealand); Gill and Peter Lucas; Mrs Pam Marshall (Australia); Miss Alison Merritt (Canada); Mrs Jean Meader (USA); Mrs Sharon Mitchell; Mr and Mrs Rhys Morgans (Holland); Miss Andrea Paccagnella (Argentina); Professor David T. Parkin, BSc PhD, Department of Genetics, Nottingham University; Miss Ruth Pickard; Mrs Chris Pickup (Carriage Dog Chronicle); Mrs Peggy Pilgrim; Mrs Phyllis M. Piper, JP; Mr Peter Rance; Dr Sidney Remmele (USA); Miss Georgiann (Peggy) Rudder (USA); Miss Frances Ryan (Eire); Dipl.Ing. Schibl Johannes (Austria); Miss Janet Simpson; Miss Monica Smith (Kennel Club Library); Mrs Julia Swinburn (British Dalmatian Club); Ms Seija Tiainen (Finland); Janet and Tom Tweedy; Femke Van Tilburg (Holland); Miss Julia Walsh (Eire); Mr Harold White; Mrs Kay White; Mrs Mary Young (Australia).

1 HISTORY OF THE BREED

Turn back through time and imagine the world as it was around 1700 years BC. Britain was in the midst of the Early Bronze Age, with great stones being manhandled across the country to build Stonehenge. Centuries would pass before the Western world discovered America, Australia and New Zealand; Europe was a vast forest. However, on the other side of the world, Greece and Egypt had already created a sophisticated civilisation. Its architecture, sculpture and art were outstanding, and it is here, in this bygone culture, that some of the first traces of the Dalmatian breed of dog can be found.

1700 BC is important as the date of the now-famous fresco, taken from Tiryns to Athens and exhibited to this day in the National Archaeological Museum in Athens. The fresco shows boar being hunted by black and liver spotted hounds. The spots have been painted on meticulously, presumably to indicate their importance. Quite apart from their markings, the overall shape and style of these hounds are so akin to our own Breed Standard that one must seriously consider whether these pictures are in fact an early record of the world's first-known

Dalmatians. What would appear to be the first spotted dog on reccord came even earlier in 3,700 BC when King Cheops or Khufu, the builder of the Great Pyramid, owned a spotted pet dog. There was little other resemblance to the Dalmatian but, nevertheless, it proves there was Royal interest in this distinctive marking.

In Greece and Crete, wall paintings and friezes have been found depicting hounds with distinct spotted markings, some liver, some black, and some with both colours. Perhaps these were the original tricolour? In Egypt, again in hunting scenes, spotted dogs are pictured in mural paintings as well as decorating the tombs of grandees.

In his recent book, *Heritage of the Dog,* Colonel David Hancock has set out details of his research and conclusions regarding the evolution of the Dalmatian and the origin of the breed's name. I am grateful to Col. Hancock who has generously given me permission to quote the following excerpts in this chapter.

"At that time (around 400 BC) there was in Ancient Greece, according to Xenophon, a hunting dog called the Cretan hound. The Cretan hound was light-boned, nimble, could run well in mountains and came in three varieties; the Cnossians –

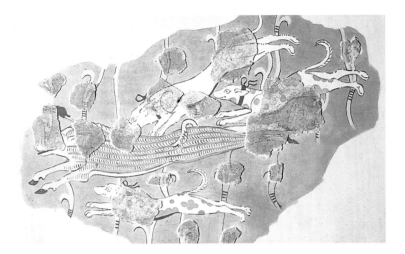

*1700 BC Fresco taken from Tirnys to Athens.
By permission of the National Archaeological Museum, Athens.*

famed for their noses, the Workers – so keen they hunted by night and day, and the Outrunners, who ran free under the huntsman's voice control only and, according to Aristotle, ran along instinctively beside the horses during a hunt, never preceding them and not lagging behind. Unlike some of the other hounds used by the Greeks in the Chase, the Outrunners were not dewlapped or flewed. Oppian and Xenophon recommended keeping them pure. They were used by the Cretans to hunt a four-horned antelope, as Aelian has recorded.

"These hounds were too special for use on hare-hunts, too valuable for use in killing the boar, biddable enough to be used as 'braches' as opposed to 'lymmers', i.e. they ran free, and hunted by sight and scent. Julius Pollux in his *Onomasticon* recommended that the colour of these hounds should be 'neither wholly white nor excessively black.' It should be noted that the Cretans were exceptional in hunting with hounds running free, both up to their time and for two centuries or so subsequently, such was the quality of their hounds and their training methods.

"I am not suggesting for one moment that the Dalmatian existed in Ancient Greece, but pointing out that there was a White Antelope Dog in Ancient Egypt which resembled the Dalmatian in size and shape; that the Greeks imported their fast hunting dogs from Egypt and crossed them with scent-hounds to give the latter greater speed and all round hunting capabilities; the Greeks pursued the boar with black and white hounds, some of them spotted; there was a variety of the Cretan hound which instinctively ran alongside the horses in the hunt and, most unusually, ran free. This was a variety used to hunt the antelope.

"Turning to the alleged Indian origin and the use of the term 'the Harrier of Bengal' by Buffon, a famous French naturalist but not an accurate source of research on dogs, I can find no trace anywhere of dogs marked like Dalmatians being indigenous to India."

"But any nation producing a breed of dog with such a remarkably distinctive coat-coloration would preserve it, prize it and trade with it. Could the classic Dalmatian coat have occurred only rarely and not breed true until comparatively recent times?"

"My own theory about the origin of the

An Iznik dish C1585, in Turkey.

word Dalmatian is that it comes from a corruption of the terms for such running dogs in the 13th century i.e. hounds *de mota (mote* = a spot or blemish, hence our word mottled – dappled with spots) or '*de meute de chiens'* meaning 'of a pack of fallow hounds'. *Dama* is Latin for fallow deer, in French it is *daim* (m) or *dain* (f), in Italian *daino. Canem daymerettum* was one expression for the running hounds which hunted fallow deer, with both *daymerettum* and *dama-chien* sounding like Dalmatian.

"In those times spelling varied even on the same page of books and '*mute de chiens'* was sometimes used for twelve running dogs and a '*lime-hounde'*. In 1216 we can read in the *Close Rolls* of John, who maintained a vast hunting establishment, reference to 'fifteen greyhounds and thirty-one Hounds "*de mota*".' They were also referred to as *Moota Canum* or *Muta Canum*. In 1213 we find reference to '114 "*de mota*" dogs and five greyhounds for hunting fallow deer in the park of Knappe' in a letter from King John to Roger de

Neville. Henry III in a letter to the Sheriff of Oxford refers to sixteen '*de mota'* dogs and one '*limarius*' or leashed scenthound. Hounds for hunting stags were different from those for hunting fallow deer; Henry III sent three men to hunt in the New Forest with '*canibus cervericus et damericus*', with deer being '*damos*' or '*damas*'. Edward III refers to hounds for hunting as '*deymerettors*', with fallow deer then being known by the name '*deyme*' or '*desme*'. Early in the 17th century Gervase Markham, in his *Countrey Contentments,* recommends for hunting deer '...the white hound, or the white with black spots or the white with some few liver spots.'

"James V of Scotland wrote to the Duke of Richmond requesting 'hounds which could ride behind men on horseback'. There are letters on record from Queen Margaret in the 16th century referring to hounds which 'will ride behind me one hors back'. Another letter from T. Magnus to the 'Quene of Scotts' mentions 'houndes of the beste kynde that woll behynde men upon horseback.' In Henry VIII's time there is reference to, in Latin, '*canum nostrarum damorum vocatum bukhoundis.*' It is the '*canum damorum*' which is of great interest to Dalmatian researchers.

"But what happened to these specialist fallow hounds, fleet-hounds or sharp-nosed hounds, as they were variously called? Firstly the hunting of fallow-deer became restricted, secondly the style of hunting changed and thirdly the coat-colouring of scent-hounds became almost standardised. The '*de mota*' hounds, like the White Hounds of France, hunted by sight principally and went very fast once the lymmer or leashed tracker had given them the right line. With the preference for 'hunting cunning' in which the unravelling of the scent by a pack of scenthounds became the admired style of hunting, the days of the '*de mota*' hounds were numbered."

"So with fallow deer hunting reduced, running hounds with their heads up no longer being required and mainly white hounds not being sought, the '*de mota*' dogs lost their role but, if my theory is correct, retained their love of running with horses to become the coach-dogs we now know as Dalmatians.

"A corruption, remembering that word of mouth was used much more as a means of communication in past centuries than in our contemporary world of books and wholesale literacy, of '*de mota*' could so easily have sounded like 'Dalmatian' and then been written down as such. I believe, in similar vein, that *epagneul* comes from the old French verb '*s'espanir*', to sett or crouch, and not from *espagnol* as so many assume. There is no more evidence of Spaniels coming from Spain than there is of Dalmatians coming from Dalmatia.

"Clifford Hubbard, thirty years ago, linked the Dalmatian with the 'Istrian Braque' or pointer, Istria or Istra being near Dalmatia. I don't know of an Istrian pointer but only of an Istrian Hound (Istrski Gonic) which has a smooth or wire coat and is a hare or fox hound, but does look like a pointer. For me however the Dalmatian is more likely to have been a Western European fallow-deerhound, a descendant of the '*de mota*' dog or '*deymerettors*' of over a thousand years ago in the mould of the Cretan 'outrunners'. If I am correct, this would be a fitting ancestry for a breed of great charm and considerable distinction."

HISTORY
There is a gap in our knowledge until the early 17th century when, we read, gypsies and wandering players in various parts of

Plate from Shugborough Armorial Dinner Service.   *National Trust Photographic Library.*

Europe adopted a number of spotted dogs, attracted by their unusual appearance. Their intelligence and sense of humour made them invaluable members of the troupe. It is also said that, following the Peace of Utrecht in 1712, soldiers brought Dalmatians home with them on their return from duty in Spain.

Books on Dalmatians invariably include reference to the Talbot hound and, as late as 1830, Watson states that "a common name for the Dalmatian was Talbot". The name Talbot comes from the Talbot family of Alton (whose estate is now the theme park Alton Towers), later the Earls of Shrewsbury and Talbot. The 6th Baron, Sir John Talbot, was created Earl of Shrewsbury in 1442. His coat of arms features two white hounds, long-eared, medium-sized, and heavy-headed. These would appear to be the true Talbot and have little or nothing in common with the Dalmatian.

However, should you be in Staffordshire with a little time to spare, do take the opportunity to visit Shugborough, the seat

Four in Hand. Painted by James Pollard. Engraved by J. Gleadah. The Dalmatian's strong physique and kindness with horses made them ideal carriage dogs.

of the Earls of Lichfield. Apart from a house full of treasures and wonderful grounds, be sure not to overlook the Armorial Dinner Service.

In 1743 the founder of the family fortune, Admiral Lord Anson, sailed his ship the Centurion into Macao with a captured Spanish galleon in tow. Stores were running low and were difficult to obtain, and Lord Anson made a personal visit to the Chinese Viceroy in Canton to appeal for help. His position was strengthened when a serious fire broke out, threatening the warehouses, which the Centurion's crew was able to bring under control.

Needless to say, there was no further delay in supplying provisions and, as an additional gesture, the European merchants presented Lord Anson with a magnificent Chinese porcelain dinner service. As was customary in those days, he was consulted about his preferred decoration and, as well as various views of Shugborough, his wife and family, spotted dogs bearing a strong resemblance to Dalmatians appear on every one of the 208 pieces.

The family archives contain no mention of Dalmatians at Shugborough, so no-one can be certain why they occupy this prominent position. They may have belonged to Lord Anson, or been brought there by his wife on the occasion of their marriage. Were they part of a tribute paid by Chinese merchants to the English gentleman's love of country pursuits?

In the 17th and 18th centuries, Dalmatians were admired and purchased by young English aristocrats, who had been sent to Europe to complete their education on what was known as the 'Grand Tour'. Many fine specimens returned with their new owners to this country, as can be verified from numerous paintings.

The Dalmatian's strong feet and legs and kindness with horses made them ideal carriage dogs, but in those days the stables were not part of the household, so Dalmatians were not normally invited into the house. Lack of human companionship, as can happen even today, made the breed appear stupid, and this perception was probably not helped by the fact that, in all likelihood, deafness was by then already a problem within the breed.

Certainly, at this time, they were unknown in Dalmatia. It was not until 1930 that Vane Ivanovic, Consul General of Monaco to Great Britain and a member of the British Dalmatian Club, took a pair

Kelly Evans driving her British Spotted Pony 'Coaster', with 'Dot' her liver-spotted Dalmatian tucked under.

Dalmatian enthusiasts still use their dogs in their original working role.

to Dalmatia as a present for his stepfather, Bozo Banac, who had expressed a wish to introduce them there.

What seems to be lost in the mists of time is why these dogs were called Dalmatians in the first place. Various reasons have been put forward, including those described by Col Hancock earlier in this chapter, but to a certain extent perhaps the name's true origin will always remain shrouded in mystery. I think, though, that most people would agree that the breed is based here in Great Britain, where it has been nurtured, bred and guarded since its arrival in the 17th century.

We can be proud that the original shape and style of the Dalmatian has hardly altered over the years, except that in early pictures the breed was shown with cropped ears, a disgusting practice now thankfully behind us.

It was not until 1882 that the first detailed breed book on dogs was published, *The Book of the Dog* by Vero Shaw. Mr Shaw included a delightful chapter on Dalmatians, together with a first attempt at a Standard. He called this 'Points of the Dalmatian' and I ran it to earth in the Antiquarian section of the Kennel Club Library, with the help of its very efficient

librarian. With the KC's permission it is reproduced in Chapter Seven, and I hope you will find it interesting to compare with that of the present day.

WHY THE SPOTS?
Long ago it was decreed that Dalmatians should have spots. The question arises – why? There can only be two reasons for distinctive markings: to attract or to camouflage, and I think an answer may be found in the latter area.

Although Dalmatians stand out so clearly against most terrains, it is interesting to find that the one place where they become almost invisible is on dunes, particularly when there are a few stones lying about. It is in the breed's nature to point, to quarter a field and to follow a scent. They have acute hearing and can move very silently, with an unexpected turn of speed over a reasonable distance. They can turn a hare without difficulty, and were it not for their fine coats, which are not practical to combat thorn and undergrowth, Dalmatians must surely have taken their place in the sporting group.

However, this same coat is no disadvantage in desert conditions. The intense white of the background colour shows up clearly against snow or normal countryside, but blends into light sand without difficulty, the spots being absorbed by various stones.

Dalmatians are shown as hunting dogs in the ancient wall paintings and friezes already described in this chapter, and their unique decoration must have made them invaluable when hunting over desert conditions with little or no natural cover. It can therefore be assumed that spotted dogs were bred to spotted dogs to fix the markings, and hence the breed has come down through the ages with an astonishing lack of change.

THE PLACE OF BREED CLUBS

Once breed enthusiasts are drawn together, by age-old custom, a breed club comes into being. In Great Britain the Dalmatian Club was formed in 1890, and, in the same year, its committee published the first official Breed Standard. Other countries followed, notably the USA in 1904, and initially the 1890 Standard served them all. Now many countries have added their own amendments (See Chapter Seven: The Breed Standards).

Undoubtedly, those who worked so hard to establish the many Dalmatian clubs, both in the UK and overseas, formed the basis of the breed as we know it today. To these people we owe a great debt of gratitude, for, without them, the breed would not exist.

In 1903 the North of England Dalmatian Club was formed in the UK, and this club adopted the 1890 Standard (with a minor exception regarding the weight of bitches). The Southern Dalmatian Club was formed by a small band of seven, and their enthusiasm was such that this gradually superseded the original Dalmatian Club. Members joining from all parts of the country encouraged the Southern Club to

widen its horizons until, in 1930, the name changed and the British Dalmatian Club came into being. The All-Ireland Dalmatian Club was formed in 1934, but it was not until 1981 that the Northern Ireland Club established its own branch. In 1970 Scottish enthusiasts initiated the Dalmatian Club of Scotland.

THE SHOW WORLD

Dog shows, which are now held in all parts of the world, owe their present system, and even their existence, to the efforts which were made on their behalf in the UK in the latter half of the 19th Century.

In 1860, the Birmingham Dog Show Society, which still remains one of the premier clubs, held 'The First Exhibition of Sporting and Other Breeds' at Cheapside, Birmingham, and a Dalmatian class was among those organised for about a dozen breeds. The judge, Mr J.H. Walsh (better known by his pen name 'Stonehenge'), was unfortunately unimpressed with the Dalmatians under him and withheld all prizes. However at Leeds the following year 'Caesar', owned by Mr G. Hutchinson, and 'Prince', owned by Mr R. Dobson, took first and second respectively in an unspecified class.

Graphic descriptions are given of the chaos that existed at that time. No pedigrees or registration system existed. Dogs were often entered in classes for the breed they most resembled. Rules were created for individual convenience, and it is not surprising that dog shows were held in ever-decreasing public esteem.

Mr S.E. Shirley, Member of Parliament for Ettrington, had organised several dog shows at the Crystal Palace and, in 1873, he held a meeting at No. 2 Albert Mansions, Victoria Street, London. From these small beginnings, the Kennel Club was formed. Mr Shirley became its first chairman, a position he held until 1899 when he became the first president.

The KC then, as now, became the UK's ruling body on all canine activities, and provided an initial role model for other organisations which grew up in many other countries. In addition to a Stud Book, which included the 14 years since the dog shows began in 1859, the KC also published a Code of Rules for the Guidance of Dog Shows, which initially was widely followed in many overseas countries as well as in the UK. Since then, the AKC and the FCI have published their own Breed Standards (see Chapter Seven: The Breed Standards), with Canada, Australia and New Zealand taking a different line again.

It was not until 1903 that the KC produced the present system of registration, and this was restricted to dogs appearing at shows. In 1904, the system was amended and registrations were extended to include all pedigree dogs. Any wayward clubs or societies were subsequently outlawed. The inevitable outcry was ignored and the dog world, as we know it, came into being.

It is fair to say the present-day UK show world is dominated by Cruft's Dog Show, now the responsibility of the KC and acknowledged as the largest and best-known dog show in the world. Mr Cruft's first Dog Show was held in 1891 in the Royal Agricultural Hall at Islington, and subsequent shows continued under his management until the 1936 Jubilee Show, which had a record entry at that time of 10,650 from 4,397 dogs. Charles Cruft died two years later and, although his widow organised one further show in 1939, she asked the KC to accept responsibility for Cruft's from then on.

Following World War Two, the first Cruft's Dog Show at Olympia was held in 1948. An entry of 137 Dalmatians was

Ch. Fanhill Faune: BIS Crufts 1968.
Photo: Thomas Fall.

judged by Mrs L.M. Gatheral, who chose Miss Whitton's Ch. Clef of the Carriageway for her BOB. Cruft's has since been held annually without a break, with one notable exception in 1954 caused by an industrial dispute.

Cruft's 1968 took the Dalmatian breed to new heights when Joan Woodyatt's Ch. Fanhill Faune (Ch. Colonsay April Jest x Ch. Fanhill Fleur of Queenwood) took BOB under Donald Stalker. Faune was then awarded BIS by Josephine Creasey, the only Dalmatian to date who has become Supreme Champion at Cruft's.

In 1990 the last Cruft's to take place in London was held at Earl's Court before the KC transferred the show to the National Exhibition Centre in Birmingham, where it has since been held. The new venue is certainly more spacious and the large rings with their smart green carpets are appreciated, but there is also nostalgia for the loss of atmosphere and sense of occasion. However, the 1996 entry of 19,711 from 13,779 dogs would most certainly have been a matter of great pride to Charles Cruft.

Looking back, one reads of shows which

13

were obviously stepping stones in breed history. The 1935 show held at Chester by the BDC to celebrate the Silver Jubilee of King George V and Queen Mary, must rank high among them. The show drew an entry of 404 dogs and concluded with a parade of 26 Champions. The Breed Standard was printed in the catalogue for the benefit of onlookers, and it is recorded that no less than 242 Specials were presented.

In 1980 the KC authorised a Special Championship Show to coincide with the first World Congress and this took place at Welwyn Garden City. The late Joe Braddon was invited to officiate, which he did with great skill in his own inimitable style. Best in Show, from an entry of 257 Dalmatians, was won by Longmuir and Scratchard's Dhulea Doodle of Randan, along with her first CC. The BOS was another first CC, this time won by Wendy Jenkins' Merrybriar Ludwig. A parade of Champions provided a fitting finale to an unforgettable day.

More recently, the British Dalmatian Club has celebrated three special commemorative shows. The Golden Jubilee Championship Show was held in April 1975, the dogs being judged by Mrs J. Agate-Hilton and the bitches by Miss I.B. Clay. Mr and Mrs Budge's Ch. Wagonette Piper Royal Lancer took BIS, with Mr and Mrs Dandy's Ch. Dandale Tudor Rose taking BCC and BOS.

In 1985, Mrs J. Rance judged dogs and Mrs G. Eady bitches at the special Diamond Jubilee Championship Show. The BIS on this occasion was won by Mrs A.G. Bale-Stock's Ch. Spring Classic by Appaloosa, with the BCC and BOS awarded to Mrs L. Butler's Ch. Dalmark Ellie the Showgirl.

It was felt appropriate to hold a further special show in 1995 to celebrate the 70th

Ch.Merrybriar Ludwig: CC and BOS winner at the World Congress Ch. Show 1980. Photo: Thomas Fall.

anniversary of the BDC, and here Mr L.M. Cutts officiated for the dogs and Mrs B. Neath for the bitches. They chose Mr and Mrs Watson's Fincham Fast Talking Tinker for the DCC and Mr and Mrs Richardson's Hyclough Cleo at Jomihvar for the BCC, with the bitch on this occasion also taking BIS.

Although it was not strictly speaking a show, the NOEDC organised and presented the first Dalmatian of the Year contest in January 1995. Karen Goff's Ch. Washakie Indian Summer won the title at seven years of age, and Mrs Gatford's Tommy Brock became Dalmatian Puppy of the Year.

RESCUE

It is a sad fact that in more recent years it has become necessary to establish Rescue Services in so many countries. In Britain it was Mrs Phyllis Piper (Greenmount) who first identified the need, and foresaw an even greater one. In 1964 she established what was then only the second breed rescue service in the UK. This became known as The Dalmatian Rescue Service, which Mrs Piper, with the help of a small committee, runs to this day. Due partly to the endless generosity of BDC members, plus

The Greenmount Tea Party: Taken the day after Ch. Lazaar's Gay Gipsy of Greenmount won Best Veteran In Show at the BDC Ch. Show in 1968.
Front: (left to right): Ch. Lazaar's Gay Gipsy of Greenmount (Mrs P. Piper), Ch. Greenmount Greensleeves (kennelmaid), Greenmount Gunner (Miss Oakley), Greenmount Granite (Mrs P. Cleggett) and Ch. Greenmount Grindelwald (Mrs G. Eady).
Second row (left to right): Grey Topper of Ascotheath (Mrs J. Cudd), Greenmount Mr Grubella (Dr Smiter), Greenmount Grenadine (Mr Wade), Ch. Greenmount Greco of Istria (Mr C. Leutchford), Ch. Greenmount Golden Guinea (kennelmaid), and Ch. Greenmount Grenville of Starmead (Mrs R. Wholey).
Third row (left to right): Ch. Hot Brandy of Ascotheath (handled by Mrs Le Grys), Greenmount Gertie Gitana (Mr Le Grys), Ch. Horseman's Partner (Mrs J. Agate-Hilton, Ch. Coachbarn Classic (Mrs M. Chapman) and Greenmount pet dog puppy (6 months).
Fourth row (Left to right): Greenmount pet dog, Greenmount pet bitch (Mrs Armstrong) and Greenmount pet dog,

voluntary contributions, a sound financial basis is maintained By the end of 1995, 2,391 dogs had been found new homes. At present about 200 dogs a year need help, but this number could escalate under the pressures of present-day life.

The NOEDC has its own Rescue Service which deals particularly with dogs from that part of the country. Countless other dogs are helped by concerned breeders and members of the various breed clubs.

In the USA, apart from the work done by individual breeders, many feel this is a question which should be addressed by the various national canine authorities. In the meantime, the many affiliated breed clubs in America run excellent Rescue Services, with most breeders prepared to help with re-homing Dalmatians in their area.

COMMUNICATIONS
The world is now much smaller, and there is no doubt that easy communication between breeders and enthusiasts is of the first priority in maintaining our standards. Many newsletters are exchanged, including

Spots of News and *The Carriage Dog Chronicle* from Britain, *The Spotter* from America, *Transcandals* from Canada, Belgium's *Spotted News,* Australia's *News Spot, Spot on News* from New Zealand, and *DAL-Magazine* from Finland, to name but a few.

These publications are read world-wide, and their editors carry a great responsibility. It is essential that correct and helpful information is passed to their own members and to those who read these journals overseas. More important still, perhaps, is the feeling of friendship and understanding that is extended to all lovers of the breed wherever they may be. We are not isolated in our four corners of the world, either as Dalmatian owners, dog lovers, or simply as people.

BEYOND THE SPOTS

The late Marjorie Cooper (Roadster) was the highly-respected editor of *Spots of News* for nearly 20 years. We are also indebted to her for the following article which encapsulates so much of our thinking in the breed today.

"BEYOND THE SPOTS"

"The Dalmatian is one of the oldest recorded breeds of dog and has remained virtually unchanged in this country for several centuries, as is shown in paintings and drawings by many famous artists.

"With its clean elegant lines and spectacular spotted coat the Dalmatian makes an instant appeal to many people who are thinking of buying a dog.

"In common with most breeds, the Dalmatian has its own very distinctive character and personality, and its own particular requirements from its owners and home if a happy and rewarding partnership is to be achieved. It is therefore wise for the would-be owner to consider carefully

before he falls for that adorable spotted bundle of charm.

"Points to ponder. Although the Dalmatian puppy grows rapidly from the chubby eight-week-old to the leggy canine teenager, full growth may not be complete until twelve or fifteen months, and even then there is a lot of 'filling out' to be done. During this period a plentiful diet of good body-building food is essential, and this will not be cheap. It is also during this time that the puppy will be at its most active and full of life and must have scope for plenty of play and free exercise. From the age of five or six months, progressive amounts of regular daily road walking must also be given to firm up muscles and feet, to teach manners in relation to other people and dogs.

"Not having the heavy coat of some other breeds, the Dalmatian, while not being in any way delicate, does need reasonable warmth, particularly for his sleeping quarters.

"Perhaps the most important thing of all for happy ownership is to understand that Dalmatians *need people*. Blessed with a high degree of intelligence and a need for affection, they are not suited to owners who regard them merely as 'The Dog', an appendage to the household to be left alone for long periods shut up, or worse still shut out, and just occasionally made a fuss of when the owner has an hour to spare. If this is what you want from a dog, please do not buy a Dalmatian.

"If, on the other hand you are prepared to value your dog as a member of your family, give him wise training, companionship and the stable homelife you would wish for your children, the Spotted Dog will reward you lavishly with his own special gift of affection and lifelong devotion."

2 *CHOOSING A DALMATIAN*

The telephone rings constantly with people enquiring how to find a Dalmatian. Some are replacing an old friend; others are new to the breed. It is to the latter I often find myself saying: "Why a Dalmatian?"

Some have a ready answer; some do not. One young man told me he had waited for years to buy a Dalmatian, until he had a home and time to spend with the puppy. Splendid, until he proudly described his high rise flat in the town centre and the job redundancy which left him with all the spare time in the world. We talked it through, but did he understand what I was trying to tell him? I will never know.

The reasons for wanting a Dalmatian may be diverse, but every now and then the fact emerges that there are many people fully prepared to take on one of this complex breed who have never known or even met an adult Dalmatian. Much as I love Dalmatians, they are not straightforward and they are certainly not everybody's dog, so I hope you will find it helpful if I try and set out some of the problems as well as the good points. Like every breed of dog, Dalmatians have faults as well as their lovely side, and, if you know the whole picture, you can make a better judgement.

POSSIBLE PROBLEMS

Firstly, you do not require a degree in hairdressing to keep these dogs tidy, but all Dalmatians have a constant shed of little white hairs. These bed themselves into every known surface and are very obstinate when it comes to removal. If you are house-proud, or live your life in navy blue or black, they are not the breed for you. More importantly, if anyone in the family suffers from asthma, then consult a doctor in advance, as these hairs can cause breathing problems.

You will need a fully-enclosed garden. Rampant curiosity will take Dalmatians through the smallest hole, under any fence or around any gate. The space may be invisible to you; it is quite sufficient for them. Have you good walking country within easy access, or are you prepared to drive to it? To keep an adult Dalmatian both well-behaved and in good health requires a minimum of one hour's free hard exercise each day, so you need to enjoy walking. Fine days, weekends and holidays apart, bear in mind bitterly cold days when you walk doubled up against wind and driving rain.

Nothing is more rewarding than the relationship between a child and a dog, but

To keep an adult Dalmatian well-behaved and in good health requires a minimum of one hour's exercise a day.

Photo: Marc Henrie.

Dalmatians are insatiably curious and a dog will explore every corner of the garden.

Photo: Marc Henrie.

there can also be problems. There is a thin line between playing, teasing and unkindness, and you cannot be watching every minute of the day. Little fingers can be cruel, and although it helps if you establish a 'get away' place for the dog, even the best canine temperament is at risk if the puppy is subjected to constant teasing. There is subsequent heartache for the whole family, even for the child itself, if the puppy has to be re-homed. Rather than put it to the test, consider waiting until your child is older and can understand.

If you are contemplating a Dalmatian before your baby is born, think ahead to what this will entail. The dog will be interested in the child and expect to be welcome in the nursery. Will you feel happy about this? If there is a thought in your mind that couples the dog with germs, dirt and unwanted mess, postpone the puppy until the baby is off the floor. When you are achingly tired, the puppy will still need attention and exercise. It can, of course, be managed – but it does need to be thought through. The same applies if you are out at work. A tiny puppy up to the age of six months or so should not be left for any length of time, any more than you would leave a small baby. An adult dog used to a good routine can be left to sleep, ideally for no more than four hours at a stretch, and then not on a regular basis. If you habitually leave a Dalmatian for longer than he can cope with, then you are likely to come back to a wrecked house.

This is not naughtiness, but is more likely to be caused by rising anxiety, which becomes fear, and then turns to panic. In panic, the Dalmatian can cause great damage both to himself and the house; punishment is pointless, only causing further distress. The remedy lies with the owner.

DOG OR BITCH
If you are new to the breed, you may find a bitch easier to handle than a dog. It is

The male Dalmatian will grow into a powerful dog, but he is blessed with a loving and loyal temperament.

Photo: Marc Henrie.

Ch. Hunterswood Georgiana: The female Dalmatian has a co-operative nature and will be ready to fit in with your lifestyle.

difficult to generalise, but there is a degree of co-operation in a bitch which is not always found in the male sex. Never let it be said, though, that Dalmatian dogs are less loving than bitches. I have kept both, and from the dogs received a total, wholehearted devotion, though this has not always deterred their ability to defy me when overcome by temptation. I always feel that bitches retain a small core of love for their puppies; on the other hand, they are much more prepared to do what they are asked and when. Neither sex, properly socialised and trained from early puppyhood, need give you any concern from a behavioural point of view.

If you own a dog already, discuss carefully with the breeder what sex of Dalmatian you should have. With a male dog at home, particularly one of dominant character, it is preferable to take a bitch. Dogs are usually less likely to fall out if they are of mixed sexes. Many bitches will also give a far warmer welcome to a new male puppy.

Regular visitors to the house who bring their own dogs should be borne in mind when you decide on the sex of your

Dalmatian. Providing your puppy is well socialised and trained to accept canine visitors from the beginning, there should be no problem. However, left to their own devices, Dalmatians can be territorial and will not always welcome other animals on to their property.

NEUTERING

Unless the dogs are being considered for a breeding programme, pet owners are often recommended to have their dogs neutered. Entire (i.e. un-neutered) dogs, picking up the scent of an in-season bitch, will disappear without trace on a walk; at home they will pine if they become aware of an 'interesting' bitch nearby. Castration prevents one possible cause of cancer of the testicles, though this is more usual in later life.

The problems of exercising an in-season bitch are manifold, together with avoiding the ever-present local Romeo. The bitches themselves go through discomfort and unhappiness with a false pregnancy after each season, and there is always a danger of a pyometra. The neutering operation itself has no after-effects and we are lucky to own a breed which changes neither in character nor appearance through being neutered. Neither, I must add, does the operation change their behavioural habits. A fighting dog does not become amiable because he has been castrated.

DEAFNESS

Deafness is a problem in this breed. We are fortunate that there is now a BAER hearing test which all litters of puppies can undergo at the age of six weeks. When a litter has been hearing-tested, the breeder receives a certificate and graph showing the hearing status of each dog and you are given this when you collect your puppy. It is as well to check that the registration number on both is the same as that shown on the pedigree.

Chapter Thirteen covers the hearing problem as it stands today. However, when considering a Dalmatian, you will do better to look for a fully-hearing puppy if you have young children, or have any plans to show or breed from your dog. Those dogs with unilateral hearing (deaf in one ear) are otherwise perfectly suitable for pet homes.

EXPENSE

Dalmatians are expensive to own. They have a healthy appetite and good-quality food does not come cheap. Remember injections, vet's bills, insurance, holiday kennelling, not to mention a suitable car if you constantly travel any sort of distance. The initial shopping list is formidable particularly if you have not owned a dog before. Details regarding pet insurance are normally supplied by the breeder.

WHAT TO EXPECT

We admit with a wry smile there is no dog more demanding than a Dalmatian. They live their life in your shadow; where you are, they are. Dalmatians do not retire to a corner, emerging only at your convenience. If you are cooking, they are in the kitchen; if you are working, they are under your desk; if you are in the bath, they are on the bath mat. Gardening is a hazard. Make no mistake, this 'togetherness' can be a mixed blessing.

Excessive demands will be made on your time, energy and financial resources. The enchanting, anxious-to-please puppy

Be Prepared: Dalmatians make demands on your money, your time and your energy.

Photo: Marc Henrie.

quickly grows into a rumbustious, destructive animal. Obedience will come in time, but not of the slavish variety to be found in some breeds.

Physical punishment plays little part in a Dalmatian's training; they meet aggression with aggression. Endless repetition and limitless patience will eventually present you with a charming and well-behaved companion, but the glint in the eye tells you it is by his own wish. They are delighted to settle down and leave you in peace, but once their unfailing internal alarm system goes off, they cannot be swayed from their purpose. It is now their time, not yours.

The Dalmatian's sense of humour is legendary, and those who actually smile are highly prized. The lips draw right back from the teeth, appearing like a fearsome snarl to the uninitiated. This breed will play tricks to make you laugh, and persist until you do so.

As a companion, the Dalmatian is so closely-tuned to your wavelength as to become almost an extension of yourself. There will be few moods he does not enter into, and few happy occasions when he does not add immeasurably to the pleasure. Few are the sadnesses he does not comfort; few the jokes he does not share. This is a commitment for the next fourteen years or so and, unless the Dalmatian can happily play its part in your life on that basis, please do not take it on.

LOCATING A PUPPY

Unfortunately, puppies do not come in specific sizes, shapes and colours. Nor, in fact, do adult dogs, and you may like to take time to visit a championship dog show, and spend the day watching the Dalmatian classes, seeing a selection of the finest dogs in the country. Although bred to one Standard, you will see there are various distinct types, and you may well prefer one to another. The breeders, as well as the owners, are given in the catalogue and you can make yourself known to them either at the show or later.

Alternatively, consult the recognised Dalmatian breed club in your part of the world, which can be found through your national canine organisation, in the UK the Kennel Club. It will put you in touch with the appropriate breed club secretary, who in turn can advise you on which breeders to approach in your locality. If you are prepared to look further afield, the breed club secretary will introduce you to the puppy co-ordinator, who will have details of further litters from recommended breeders.

There is no-one more fanatical than a responsible breeder in his or her search for the best homes, and in this way you will be buying a Dalmatian from someone who has a vested interest in ensuring that you are the right owner for one of their puppies. Such breeders give you endless back-up and help, and you have the added advantage of knowing that behind them lies the authority of the breed club. This is infinitely preferable to buying from one of the various commercial selling operations.

At this point I would say *do not rush*. Most reputable breeders have advance bookings and their puppies are often sold before they are born, so you may have to be prepared to go on a waiting list. Make a point of asking whether you may meet the adult Dalmatians, particularly the mother of the puppies and, when you go to see them, do take your children. The adult dogs are what your puppy will very soon become, and it is important to gauge the children's reaction.

Pay particular attention to the temperament of the adult dogs. Be wary of any form of nervousness or sign of

Taking on a Dalmatian puppy is a big responsibility so give yourself plenty of time to find the right puppy.

Photo: Marc Henrie.

Make sure you see some of the adult dogs at the breeder's home. This will give some idea as to temperament as well as overall type.

Dalmatians may be black-spotted or liver-spotted.
The colour you choose is entirely a matter of personal preference.

aggression either towards each other, the breeder, or to you and your children. Make sure that the breeder will give you all necessary guidance on feeding and care of your puppy until he reaches maturity.

All breeders have their own way of dealing with enquiries. Some will merely take a note of your details and arrange to contact you after the arrival of the litter. Others may suggest you come and see them before the litter is born to meet the adult dogs. Common to all breeders is the wide-ranging list of questions they will ask. Remember they have put their whole heart into breeding this litter, and their first priority is to find suitable and loving homes for their precious puppies. In turn, ask all the questions you can think of, and never be afraid to turn away if you are not satisfied with the answers.

COLOUR AND FAULTS

As to colour, you may choose between black and liver spotting, but as in all pigmented breeds, nature does occasionally make mistakes. Colour is sometimes missing from eye rims and noses, leaving areas of pink. An experienced breeder is normally able to tell whether these will grow over in time. Animals with large areas of missing pigmentation, which will remain in adulthood, are not normally suitable for showing or breeding.

The actual colouring of the puppies can also come up wrong, with the result that they have either lemon or orange spots. Occasionally a Dalmatian will have one or two blue eyes. This does not affect their eyesight but is undesirable because it alters the characteristic expression, so much admired and sought-after in the typical

Dalmatian. 'Patched' Dalmatians are sometimes offered for sale. A patch is a solid area of colour, present when the puppy is born, as opposed to the spots which arrive 10-to-14 days later. The fur is slightly different, and gives an appearance of satin as opposed to silk. Unlike the spots, a patch may well grow on and, as the animal becomes adult, it can cover quite a large area. You must be sure that you are happy to go ahead if you are offered a puppy with this marking.

Puppies with any of the above defects make acceptable pets, but they are not suitable for the show ring, nor should they be used for breeding.

DECISION TIME
Once you have met a breeder with a line you really like, discuss the sex and colour of the puppy you prefer, whether you want a pet or are prepared to have a go in the show ring, and whether you feel you would like to breed a litter in the future.

If there are no puppies immediately available you may like to be put on the breeder's waiting list, particularly if there is a litter due. As I said earlier, do not be in a hurry. Remember, if you are not completely happy, there will always be other puppies to see.

Assuming a litter is on the way, the breeder will contact you shortly after the bitch has whelped. Although you will know then that there is a puppy available, you may possibly not see the litter until they are about five weeks old, partly to avoid the risk of infection and partly to avoid agitating the bitch.

Most breeders have a good idea of which dog they would like to offer you, and do take note of their advice. There is always a particular puppy which is the right type and character for your circumstances, and the breeder will be the person to point this out. Once the puppy of your choice has been booked then you are into preparation time. The breeder will give you a shopping list and, from then on, it is just a question of spending rather a lot of money, reading the right books and waiting for the new arrival.

FINDING A RESCUE DOG
Dogs need re-homing for various reasons. Some are homeless through the death or chronic illness of an owner. Retirement homes all too often ban pets, causing much unhappiness to elderly folk. Other causes

Ch. Washakie Indian Summer: Winner of 18 CCs, 18 RCCs, BOB Crufts 1994 and final 6 in Utility Group, BOB Crufts 1996 with group 2; Top Dalmatian Puppy 1989, Top Dalmatian Bitch 1993 and 1994, Dalmatian of the Year 1995.
If you are planning to show your dog, the colour and markings must be correct.

are the breakdown of family life; the arrival of a baby; an owner going abroad or moving to a city centre – all of these reasons and many more. Very few dogs are abandoned, and cases of cruelty are thankfully few and far between. Unkindness, even physical or mental damage, are more often caused through ignorance than any desire to inflict pain.

A sad fact of life today is the existence of puppy farms and unscrupulous breeders who sell all too many Dalmatians into homes totally unsuited to them. The puppy is bought in all good faith, and it is a matter of distress to many owners when they are forced to bring the animal back on rescue. Amazingly, whatever the past experience of these dogs has been, in the vast majority of cases they settle quickly and well, giving their new owners untold pleasure.

LOCATING THE RESCUE DOG

In the UK, the Dalmatian Rescue Service and the North of England Dalmatian Club Rescue, with wholehearted help from club members, work hard to re-home all Dalmatians which come to them. This is true of breed clubs and Dalmatian lovers the world over. Rescue Services, like breeders, always give a warm welcome to offers of suitable and loving homes. Again, like breeders, they tend to ask a lot of questions, and it is important that they have accurate information from you, and that, in turn, you receive a careful report on the dog under consideration.

You will be asked, for instance, if you have a fully-enclosed garden, and whether you have time to give the dog the regular exercise and care he will need. With your children in mind, you will want to know whether the dog has been accustomed to youngsters. If you already have a dog, or a dog comes regularly to your house as a visitor, it is worth discussing this with the Rescue Service, as it may have some bearing on the sex and age of the dog you are looking for. Take into account cats and other domestic pets. The amount of time the dog will have to spend on his own at any one time will need to be considered – an unhappy Dalmatian is a destructive and naughty animal.

It is normal for the rescue Dalmatians to come for a period on approval, and an absolute joy how seldom they fail to prove themselves indispensable members of the family. Most questions concerning the care, feeding and training of Dalmatians are covered in the various chapters of this book. However, over the years, certain questions have arisen concerning rescue dogs in particular, and I will cover some of these points in the hope that you will find them useful.

EARLY DAYS

There is a certain insecurity in all rescued animals when coming to a new home, which one hopes will be of short duration. It will help enormously if the dog is allowed a few days' grace with you and your family before being introduced to your friends and neighbours. Dalmatians love young people, but at first ask the children to sit down and let the dog come to them. This is much less confusing, and easier for the dog to deal with.

If there is already another dog at home, ensure the two meet for the first time out of doors and have a walk together, even if your rescued dog must stay on an extending lead. You can then let them run free in the garden, and they will make their way into the house together in their own time.

The future relationship of the two dogs is all-important, but there should be few problems if your first dog does not feel jeopardised and is given preference generally over the newcomer. Dogs are pack animals and are happier with a set hierarchy, but never let familiarity breed contempt. If they tease each other too much, or play too roughly, it can so quickly end in tears.

FEEDING

The dog's previous diet will almost certainly have been passed on to you, and initially it is better to keep to this and avoid a possible tummy upset. If you have a strong preference for an alternative, make the change-over gradually and you should not experience any great problems.

You may need special advice for dogs that are under- or overweight, but an average healthy adult will eat approximately one-and-a-half lbs of food a day. This is best given in two meals, in the ratio of one-third in the morning and two-thirds in the late afternoon, with a couple of biscuits to go to bed with. Whether you feed fresh food or dry, always scald it with boiling broth or water half-an-hour before feeding. This ensures that it expands to its full size before entering the dog's stomach, helping generally with digestion.

Clean water should always be available and like most Dalmatians, including mine, they will adore a drop of milk diluted with hot water after breakfast. If possible, exercise the dog before feeding and then ensure he has a couple of hours' rest to let the meal digest. Dalmatians have a difficult digestive system and, if you need advice, do go back to the Rescue Service with any queries.

TRAINING

Your rescued Dalmatian will flourish on a set routine, particularly for the first few months. Any lack of security will be greatly helped if the dog knows what is expected. You may be lucky and have acquired an obedient dog, but equally he may know nothing. However well-behaved, there is no harm in starting a behaviour training programme, and each new rule can be learned in the same way as a puppy would.

Training, as always, is a matter of bribery,

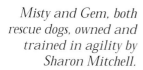

Misty and Gem, both rescue dogs, owned and trained in agility by Sharon Mitchell.

and your early obedience lessons can be held in the house and later the garden. Continue them on your first walks while the dog is still on an extending lead and, once you have bravely let him off, use the same tactics.

If inviting new smells prove too tempting, and answering your call is delayed, still produce a tidbit and a lot of praise when the wanderer returns. This seldom fails to work – the most disobedient Dalmatian will quickly learn that coming back when called brings its own reward. Mistakes will be made, and while the dog must know they are wrong, try not to make too much of them. As for a puppy, it helps to start with just a few rules and add to them over the ensuing weeks.

PROBLEMS
1.Pulling on the lead.
Training a young puppy to walk quietly to heel on the lead is relatively easy. A strong adult, with little or no training and a tendency to pull you off your feet, is another matter. At this stage, a choke chain is seldom helpful and will only hurt the dog. There are various aids on the market to a trouble-free walk, including the Easy Walk training harness from Pet Brands, which is available in the USA from Four Paws. The harness does not hurt or rub the dog sore, but it does work.

2.Guarding Food.
Food may have been the major comfort in this dog's life. If there was not enough to go round, there may have been constant battles to get a fair share. It will take time for your rescue dog to learn that in his new life there will always be good meals, that you share in this pleasure and will not wilfully remove them.

Always say "Wait" before you put the food bowl down. If it is practically snatched out of your hand, leave it with the dog but remain in the room and, without watching, talk gently to show you are still there. Good, regular meals for a few days will go a long way towards solving the problem but if the guarding and snatching continue, the most effective punishment I know is to put the dog out of the room for five minutes.

Perhaps you are about to put the food bowl down and can foresee there is going to be a problem. Put the bowl back, well out of the way, take the dog firmly by the collar saying "Wait – you can just go outside now and wait there." Put the dog outside the door for not more than five minutes and when you let him in again say "Wait" very firmly and put the bowl down on the floor. Repeat this each time the dog grabs at the bowl. No Dalmatian appreciates being put outside the door and will understand very quickly why you have done this. With luck there will be an almost immediate improvement.

When the dog has become totally adjusted to having a meal in a civilised manner, take this a step further. Offer the first half of the meal while you are still holding the plate and then put it down on the floor for the dog to finish. This will develop trust between the two of you because the dog now knows that the food which comes from you will not be taken away. Greet all signs of improvement with warm praise.

Try, if you can, to think yourself into this dog's mind. You will never know how many times people have let him down, so, though you will make friends, the deep-seated trust which is such a joyful gift from an animal may take a little time in coming.

3 *THE NEW PUPPY*

The breeder, I am sure, will advise that you continue with the puppy's present feeding routine, and will tell you precisely what to buy. In addition, there are quite a few items which you will need and, once again, your breeder will probably provide a shopping list. However, it may interest you to see a sample list I sent recently to new puppy owners, and I have also added a few words of explanation in case you are totally bewildered.

Two medium size Vet Beds.

Dog bed: large size bean bag or 32 ins. fabric quilted bed.

Rubber grooming glove.

Soft rubber brush.

Jumbo-size guillotine nail cutters.

Strong metal nail file.

Smokers' tooth powder.

Soft toothbrush.

Tube of Germolene or similar.

Packet of commercial Epsom salts.

Teething gel (babies' brand from chemist).

Gripe water.

Anal thermometer.

Bottle of kaolin and morphine.

Rolled leather collar – medium size for now.

Long leather training lead.

Soft webbing house collar.

BEDDING

Vet beds, if you have not met them before, are one of the joys of a modern world. They come in a variety of sizes, fit snugly into any bed, go straight into the washing machine and dry in minimum time; they do not harbour germs, and dampness goes straight through – the dog is therefore always on a dry, clean bed and looks very glamorous against the shining white. Beds themselves are a matter of personal preference. Bean bags are a favourite with my dogs, but I do warn you to get a really large size. The amount of space taken up by a Dalmatian circling round to make a nest in the middle is surprising.

Fabric quilted beds are also excellent and easy and light to carry in and out of the car when staying away from home. However, your puppy is going to grow very quickly, so do not be persuaded into getting anything less than size 32 ins. A Vet bed in the base will keep the interior clean, though an advantage of this breed is the small amount of dirt they bring indoors.

GROOMING EQUIPMENT

You will find a rubber grooming glove is admirably suited to a Dalmatian's short, fine coat and, used daily, it helps not only to contain the everlasting moult but to build up the underlying muscle. The soft rubber brush is used for the head and a general finish.

Your breeder will have advised you on keeping your puppy's toenails trimmed. Overgrown nails are not only ugly in themselves, but they also ruin the dog's feet. There are two types of trimmer; the guillotine and the clipper. I find the former easier to use and less likely to crush the bed of the nail.

Before you start, the dog should sit or lie with his feet against the light (the sofa comes in handy here) and you can then see quite clearly where the quick joins the dead nail. Trim off just the tip and smooth the edges with your metal file. Black nails are more difficult, but take the same amount off as the white nail alongside. Above all, avoid cutting into the quick. Once hurt, the dog will be most reluctant to let you try again, and it takes a while to re-establish confidence.

Nail-trimming is usually a once-a-week task, though some owners are blessed with dogs whose nails never grow. If a second pair of hands is available, accept assistance with alacrity; it is particularly helpful to have someone hold the dog steady and keep its attention with a small biscuit hidden in the hand.

Gleaming white teeth can discolour with age. Cleaning them with a soft toothbrush is easier than it sounds, and a (human) smokers' tooth powder is ideal. Wrap a towel around your dog and, with plenty of powder on the wet toothbrush, lift the top lip and gently brush the teeth up and down and from side to side, both in front and at the sides. I find my dogs quite enjoy it. Once brushing is finished, wipe the excess tooth powder away with the towel and your Dalmatian is left with a nice clean mouth.

Before you collect your puppy, you will need to prepare your home for the new arrival.

MEDICINE CUPBOARD

An antiseptic ointment such as Germolene is indispensable. Any cut or wound is first bathed in hot water with a handful of Epsom salts added, and then a touch of Germolene applied.

Teething is likely to be one of your first problems and Dalmatian puppies can react badly, some going right off their food. Keep an eye open for red, swollen gums and, at the first sign, rub them gently with a little ordinary baby teething gel which usually gives instant relief. The second teeth occasionally come through before the baby teeth drop out, and for a few days the two together can look quite alarming. If the situation persists, the vet may decide to extract the baby teeth, but this is seldom necessary.

Indigestion and subsequent loud hiccups

Make sure you provide safe, sensible toys for your puppy to play with.

sound alarming and can distress the puppy. A tablespoonful of gripe water can be a great help. All puppies, not to mention adult dogs, eat disgusting horrors with every appearance of enjoyment, and usually very few after-effects. However, if they do have an upset tummy of which you can trace the source, a dose of kaolin and morphine will often work wonders.

COLLAR EQUIPMENT

Collars and leads are a matter of personal taste, but a Dalmatian looks very smart in a rolled leather collar with a nice length of leather training lead.

Dalmatians have a bad tendency to hang on their collars and pull on the lead and, in this case, a choke chain can be a great help. I have never found it necessary to use this as a 'choking' mechanism; I simply slip it over the dog's head, and find they drop back at once to walk to heel (more or less!). If the dog is trained at an early stage, he will not pull against a choke chain, although I find most of them lean against an ordinary leather collar. For an inveterate 'puller', try a specialist training harness.

TOYS

Buying toys for the new puppy is very beguiling, but the squeaky or soft variety have a two-minute life at most. There is no

need to spend a fortune; a hard rubber toy and perhaps one of the new 'raggers' are always very acceptable. An old tea towel, knotted in the middle, is a favourite. The knot will hold it together and distinguish it from those you might use for drying up.

A long sock, with a hard rubber ball down one end and a knot in the middle to prevent it coming out, is one of the best toys I know, but make sure the ball is too large to swallow. Discarded trainers (athletic shoes) are also very popular, or an old glove or slipper – and, if you leave the loo door open, lavatory brushes tend to disappear down the garden path in the jaws of a triumphant young Dalmatian.

A cardboard carton made without metal staples, found usually in the local supermarket, is very useful as a toy box. Unpacking it gives the puppy enormous pleasure and interest, particularly if occasionally there are one or two new surprise items. It also provides a place for you to throw the puppy's rubbish when you want it out of the way.

I have been asked: "Surely if you provide a slipper or glove this will tempt the puppy to steal from the owner's wardrobe?" I think the opposite. The objects are now familiar rather than an inviting novelty and, if the puppies pick up the wrong ones by mistake, they are happy to have them replaced by those in the toy box. They learn the lesson 'That is yours, this is mine' in a surprisingly short time.

DAILY ROUTINE

You will find it a great help to ask the breeder for an outline of the puppy's current day-to-day routine. Keep to this for a while and it will help your puppy to settle down. You can always change things slowly to fall in with your own ways, but it is helpful if the puppy has to face as few changes as possible during the first weeks.

The basic routine for the puppy remains the same throughout his life and is best understood by equating it with an animal in the wild.

The dog is a carnivore, and his inside works as one. A wild animal goes out to hunt, returns with its kill and devours it and, with a full stomach, settles down to sleep. Transferring this to a domestic scenario, the dog should be exercised, fed, and then allowed to sleep. The rule in our household is that no dog is fed before it has been exercised, and no dog is exercised for a minimum of two hours after it has been fed.

Therefore, as a tiny puppy, your Dalmatian should have a game in the garden before breakfast and, after the meal, settle down to sleep. The same can happen at lunch, tea and supper time, and again before the puppy goes to bed. At this stage good food and exercise are vital, but regular and uninterrupted sleep is also of the utmost importance in the correct development of your dog, both physically and temperamentally.

THE VET

Make an appointment and take the puppy to your vet a day or so after arrival. You will want to satisfy yourself that all is well, and you may wish to discuss insurance. As far as injections are concerned, the present thinking is that if they are given too early this can interfere with the immunity passed on by the dam, so your vet will advise on the first injection, taking into account local conditions.

JOURNEY HOME

There are three traumatic events in the early life of a puppy; getting born, being weaned, and leaving home. Leaving the breeder's home is possibly the most upsetting of all, so, if you can, arrange for someone else to drive the car. You will then hold the puppy and be there yourself to give initial reassurance. For the actual journey you are going to need a large bath towel and loads of kitchen paper, though with luck the puppy may simply curl up on your lap and go to sleep. Much will depend on the skill of the driver, who must have the patience to take the first mile or two very slowly indeed, and go round corners as though driving on glass.

The breeder will normally help by sending you off with the puppy's meals for the first two days, but if you are facing a really long journey you may need some extra provisions. With many hours to go before arriving home, you will need to stop at a convenient place, allow the puppy to be clean and have a short run, and possibly eat a small meal. The puppy may not eat, but is likely to welcome a drink of warm milk.

INTRODUCTION TO THE HOUSEHOLD

With luck, you will arrive home in good order. Put the puppy down straightaway in the garden. That is also the time and place to introduce any other animals from the household. Everybody can meet on outside territory and, in their own time, go into the house together.

Your puppy will feel quite bewildered when he first arrives home. Give him a chance to explore and to find his feet.

Once the excitement has died down and you have had time to collect yourself, unpack the appropriate meal and offer it to the puppy. It may well be ignored, in which case just take it up and forget it. A little warm milk in its place may be acceptable. A missed meal is unimportant, but wait until the correct time before offering the next. By then, hunger will prove to be a great inducement. Although there will be many friends longing to see the puppy, try to keep the numbers down for the first couple of days. The little one has a great deal to learn and can only take in so much at a time.

THE FIRST NIGHT

This is a very frightening time for a puppy. Coming into the new home has created great excitement, but this may well be the point when realisation dawns that mother and siblings are missing and there is nothing familiar to provide comfort. If you have a dog already, with luck your puppy will find a friend and will tuck up alongside. However, I am no believer in leaving the puppy to cry on his own in a kitchen or bathroom surrounded with newspaper,

however warm and comfortable the area. It is companionship and reassurance that the puppy needs and this can only come from you. I know some people take a mattress and sleep with the new puppy, but I cannot help feeling they are making a rod for their own backs.

My own suggestion is that, for the first two or three nights, you put the puppy down to sleep in a box beside your bed. If he stirs in the night or cries, you can put a hand down to give reassurance, at the same time establishing a very real bond. You will also hear him stir first thing in the morning and can carry him straight downstairs and into the garden without further ado. Once you have the puppy's confidence, he can be transferred to his normal sleeping place and you may like to leave a light burning with a very low-voltage bulb. If the puppy cries out, then it will be from exasperation rather than fear, and a quick visit from you to re-establish confidence should eliminate this very quickly.

HOUSE TRAINING

If the puppy has been reared in a home, he may well come to you almost house-trained. At this early age, a puppy cannot control his bladder for any length of time, so at night put some newspaper down near the door and if the puppy cannot wait he will use it. If you manage to wake really early, catch the puppy as he first stirs and take him to the garden immediately with a little warm milk for encouragement. An unused newspaper and an early visit to the garden is a major bonus, and sets the trend for the day.

Initially, apart from first thing in the morning, the puppy should be taken out before and after every meal, immediately on waking from a sleep, and last thing at night. Keep a good look out at all times and, at the first sign of hunching up or circling round, put the puppy straight outside and stay there yourself (under an umbrella if necessary) using whatever word you choose as encouragement to be clean. As soon as he responds, praise the puppy warmly and bring him inside again immediately. I am afraid that accompanying the puppy at these times is obligatory. No puppy and few adult dogs will stay on their own; they merely come back in without having obliged.

The word you use for encouragement to perform is all-important. There will come a time when it is a tremendous help in persuading your Dalmatian to use an available piece of grass at a time to suit your convenience – stopping at a motorway service station, for instance, on a long journey. Your house will be unfamiliar to the puppy, so make the early geography as easy as you can. The doors will all be in different places from those he is used to; this is bewildering at eight weeks of age and some mistakes are inevitable. At first, spread some newspaper in the corner of any room you are using, particularly at night. After a week or so this should no longer be necessary, providing you continue to keep a

careful watch on the puppy.

If a mistake is made, show it to the puppy (do *not* rub his nose in it), take the puppy straight outside and point out where he should have gone. Dalmatians are clean by nature and intelligent, and will very quickly learn to behave.

FEEDING
An adult Dalmatian, having reached full maturity, is a strong, well-boned animal of great substance. At eight weeks of age, this is all to come and good feeding plays a major part. The degree of growth in a relatively short space of time is prodigious, and this in turn makes it necessary that everything the dog eats should do the maximum good. Filling the puppy up so that he is not hungry is no answer. There are two methods of feeding, dried food and fresh, and I hope that the information in Chapters Four and Twelve will prove useful.

RELATIONSHIP WITH EXISTING PETS
It is essential for their future relationship and happiness that your existing animals should not feel at risk from the puppy. There should be little problem if you are tactful and give the older animals priority at all times. My own dogs are dealt with strictly in age priority: the oldest comes first, and the youngest last. I will not say there are no arguments but that is the rule, and it is interesting to find that if I am absent-minded enough to put the bowls down in the wrong order, the younger animals step back at once.

The arrival of a puppy at home is always greeted with enthusiasm by the other animals because suddenly there are five meals a day instead of two. The fact that, for three meals out of five, the adult bowls only contain a couple of tiny biscuits with a little broth is unimportant, so long as they do not miss out. Jealousy, once it rears its head, is very hard to eradicate, so it is worth taking trouble to ensure it never arises. However adorable your Dalmatian puppy may be, let everyone realise that his place is last in the line.

EXERCISE

For the first four months avoid formal walks; playing is all that is required. If you only have a small garden and need more space, find a nice field where you can sit and let the puppy play around you.

From four months onwards the puppy will be strong enough for regular walks. Start off with about twenty minutes and gradually increase this to an hour, with shorter walks at other times of the day. Avoid road work until the dog is a year or so old. Until then bones are too soft and can easily be damaged.

HOUSE RULES

Once you have got house training established, then house rules can be introduced. These will be different for every one of you, but establish what you really want the dog not to do and then make sure he does not do it. It will help you always if you can incorporate the puppy into your own lifestyle.

Initially, perhaps the first priority is to make sure your puppy will answer to his name. Try getting down to the puppy's level, calling his name and holding your hand out, if necessary tapping the ground with your fingers to attract his attention. Once your puppy responds, praise is high on the agenda – Dalmatians thrive on limitless affection. If you decide on a name in the very early stages, ask the breeder to use it beforehand and you will have won half the battle.

Obedience is really instilled at any level

To begin with your puppy will get all the exercise he needs playing in the garden.

Photo: Burrows.

with bribery. Both in the garden, where the puppy will come to you happily, and on a walk, where diversions can be so tempting, keep a rustly paper bag in your righthand pocket, filled with tiny pieces of biscuit, etc. Every time you call the puppy, rustle the paper bag and, when he comes, produce a tiny piece out of it. Make a tremendous fuss when you give him the tidbit, and you will shortly find that all you need to do is put your hand in your pocket. Wait until you see the look of astonishment on your visitors' faces when they accidentally put a hand in their pocket and are instantly surrounded with 'obedient' Dalmatians.

Another early lesson is to avoid damage to your possessions and furniture. You already have the toy box and, at this stage, will find it very useful. Each time the puppy picks up one of your possessions, remove it at once, saying "No, that's mine, *this* is yours", and produce a diversion from the toy box. As with a small child, you need to distract your puppy's attention with an alternative; otherwise he will go straight back into the attack. This is not usually naughtiness or obstinacy, purely that, to a young Dalmatian, removing the object becomes part of the game.

Dalmatian puppies are no respecters of Georgian chair legs. Diverting their attention may be all that is needed, but puppies are tenacious little animals and, if something proves hugely attractive, I suggest you remove the object for a time, or else exclude the puppy from the vicinity for a week or so. If he returns to the attack, remove the object once more for a few days. Puppies loathe to be thwarted but, if they cannot win, they will eventually give in gracefully.

GROOMING

As owners of horses will know, short hair is no good reason for a grubby coat, and a Dalmatian repays regular daily grooming a hundredfold. Dalmatian coats vary enormously, from a short tight coat where the white gleams silver in the sunlight, to those which are slightly longer. Some are soft and some much coarser. All are improved enormously by daily brushing with a rubber grooming glove, finishing off with the softer brush and maybe a polish over with a silk scarf.

Hand stripping with your hands wet from dew is another good tip, given to me many years ago by a good friend. First thing in the morning, drench your hands in the dew and then hand strip your dog, i.e. brush

him with your wet hands. It is surprisingly hard work but, as your hands dry, the pressure pulls dead hair plus an amazing amount of dirt from the dog, and imparts a shine that you never seem to achieve otherwise. It is well worth the effort, but it has to be dew; unfortunately tap water does not have the same effect. Nails and teeth we have already discussed. Any snags in the coat, thorns from passing brambles, or other problems, are usually discovered while you are grooming the dog.

SOCIALISATION

This is a very important aspect of your puppy training, and is well worth your time and trouble. Some vets and canine clubs have taken the initiative of organising 'puppy parties' and these are an excellent idea. A group of puppies, of all sizes and breeds, meet on neutral ground to play and get to know each other. I have a riveting photograph of a puppy of mine who recently met a young Shar Pei at one of these parties. Spots versus wrinkle: the astonishment was mutual.

Failing this, a card on your vet's notice board asking owners of puppies to contact you will usually elicit a number of answers. In whatever way you can, find some local puppies and see that they meet your own. Your Dalmatian puppy must be socialised to cope with all sorts of people and situations.

TRAINING CLASSES

Following on from puppy socialisation, your local canine society will be able to direct you to training classes in your area which will almost certainly have a puppy section. Such classes are normally divided into obedience or ringcraft, and both are excellent.

Take the puppy to a class when he is about four months old, and hold him on your knee just to watch. Join in for a short time on your second visit, and perhaps rather longer on the third. Five or six sessions in all may well be enough – you can always go back for more later if you wish.

Dalmatians have a low boredom threshold and may lose interest after a while. However, by then, they have usually learned the basics. If destined for the show ring, they will carry on with ringcraft lessons at home and in the show ring. Apart from general usefulness, basic obedience is essential if you want to try your hand at Agility.

As far as training in the home is concerned, Dalmatians do not respond well to aggression. A good telling-off in a really cross voice, or a smart tap with a rolled newspaper, is usually enough. If there is a real transgression, and I am thinking here of something like chasing livestock, try picking the dog up by the skin over the shoulders and giving it a good shake. This humiliates rather than hurts, and is far more effective than any beating.

The Dalmatian's legendary smile: The lips draw back from the teeth, appearing like a fearsome snarl to the uninitiated.

BRINGING UP A SHOW PUPPY

If you keep to a strict daily routine, this will help to establish normal events like meals and walks on a day that is disrupted by a show. Try to feed your puppy standing up, so that he does not go over at the shoulder when stretching down to the bowl. Before offering the meal, see that the front legs are nicely placed, straight and near together, and that the back legs are not bunched up. Hold the bowl at a height where the food can be eaten easily but slightly in front of the puppy so that the neck is stretched forward a little. This also teaches the puppy to stand happily in front of you, just as he will in the show ring.

If you are carrying the puppy, take particular care, when putting him down,

that all four legs are carrying the weight evenly before you let go. Be on the lookout to avoid any sort of injury, particularly with steps or stairs. Keep an eye out for any high 'platforms'. Puppies have a wicked instinct to climb such things and hurl themselves off, and a shoulder injury can take months to heal.

As discussed earlier, keep a rustling bag of tidbits at all times. The puppy will watch your hand in that pocket and be alert to see what comes out of it. On a walk, in the garden, at any odd time, rustle the bag, call the dog and say "Now, what have I got here in my pocket?" Puppies learn very quickly.

The puppy must be happy to stand still while the judge 'goes over him'. This entails the judge running his hands over the puppy's back and sides, picking up a foot, feeling the pads and gently checking that a male puppy has two testicles. Ask all your friends to do this while you hold the puppy on his show collar and lead, and your Dalmatian will soon become accustomed to this.

The judge will wish to look at the puppy's teeth, so he must be happy to have these examined. Practise by gently lifting the lips away from the teeth so that the judge can see the 'bite'. Do not make an issue of it, and always accompany the action by saying something like "Teeth". Thus, when the judge wishes to look, all you have to say is "Teeth" and the puppy will know what to expect. If you prefer, you may always show the dog's teeth to the judge yourself.

It is particularly important to keep nails trimmed without fail. Do not keep a collar on the dog, except for walks, and then use a rolled leather collar not a flat one (which will mark the coat). A webbing house-collar can be used if you wish. Once accustomed to a collar and lead, teach the puppy to run quietly at a trot beside you, up and down. If he pulls away, run the puppy beside a fence or wall so that it keeps straight of necessity. Once again, these exercises should be kept to a minimum; boredom is a constant menace and a few minutes is quite sufficient.

It is difficult to judge your dog's best pace on the move, so ask an experienced exhibitor for an opinion. It is all too easy to encourage the dog to move at your own best pace, rather than the reverse. It is better not to teach the puppy to "Sit" but, if you wish to do this, then teach him also to stand on command and stay standing. Your share of the judge's time is minuscule, and it is a terrible waste if your puppy spends most of it sitting down.

PREPARATION FOR THE RING
We have already discussed teeth cleaning. If the puppy has been groomed regularly, with a dew bath when possible, you can almost certainly avoid a complete bathing session. Stand the puppy on a rubber mat in the bath in ankle-deep warm water and wash his feet and lower legs only – a proprietary baby shampoo is excellent.

Having dried off the feet, soak a towel in very hot water, wring it out as tightly as possible and rub the puppy all over with this hot dry towel. This takes off any surface grubbiness. Nails should have a final trim-and-file two days before the show. If the rubbish dump has proved irresistible and a complete bath is necessary, do remember to cover the dog with a towel before he jumps out and drenches you with the inevitable shake. Dry your young dog really well – make sure that all the bedding is clean and there are no draughts to cause a chill.

Do not over-exercise the day before a show, and keep to a well-known and hazard-free route. Finally, enjoy the day and good luck to you both!

4 ADOLESCENCE TO ADULTHOOD

F irstly, perhaps one should ask: where does puppyhood end and adolescence begin? If you suggest it is at the age of six months, there will be many owners ready to point to their ten-year-old 'puppies'. Dalmatians, it would seem, are forever young, or it could be that their delight in life and sense of humour makes them seem so?

During the first few months with your puppy, you will have begun to appreciate the many sides to owning a Dalmatian. You will have gained a large number of new friends, but you may also have lost one or two along the way.

You will have winced at the sound of angry shouts from invisible fishermen, and become adept at retrieving half-chewed packets of sandwiches laid at your feet with loving pride. My own cringing embarrassment over a Dalmatian leg lifted inappropriately in Hyde Park is indelibly imprinted on my mind; a young man looked up from his book with the expression of one who could feel a warm trickle between his shoulder blades. My words "he has never done such a thing before" sounded lame, even to my own ears.

Never mind. The countryside is more

beautiful foot-slogging in the rain than when seen from the car window, and you may comfort yourself in the sure knowledge that there is no owner born who cannot cap any Dalmatian story you have to tell.

However, the purpose of this chapter is to deal with everyday care rather than quirks of character, so perhaps it is realistic

As your Dalmatian matures, his nutritional needs will change.
Photo: Marc Henrie.

if we now draw a line under puppyhood at six months. Some breeders will have been very thorough and given you information covering every stage through to adulthood. If not, I will set out some ideas which I hope you will find helpful.

FEEDING

THE STOCKPOT
A dog stockpot is a 'must' in any doggy household. Commandeer an old saucepan with a tightly fitting lid, and scrape in all the bones, meaty bits, anything off the plates that you would normally put in the bin. Avoid green vegetables which may make the contents smell, but drain in any vegetable water and top up from the tap as necessary. At the end of the week throw it out and start again.

Boil up the stockpot every day and pour a good ladleful or so of the scalding broth over any biscuit or complete food. The liquid is quickly absorbed and enlarges the biscuit to the size it would have become in the dog's stomach. This reduces the chance of a dog eating more than it should, and can even lessen the chances of a possible case of bloat.

SIX MONTHS TO ONE YEAR
At this age a Dalmatian will be on three meals a day, plus biscuits at night. There is still a lot of growing to be done, a lot of substance to be put down, and general 'bodying-out', all of which needs good, nourishing food. It is true that some youngsters abandon the third meal of their own accord, but it is better for the animal if it can be retained throughout the first year.

At whatever time it is fed, this third meal is very light, which makes it easier to dispense with when the time comes. If your Dalmatian is a glutton (not unknown), simply reduce the amount gradually at

about 12 months until the meal disappears altogether.

FEEDING AT ONE YEAR
Apart from bedtime biscuits, a Dalmatian from 12 to 15 months of age should be on two meals a day for the rest of his life. For my convenience, I make these breakfast (one-third) and tea (two-thirds).

Two meals are recommended for many reasons. It is easier to digest two smaller meals than one large one, and this method prevents the feeling of starving hunger by the time a single meal arrives. I love to see a good appetite but do not like it when dogs fall on their food as though their last hour had come. There is some leeway too if, through no fault of your own, a meal is late. The type of food you use will probably have been instigated by the breeder, and it falls into two categories – either one of the varieties of complete food or fresh food.

COMPLETE FOODS
If your puppy has been reared on complete food and you wish to continue with this, you will find most different brands are available in 'age' categories. Thus, you can start with the puppy version and, at the appropriate time, transfer to a more adult mixture. The quantity is geared to the weight of the dog, and all details are given on the package. The makers include whatever vitamins, etc., they consider necessary, and do not normally recommend that you add anything further yourself. For a Dalmatian, dried food should always be soaked, so use the broth from your stockpot which will also make it a little more tasty.

FRESH FOOD
Like myself, many owners prefer to feed their Dalmatians on fresh food. They like to know precisely what the dogs are eating,

and to be able to vary both diet and additives from dog to dog. It takes more time and is slightly more expensive, but the interest generated through the necessary study of animal feeding and husbandry is immensely rewarding.

LOCATING FRESH DOG FOOD
Back in 1972, I used to go down to London's Smithfield Market at 4.30am, and collect an order of 100 1bs. of cow meat at 10d. per lb (about two pence in today's money). The porters had a glorious time at my expense, and 'my hungry boyfriend' became a well-known figure. I bought boxes of chicken too, and the dogs then took on the alter ego of my 'caff'. "Is this for you or your caff?" the butchers would ask, adding "It's fine for your caff, but don't eat it yourself."

Sadly, neither cow beef nor horsemeat for animals are readily available nowadays, and it is difficult to find suitable substitutes. Nothing, of course, quite takes their place, hence the need for extra vitamins and various additives. Study of the Yellow Pages in your local telephone directory will probably locate an animal cash and carry warehouse where you can buy in bulk at competitive prices. It will stock, among other things, frozen packs of tripe, fish, mince etc., plus fresh turkey fillets, minced raw ox cheek (minus skin and lip), along with the better brands of tinned meat and complete foods. You can also buy excellent makes of wholewheat biscuit meal, in the terrier size suitable for our adult Dalmatians. All sorts of large, hard biscuits are on the market and Dalmatians are adept at sorting out the ones they like the best.

As for additives, try sterilised bonemeal and corn oil (fed together), garlic and greenleaf tablets, and a mineral/vitamin additive such as Canovel or Stress. Small quantities of grated carrot or parsley are excellent, and other additives are available as and when the occasion demands.

MAKE-UP OF MEALS
I hope you will find the following suggestions helpful. Quantities are obviously approximate, and you must use your own judgment for each dog individually. Pay particular attention to the feeding of a dog being used at stud or a bitch for breeding.

Breakfast: Equal quantities of biscuit (dry weight) to protein (boiled fish, turkey breasts, raw egg, etc.) plus additives. Soak the biscuit meal before you add the remainder. Follow the meal with a small cup of milk diluted with hot water – more because the dogs love it than because it does them good.
Quantity: At six months, about five oz biscuit plus five oz protein. Increase gradually until at 12-24 months the meal will consist of eight oz biscuit plus eight oz protein. This is normally a maximum amount and will gradually decrease until, at about four years of age, four oz biscuit plus four oz protein will be about correct.

Lunch: One scrambled egg mixed with unsweetened cereal (Ready Brek or similar) and milk.
Quantity: This is correct at six months but can be discontinued when considered appropriate.

Tea: Raw beef, ox cheek, or healthmeal, plus added vitamins.
Quantity: At six months, about 1lb of meat is sufficient. Increase very gradually until, between one and two years of age, you are feeding about one and a half lb of meat. Over the years, I have found this to be a maximum amount. Adolescent dogs, like teenage children, have hollow legs but,

ABOVE: Regular exercise will help to build up muscle in the growing Dalmatian. Photo: Marc Henrie

BELOW: Many Dalmatians enjoy a swim!

when this period is over, the quantity will reduce gradually until, from about three years onwards, you will be back to feeding approximately one lb of raw meat.

Supper: Rice pudding, to be followed at bedtime with hard biscuits.
Quantity: About two tablespoonfuls is sufficient, but supper will be discontinued shortly after the six-month birthday.

Never forget that clean water must be available at all times. Directions on additives are given on the containers and, leaving aside a Dalmatian's propensity for stealing, this should constitute a more than adequate diet. Plan the timing of your dog's meals to suit your own convenience but, if you can, keep to that time as accurately as possible. A Dalmatian flourishes on a strict routine and, right through his life, will do best when exercised before a meal, fed at a regular time, and then given the opportunity to rest while digesting the food. Tempting a dog to eat when he is recuperating from an illness is a testing experience. You will find various suggestions which may help in Chapter Five.

GROOMING
Grooming, nails and teeth cleaning have already been covered in Chapter Three.

EXERCISE
From six months onwards it is almost impossible to over-exercise a fit adult Dalmatian, but an hour to an hour-and-a-half a day will keep your dog both healthy and happy. With this sort of regular exercise there will be a gradual build-up of muscle, which is so essential to correct movement. Twenty minutes a day steady road walking does wonders for feet and legs, but correct, thick pads make it unlikely that the nails

will be affected. Walking on an extending lead is greatly to be preferred than on a tight leash, but it is important that Dalmatians should have free-running exercise every day. There are few areas where this cannot be found, even if it means a short drive to get there. It is well worth your trouble, the delight of the dogs being thanks enough.

WALKING HAZARDS
When you are new to owning a dog there are certain hazards worth bearing in mind. The first time you walk over unfamiliar country, for instance, it may well pay you to keep the dog on the lead. Nothing is worse than finding yourself in the middle of unexpected livestock, roads that come from nowhere, or game preserves and it is always worth checking this out. If you walk in a dream and take your mind and eye off the dog, the chances are that you will soon have no dog in sight or one who has found a flock of sheep.

A dog who constantly runs too far ahead or disappears over the horizon is a real problem. From the beginning, never let your Dalmatian be certain exactly where you are or assume that you are following a definite path. Call or whistle once, turn and walk quickly in a totally different direction; hide, if you can, behind a convenient tree and wait. When the whirlwind of anxiety rushes past, call again, make a great fuss of the dog once he finds you and produce a tiny reward from your pocket. Then walk in a different direction yet again. Your Dalmatian will quickly learn that he must keep an eye on you or risk losing you altogether.

When there are obvious difficulties ahead, an aggressive dog for example, call yours very firmly and walk away. This is more likely to avoid trouble than if you go hurrying up to try and prevent it, and your

A Dalmatian at full stretch, enjoying a spell of freedom.

dog will be able to follow you without losing face.

An entire male dog will almost certainly disappear if he crosses the scent of a bitch in season, and all you can do is follow as best you can, calling frequently. With luck, he may give up and retrace his steps. Praise him warmly when you finally get him back – this is nature and not his fault – but put him firmly on the lead and give that area a miss for the next couple of weeks or so.

Permission is often needed when walking on privately-owned land but, wherever you are, you will find you are asked to clean up after your dog. On a country walk you can easily bury any mess, but in a park or public place you are now asked to remove it, so habitually keep a strong plastic bag in your pocket. Most public parks now provide bins in which to deposit the contents.

Even sea birds on the shore are now protected, so avoid disturbing wild life of any kind and assiduously obey any notices you may find regarding your dog. However irritating it may seem, if there is a notice for them to be kept on the lead there is usually a good reason for doing so.

GENERAL TRAINING

Dalmatians are creatures of habit. There is nothing they cannot learn, but they need constant practice. It is a waste of time and effort to instil lessons you are never going to use, so concentrate on those which will fit in with your particular way of life, and work out commands that you can remember and the dog will understand. I have suggested a few here which I have found useful and, no doubt, others will occur to you as time goes by.

"WAIT"

Learnt from the cradle. Practise when you put down a food plate, before you give a tidbit, before you put on a lead, and before you move off for a walk. In this way, young dogs become accustomed to the word in different situations.

Extend this in time to a wider application. Make the dog lie down, take a few steps back telling it to "Wait." Return after a few seconds, with much praise and reward. Practise each day, always in a different place, and then try it with the dog standing. Not so easy, but your Dalmatian has now become used to the word, and you will find instant obedience comes in time.

Train the dog to stay in the car when you open the door, by saying "Wait" very firmly and putting the flat of your hand against the window as you open the door slightly. Bang it back several times loudly until, gradually, you can open it sufficiently to catch hold of the collar. Then make the dog wait for a few minutes before he jumps out. Repeat this ritual whether you are in the garden, the middle of a field, or in a town centre. It is immensely useful and, once trained, dogs will step back as soon as they see your hand on the window and they hear you say "Wait."

"COME HERE"

This command should always be prefaced with the dog's name and taught without difficulty with the use of a little judicious bribery. Lavish praise and a small tidbit will instil the habit. Dalmatians are normally obedient though, like some children, they behave better away from home. They come immediately they are called on outside territory; at home they give it due consideration.

"LEAVE IT"

This is particularly useful when disgusting objects are found on a walk; when a much-

Practise makes perfect, and a regime of fair and consistent training is needed to produce a well-behaved dog.

prized possession is disappearing down the garden; or when your Dalmatian's natural instinct to steal is about to surface. Because it is so easy to laugh when they are being wicked, this is the most difficult lesson to teach a puppy. However, in the case of an adult dog it is a perfect nuisance when this command is not obeyed.

Start at the earliest age possible by putting a toy down in front of the puppy, and holding the puppy back saying "Leave it." After a few seconds, reward the puppy and let him play with the toy. Repeat this at different times in different places with different objects and, once the puppy is old enough to go for walks, be sure that on every occasion you try at least once to incorporate the lesson in some way.

"LIE DOWN"

This is so useful in a variety of situations, particularly if you are in strange territory and you want the dog to settle down quietly. Once again, if the lessons start early they are easy to learn. If your puppy is on a collar and lead, pull down on the lead and gently press the hindquarters towards the ground at the same time. The dog should go down without difficulty and will enjoy the praise and reward that follows. "Lie down" can be followed by "Wait" in due course, and this too can be extremely useful. Remember, however, not to let the dog slip your mind – my grandfather once had to make a six-mile round trip to collect his old Setter.

"ON YOUR BED"

If your Dalmatian has the run of the house and accompanies you to a variety of houses, hotels, etc., as mine do, then you need to be able to send him to his own bed wherever that may be. Again, this is an easy lesson if taught from an early age. In my case it is also a punishment and, if I roar "On your beds", there is a general stampede for the nearest bean bags where they remain until they think I have returned to sanity.

"DON'T JUMP"

This is one of the most difficult. Where do you draw the line between a joyous welcome and an unwelcome onslaught? Again, it must start with early puppyhood, difficult though that is. As the puppy comes towards you, put your hands on his shoulders, saying "Don't jump", and come down to the puppy's level yourself.

It is a lesson which must be learned, for, as your Dalmatian grows older, jumping up at old people or young children can cause accidents, and with quantities of mud added to the clothes of an immaculate stranger, embarrassment to say the least. A sharp tap on the nose with a rolled-up newspaper will often help to enhance the command and, for a really

obstreperous male, you can raise your knee and catch him on the chest, but I would only suggest this as a very last resort.

"ON YOU GO"

There are many occasions when it is very useful to send the dog straight ahead. If you wish to avoid a muddy pond; a picnic party; a group of joggers; somebody on a horse; or a cyclist. It works in most cases, except possibly for a dead rabbit. For my dogs, these commands work well, but your life will dictate other requirements. Without exception, dogs benefit from early training classes. They learn to socialise, and both owners and dogs acquire the rudiments of Obedience, Agility and/or Ringcraft. All this is learned so much better in person than from books.

Particularly in the present political climate, canine obedience is of prime importance and, as has been said, bribery plays an all-important part. Outside influences need to be counteracted, so train each puppy on its own; another dog in the background will prove too much of a distraction. Avoid confrontation unless you are going to win, and never let the dog feel he has the better of you. I have always found there is a strong incentive in constant reward for obedience. In whatever training you undertake, always remember the Dalmatian has a very low boredom threshold, so keep your lessons short and vary the time and location.

HOLIDAY ARRANGEMENTS

There are two ways of handling holidays when you cannot take the dog: either employ someone to live in the house and look after everything, or else find a good kennels.

HOUSE SITTING

House sitting is a growing occupation, and

good people have to be booked well ahead. Look out for advertisements in magazines, and there are also agencies. There is a daily fee, plus food, and a charge for petrol – normally one journey only. There are obvious advantages because your home is also occupied and looked after, and the dog has the comfort of his own home.

KENNELS
Some owners prefer to know that their dogs are safely confined, with no possibility of getting into any sort of trouble, so they must look for a good kennels.

Do not leave this to the last minute and then try to book in at the nearest kennel. If it is any good, it will probably be full. Think ahead, take time to go and see all the local kennels, and ask to be shown round. Notice whether the dogs seem content and quiet, have clean water, adequate bedding, heat lamps, and whether the kennels themselves are clean. You may find the kennels will follow your dog's normal diet but, if not, ask for full details regarding feeding. Enquire at what time the kennels closes down for the night. Your dog is used to being let out last thing at night; some establishments shut at 5pm, and the dog is then left until the following morning. Check on arrangements for exercise and security, and whether there is insurance cover. You will find that they ask you for up-to-date inoculations, and many kennels require a Kennel Cough certificate. There is normally a daily charge which varies according to the location.

THE OLDER DOG
Dalmatians are so young-at-heart that old age comes upon them almost unawares. No grey muzzle gives an early warning, and a faint indication of cataract across a bright eye is often the first sign you have. Suddenly the dog seems fragile, with back legs that have become a little unsteady. You look back, and thirteen or fourteen years have gone by in a flash.

Walks are still the chief delight and these, together with warmth, comfort, love and your company, are what the older Dalmatian needs. Avoid soaking rain and cold winds and, if the weather is really harsh, do not despise a dog coat. You may receive a look of outrage at first but, very quickly, the old dog will begin to welcome it. Warmth is extremely important, and veterans will quickly shiver at sudden drops of temperature, particularly at night. Dampness after a walk must be towelled off and you will find that Vet beds are, yet again, a blessing. Just occasionally, you may find the younger dogs are a bit rough, even bullying, in their behaviour, but they will stop this as soon as you make it plain it is unacceptable.

In old age, your Dalmatian deserves special care and attention.

Photo: Marc Henrie.

Ch. Spring Classic at Apaloosa: A great show dog, pictured in retirement, aged eleven years.

A regular check-up by your vet is never wasted, and he will advise on any treatment or extra vitamins etc., that are needed. You may find that three small meals a day go down rather better than the customary two. Deafness, convenient or otherwise, can also begin to be a problem. When older Dalmatians are asleep, you may find you have to touch a shoulder to attract attention and, when you are on a walk, be sure to keep yourself within sight to avoid agitation.

DEALING WITH DEATH

Dogs die for many reasons, in sickness and in health. Terrible accidents happen. Disease strikes at them in the same way as it does at us, and the most clever vets in the world cannot save them. If illness strikes in extreme old age, do not subject your dog to operations and lengthy treatment. Dogs have great natural dignity. Their pleasure is being with you, taking part in your activities, being able to follow you, and, when their quality of life becomes impaired,

it is no kindness to ask them to live on.

There comes a time where the decision is yours. I am asked so many times – how can you tell? I can only say that if you have the eyes to see, the dogs themselves will tell you. It was Kipling who wrote: "Master, there is no heat in the mid-day sun". A flash of fear crossing a dog's face will often give a clue. Pain is recognisable in a dog just as it is in a human being.

The kindest way for you both is to arrange for the vet to come to the house. If the dog is held safely in your arms, this will avoid all feeling of anxiety or separation, and it is a great comfort afterwards to know that you were there for the dog to the end. The anaesthetic injection takes a split second to work, but it may be a few minutes before you yourself feel the dog has gone. The vet will either leave your Dalmatian for you to bury, or will take the dog away to be cremated and return the ashes to you later. If you prefer, he will simply remove the dog altogether.

You will perhaps choose to bury the dog in your garden, in which case have the grave dug beforehand. It should be two feet deep. Water the bottom well with a full can of strong diluted disinfectant. Lay your dog at the bottom in a comfortable position that you can remember with pleasure, and place flower petals, leaves or grasses across so that no part of the animal can be seen. Replace the earth and, having firmed it down, water the top with another can of strong disinfectant. I have never had a grave disturbed, prepared in this way, and I have been very happy to know that my dogs are still around me.

This is a time of great sadness, but I can only repeat the very comforting words said to me so many years ago, which I have remembered ever since: "A dead dog is not an unhappy dog. The pain is yours, and that is as it should be."

5 *HEALTH CARE*

Keeping your dogs healthy and happy so often depends on a good early-warning system. That is why, when an animal has emptied out, you will find so many committed owners peering, prodding and poking to ensure that nothing untoward has been passed.

The longer you own your Dalmatian the more you will feel able to deal with certain problems, at least in the early stages, and there is always advice to be had from experienced friends. The important thing is to recognise the symptoms for what they are, and to consult the vet without hesitation before the illness escalates and gets out of hand.

FINDING THE RIGHT VET
The relationship you have with your vet is all-important. He or she should be easy to approach and even more to talk to. If you are worried by your vet's attitude towards you or your dog, then however good the practice's reputation, find another. In this day and age it is not necessary for your vet to be a fount of all knowledge on all subjects. As with human medicine, there is an active referral system and, if your dog is seriously ill, a second opinion may be sought from the top authority in that field.

The Dalmatian is a lively active dog, and with the correct care, exercise and diet, it should experience few major health problems.
Photo: Skurray.

Much more important is a vet who will be on good terms with you and your dog; who will be prepared to make house calls when necessary and take time to discuss a problem thoroughly and explain the treatment. Vets are busy people and their time must not be wasted, but they should be prepared to listen if you have a point to make. Look for kind and gentle handling of

the dog, particularly a puppy. Some vets are better equipped than others and appear to offer wider facilities, but sympathetic, gentle handling is, to my mind, more important.

ALTERNATIVE MEDICINE

Alternative medicine, notably homoeopathy and acupuncture, plays an ever-increasing role in animal medicine. Homoeopathy is now widely accepted by the veterinary profession and is offered as an alternative treatment in many traditional practices.

As far as acupuncture is concerned, many of those treating human patients are also happy to take on dogs and horses, and some are now specialising in animal treatment. Your vet will normally be happy to refer you on when this is advisable.

SAMPLES

Even in these days of super-efficient blood tests, the vet will still ask for urine or faeces samples. Needless to say, dogs seem to know instinctively when this is required and either refuse point-blank to oblige or retire instantly to the nearest overgrown swamp.

Collecting a urine sample is the more difficult and I have always found the easiest approach is with the bottom half of an egg-poacher. It is shallow, easily sterilised, has a long handle and is about the right size to fit between the back legs of a bitch, or to be held as appropriate for a dog. Guests to the house need not worry – I have acquired a new one especially for people.

Unco-operative dogs should be taken out first thing in the morning on the lead and walked patiently round the garden until eventually they can hold out no longer. One tip regarding the collection of urine: the sample should not come from the first few drops – only start collecting when the animal is in full flow.

MEDICINE CUPBOARD

Almost without your noticing, your medicine cupboard will gradually evolve. It goes without saying that this should be kept well out of the way of both dogs and children. Taking a look in my own cupboard, I thought you might find some of the items of interest. I have added a note on what they are used for.

Two jersey socks with soft leather soles; packet of strong rubber bands.
(To cover bandaged feet out of doors; plastic freezer bag covers sock in wet weather)
Teething gel.
(Teething puppies)
Antiseptic Cream.
(Used for all sores)
Eterna ear drops.
(Use initially but call vet if problem persists)
Anal thermometer.
(Taking temperature)
Glucose and Complan.
(A liquid protein food for invalids)
Bottom of egg-poacher.
(Collecting urine samples)
Commercial Epsom salts.
(Add to hot water for cleansing)
Liquid Antiseptic.
(Good disinfectant)
Sherley's deodorant tablets.
(For in-season bitches)
Veterinary wound powder.
(Treating open wounds – obtain from vet)
Powdered starch and boracic powder in equal parts.
(Apply to Dally Rash pustules)
Plastic syringes of various sizes.
(To measure medicine accurately; give dose through side of mouth – keep fingers loosely around nose and inject only a little at a time or dog will choke)
Primapore adhesive wound-dressing,

**crepe bandage and fastener, scissors,
lint, cotton wool.**
(For wounded Dalmatians)

TEMPERATURE
The easiest way to take the canine
temperature is to stand the dog beside you.
Shake the thermometer down, apply
Vaseline or spit on the end and insert very
gently into the dog's anus, holding the
hindquarters steady with your other arm.
Talk encouragingly, count up to 60 very
slowly, and then draw the thermometer out
again. This can also be done if the animal is
lying down and you do not wish to disturb
him.

The normal temperature of a dog is
100.5° F, and anything much above or
below that is a matter for concern.
However, if you can take the temperature
without difficulty, it will not only set your
mind at rest but give you sufficient courage
to ring the vet at 4am without
compunction when it is necessary.

TYPICAL DALMATIAN AILMENTS
It is worth bearing in mind that fear is
probably the greatest enemy of all. Pain
frightens animals, and their owners are
frightened for them, so it becomes a vicious
circle. However terrified you are, remaining
calm will do more to help than anything.

There are various troublesome ailments
to which Dalmatians are prone and for
which experience has taught us various
forms of treatment. I have set these down
in the hope you may find them helpful.
However, common sense will tell you that,
if the dog is seriously ill, you must consult
your vet. I have also tried to describe
symptoms of some of the more serious
problems you may encounter, so that you
will recognise them and be able to take
swift action. If you need veterinary
treatment, the earlier the better is a

standard rule.

DALLY RASH
Best described as bumps under the skin,
appearing on the head or body and
occasionally even down the legs. Pustules
often form, headed with pus. The hair
looks rather grey and eventually comes
away leaving pink skin exposed.

This is often attributed to a blood
disorder or over-heating of the blood and
can be greatly helped with a carefully-
balanced diet. Vitamin B, greenleaf and
garlic tablets, should be given daily, plus
chopped parsley or green bean parings cut
up into small pieces. White meat or fish can
be fed in place of red meat or, if on
complete food, try one with a lower protein
level. Piriton tablets (anti-histamine) can be
helpful, and your vet will recommend the
correct dose. Cut down on additives and
vitamins as far as possible.

Postpone bathing or washing the dog,
and do not groom the affected areas.
Sponge any pustules with a light solution of
Epsom salts and warm water, morning and
evening, and apply a mixture of equal parts
of starch and boracic powder. Keep the dog
out of the sun as much as possible and
exercise only when it is cool and shady.
Dally Rash is sometimes mistaken for
mange. However, if mange is suspected,
consult your vet immediately.

BLEEDING TAILS
Dalmatians wag their tails with such
ferocity that some damage may occur. Once
the skin is broken, blood splatters far and
wide; inevitably the dogs lick the wound,
thus opening it out still further.

Initially, soak a towel in iced water and
hold the tail gently in the dripping cloth.
Repeat several times and this will often
work on its own. If not, try applying Friars
Balsam, surgical spirit, or a saline solution.

If the bleeding persists, you are faced with protecting the wound from further damage during healing and from the attention of that all-invasive tongue. Many ways are suggested for protecting the tail: the inner portion of a toilet roll, baking foil, clingfilm, a hair curler, etc. The difficulty lies in finding a means of keeping these in place.

More recently, I have good reports of a very lightweight filament tape which can be bound over a cotton wool dressing. This is sufficiently strong to prevent the tail from being hurt when it wags or hits the furniture, but is light enough to avoid attracting unwanted attention from the dog. The wound can be protected while healing takes place, and it even allows for re-growth of the hair. The threat of amputation is always present, so it is worth making extensive enquiries and trying every alternative.

CAR SICKNESS
This may be caused by nervous tension, or possibly triggered off by a traumatic first journey. Usually, a few days spent quietly at the new home, followed by some short journeys in the car, will sort the matter out. However, there are some Dalmatians who find it much more difficult to settle in the car; as soon as they are inside they tense up, start to salivate, and once the car is in motion they are sick.

The chemist will offer patent travel sickness remedies and the vet can prescribe sedatives, etc., but these tend to make the dog 'dopey'. The following routine is rather long-drawn-out, but you may find it helpful.

Travel sickness can become a habit and, to break this, leave the car alone for two or three days to let the bad memories recede. For the whole of this training period, feed one of the dog's meals in the car each day

and for the first two or three days do no more than that. As soon as the meal is finished, praise the dog warmly and take it out of the car again at once.

For the next stage, put a rug in the back of the car, lift the dog on to it and let him sit there for a few minutes while you talk to him. Lift the dog out at once if there is any sign of salivating so that, with luck, you actually avoid it starting.

When the dog will sit in the car for ten minutes without a problem, shut the door and leave your Dalmatian inside for a short time. If there is no adverse reaction, walk round and get in the driving seat. Run the engine for a few minutes without moving the car at all. Once the dog can tolerate the running engine without distress, drive for a few yards only and stop the car. Praise the dog once more and let it out at once.

This will take about a week, and the time then comes to go for a short drive. Try for a destination not more than five minutes from your house – someone else's garden or a field – somewhere that is a special treat and where the dog can have a run. It is most important that you manage to stop the car before there is any sign of distress, and that there is a treat waiting for the dog as a reward. Keep initial journeys short, be particularly careful going round corners, and keep the speed right down.

Be prepared to go back a stage at the first sign of trouble. However, if you persevere, the nervous tension will disappear and within about three weeks the whole problem should have resolved itself.

WORMS
Garlic given daily provides a safeguard, but nevertheless you will occasionally find evidence of tapeworm (flat white segments) or roundworm (long, thin and wiry) in the faeces. An immediate dose supplied by the vet is required. A bitch to be mated should

be wormed well before she comes into season.

KENNEL COUGH

You hear this as a little dry cough and, although for the healthy animal it is a fairly minor infection, for an old dog or one with respiratory problems it can be dangerous. It is extremely infectious and any animal suffering from it should be kept away from others and should not, under any circumstances, be taken to a show.

Serious cases should be treated by the vet, but normally the main problem is trying to stop the cough. Honey is very popular by the spoonful and many find a proprietary cough preparation, such as Benylin, a great help. Reduce infection as far as you can by changing all bedding etc. on a daily basis.

There is a vaccination for Kennel Cough which is taken by the dog through the nose into the respiratory tract, and provides protection for six months at a time. Many kennels now insist on this, but remember the vaccination only becomes effective after ten days.

FALSE PREGNANCY

All bitches experience the phenomenon of a 'false pregnancy', but to varying degrees. The normal life cycle takes place in a bitch usually twice a year and, if she is mated, the process continues until the puppies are born, reared and weaned. False pregnancies occur, firstly, when the bitch has been mated but no puppies result, in which case the bitch is said to have 'missed'; and, secondly, when no mating has taken place at all. In both cases, the bitch will go through the whole cycle, even to blowing her rib cage and producing milk, sometimes in vast quantities.

The two cases are a little different. Where the bitch has been mated and missed, she will have been fed on especially good food, with the quantity increasing as the time of 'birth' draws nearer. With no puppies to absorb some of her substance, and later take the milk, the physical difficulties can be vast. If at all possible, let nature take its course, but when the case is particularly bad, consult your vet. There are various injections available, but these are never ideal and should be avoided if possible. Reduce the protein in her diet in favour of added carbohydrate, and otherwise treat her in the same way as described below for the unmated bitch.

When the bitch, although not mated, has a tremendous reaction after her season (usually around the 63rd day from when she would have been mated), becoming 'broody' and soulful, making nests, and producing milk, then you can do some things to help, but mostly you just have to live through it.

If you know from past experience that your Dalmatian bitch is going to suffer from this problem, reduce the protein in her diet immediately she comes into season, and continue until she would have weaned her puppies. Do this gradually or she will lose condition, but eventually she can have one-third of her normal meat ration replaced with biscuit soaked in broth.

Add two raspberry leaf tablets to the bitch's food twice a day from day 1 of the season, and increase this to four tablets twice a day from when her puppies would have been born. Continue until the puppies would have been weaned, i.e. a total of 17 weeks. In addition, add three garlic and three greenleaf tablets to her food each morning, plus about one tablespoonful of either raw parsley or grated carrot. Some people add a pinch of Epsom salts to each meal.

Hard exercise is essential, with longer walks than usual, and no opportunity to hide in corners and become sentimental. Try and take her with you most of the time and 'jolly' her along. It is important to watch for mastitis (hard swelling in the teat area, usually with red inflammation) and any sign of this should be treated at once with Germolene or similar. If, in spite of your efforts, mastitis occurs, take her straight to the vet for antibiotics, or it can escalate into a real problem.

Milk may escape from the teats and run down to make damp patches on the bedding etc., and some bitches lick their teats to stimulate the milk. Unpleasant tasting preparations are sold to combat this. One good one comes in an ozone-friendly aerosol, but you will find it easier to spray on to cotton wool and then apply.

The bitch can also become very swollen behind, and often has a pronounced scent attractive to male dogs. She may regurgitate food at a later stage, as though for feeding puppies, and she will become very protective and even aggressive about an area where she imagines she has put her puppies. She is not being naughty, so please do not scold or punish her. Remember, she is feeling wretched and cannot understand what is happening to her.

Remove any soft, squeaky toys at this time as they can become puppy substitutes and prolong the false pregnancy. Other dogs in the house seem to understand, and refrain from retaliating if she reprimands them for inadvertently sitting on her non-existent puppies. When banished from her sofa at these times, my older bitch wears an expression of resigned indignation.

ANAESTHETICS AND ALLERGY TO INJECTIONS
It has been found that Dalmatians can be peculiarly sensitive to general anaesthetics. It is worth discussing this with your vet before the dog undergoes an operation, as they appear to have a higher vagal tone or a lower pain threshold, which leads to a pronounced reflex slowing of the heart. It has been suggested that atropine should be given routinely as a pre-medication to Dalmatians.

POST-OPERATIVE TREATMENT
Let us say your dog has had an operation and you are to collect it from the vet. Put a strong sheet in the car, with a Vet bed on it where the dog can lie. When you arrive home you will avoid hurting the dog if you carry it in on the sheet. Two people are, of course, ideal but if you are on your own you will find it is easier to gather up all four corners and carry the dog on your back.

Keep the sheet across the bottom of the bed for the time being in case you need to carry the dog outside to be clean. However, most Dalmatians are very resilient and stagger to their feet in a remarkably short space of time.

Dehydration is the first enemy. If the dog will not drink at all, crush some ice cubes in a cloth and slip an ice sliver under the side of the lip, just a small piece at a time. It will melt and trickle down your Dalmatian's throat without fear of choking. You can make up some ice cubes with glucose added and use those in the same way.

Though unlikely to have an appetite, the dog will sometimes welcome white of egg beaten up very stiffly, again with a little glucose, fed from your fingers. It gives a lining to the stomach and can prevent sickness. Liquid food-substitutes, available from the chemist, will often prove tempting and are very easily digested. Brands Essence is full of goodness, boiled chicken is easy to digest and a little rabbit added makes it less bland. Farex (now sometimes called children's rice), Ready Brek or similar cereal and rice pudding are all good standbys.

While recuperating dogs have little appetite, so everything you offer should have maximum food value, but sometimes in desperation you will be reduced to trying everything in the cupboard, from the cat's food to Marmite sandwiches.

You may prefer to sleep downstairs with your Dalmatian for the first night or so. If the dog seems restless, try and encourage him to lie on the other side. Dogs naturally change sides frequently, and are uncomfortable unless they can do so.

INTERDIGITAL CYSTS

This is another name for cysts between the toes. They look like small boils or sheep ticks, and are extremely painful. If they occur between July and September, the problem is usually due to grass seeds. In the early stages you can treat this yourself, sometimes with success.

Three times a day, morning, afternoon and evening, after exercise, soak the affected feet in hot water with a good handful of Epsom salts added. The water should be as hot as your hand can bear. After soaking for about ten minutes, dry each foot very gently, always on a clean towel. At night, after the last wash, apply a little Germolene to each boil, using a cotton wool bud, a new one for each boil. In addition, get the strongest Vitamin B tablets available from the chemist, and give four times the suggested dose three times a day.

Once you get rid of the cysts you may be disappointed to find that sometimes they re-appear a few weeks later. Just start the treatment again, and with patience you will find that eventually they stop altogether. If the condition does not improve, you will need to consult your vet.

URIC ACID AND KIDNEY PROBLEMS

Kidneys act as filters. Blood containing waste products passes through them and is purified, and the by-products are filtered out and manufactured into urine which is later excreted. Alone of all mammals, Dalmatians (together with human beings and apes) have a high uric acid content in their urine, coupled with a low percentage of allantoin. This can lead to uric acid crystals forming which, in turn, result in kidney stones.

Symptoms of kidney or uric acid problems are excessive drinking: frequent urination; obvious difficulty and pain while urinating; presence of blood in urine; dog assuming hunched-up position obviously due to pain.

Immediate veterinary attention is needed to deal with the infection. Medicines are available, but I prefer herbal remedies where possible. Prostate disease can present in a similar way. An obstructed urethra needs immediate surgery. As far as diet is concerned, it is sometimes recommended that red meat be replaced by white, and the overall protein content reduced in favour of added carbohydrate and vegetable. Some people even advocate a vegetarian diet. In my own experience, greenleaf and garlic tablets given daily, with small quantities of chopped parsley and grated raw carrot, help to keep the dogs clear of trouble.

INCONTINENCE

This is a problem which comes to a great many dogs and bitches in later years, and is caused when the muscles which control the bowel and bladder relax, causing unconscious leakage. As far as the bowels are concerned, I have not found this too much of a problem. If the dog is regularly exercised, mistakes will not be made too often and can be removed fairly easily, but do remember that these happen without the dog's knowledge. There is no point in punishment or pointing out the error of your Dalmatian's ways. This will merely cause the dog additional distress and worry.

The loss of urine is much more of a problem, not least because of the unpleasant smell. However, drugs are available which can alleviate the problem. Stilbaestrol for bitches and Propalin syrup for dogs or bitches can both be recommended, and a visit to the vet will produce the correct advice. It will certainly help if the dog is not overweight, and if he is taken out last thing at night and before being left alone. Once again, remember this is happening without the knowledge of the dog and cannot be controlled voluntarily.

ENTROPION

This problem seems to have subsided in our breed to a certain extent, but you should still be watchful. If there is a marked staining under the eye and you notice a runny discharge, check immediately with the vet.

Entropion is caused when the eyelid turns inwards and the eyelashes thus brush against the eye, causing ulceration with much pain and discomfort. An operation will correct the fault but these dogs should not be shown or bred.

EPILEPSY

The genetic factor of epilepsy is one which must be addressed with great care by the breeder. I am indebted to Janet Harding for the excellent notes she wrote for me when I was researching this subject previously and, with her permission, I am quoting from them now.

"Epileptic fits can be very frightening for owners, and a few lines on how to recognise that your dog is having a fit, what may happen, and how to help your dog, may be useful.

"Epilepsy is a severe nervous disorder affecting the central nervous system. It may result from a head injury, and can occur when scar tissue is formed on the brain. Puppies can 'fit' when getting their permanent teeth at about two to six months, or when heavily infested with round or tapeworm, but these are not epileptic fits, and after teething or worming they often disappear.

"Attacks of epilepsy start without warning. The animal falls to the ground unconscious and has convulsions. The limbs can be held stiffly, and sometimes move as if the animal is galloping. The animal champs its jaws, often salivates heavily; the eyes may be fixed and staring, or the eyeballs may roll. The pupils are dilated. The rectum and bladder usually evacuate involuntarily. These fits normally last between one and two minutes, and generally occur between the ages of one and three years.

"*Warning:* Do not touch the dog around the mouth during a fit, as it may bite you accidentally. After consciousness returns, the dog should be placed in a quiet, dark room, away from other animals on a blanket or rug, and allowed time to recover, as the whole experience is very exhausting for the dog. Comfort the animal with a gentle voice, calling its name. Keep the curtains drawn, have absolute quiet and in particular ensure that the television is turned off. Dogs can react very badly to the light coming from the screen.

"Epileptic fits can be diagnosed by an EEG, assessed and kept under control by your veterinary surgeon, who will monitor the progress and treat the condition with tablets such as Largactol or Mysaline."

BLOAT OR GASTRIC TORSION

Opinions exist in plenty, but no definitive reason has yet been established for this condition. Symptoms are: acute discomfort after a meal; restlessness; repeated retching; the dog showing signs of trouble with breathing and of being in shock. Sometimes they seek relief by lying in wet grass and salivating, even digging holes in the garden and hiding in them. Generally, there is erratic behaviour coupled with great distress. The next sign is of a distended stomach and, by then, you must immediately contact your vet. There is no time to be lost, as in many cases you have only 30 minutes before treatment will be too late.

Because the sequence of events is not yet properly understood, it is difficult to offer anything other than a commonsense view of avoiding the problem. Feed two or even three small meals a day rather than one large one; always soak any form of biscuit; insist on adequate rest after each meal and ensure good daily exercise. Care should be taken that food is at blood heat, neither straight from the fridge nor the saucepan. Avoid feeding when the dog is excessively tired – delay the meal if necessary.

Checking your dog throughout his life will become second nature for many reasons, none more important than bloat. Seek help irrespective of whether it is day or night; all veterinary practices have a 24-hour service and this is the time to use it.

HIP DYSPLASIA

Hip Dysplasia is an hereditary disease. It is caused by the ball and socket joint of the hip not fitting properly, in severe cases inhibiting the free movement of the dog. Slight cases cause little discomfort, but for those severely affected an operation will be necessary. Although basically an hereditary fault, poor rearing, unwise over-exercise at too young an age, or over-feeding can exacerbate the problem without necessarily causing it in the first place.

The only sure method of diagnosis is an X-ray and the results are shown in a points system. The best score is 0 and the worst is 106, these being made up of the two hips totalled together, i.e. if you score two on one side and three on the other your overall hip score is five. In the UK a dog can be scored from the age of 12 months.

In the US, the Orthopaedic Foundation for Animals (OFA) uses the following grades in reporting the character of hip joints:

1. Excellent conformation: Superior hip joint conformation as compared with other individuals of the same breed and age.
2. Good conformation: Well-formed hip conformation as compared with other individuals of the same breed and age.
3. Fair Conformation: Minor irregularities of hip joint conformation as compared with other individuals of the same breed and age.

The following categories are not eligible for an OFA breed number:

4. Borderline conformation: Marginal hip joint conformation of indeterminate status with respect to hip dysplasia at this time. A repeat study is recommended in 6-8 months.
5. Mild hip dysplasia: Radiographic evidence of minor dysplastic changes in hip joints.
6. Moderate hip dysplasia: Well-defined radiographic evidence of dysplastic changes in the hip joints.
7. Severe hip dysplasia: Radiographic evidence of marked dysplastic changes of the hip joints.

Breeders are encouraged to have their stock X-rayed so that no animal knowingly carries hip dysplasia and is the means of passing it on. The dog is placed on its back with both hind legs pulled as far as possible down the table, the legs kept parallel to each other and the femurs rotated inwards. Because the dog must be kept absolutely still, and for safety regulations, it is usually necessary to give a light anaesthetic. For this reason, some owners wait until an anaesthetic is otherwise necessary before having their dogs X-rayed.

In the USA, the Dalmatian Club of America research committee report, *Hip Dysplasia in Dalmatians* by Raymond F. Fitzsimmons, expresses some concern at the rise in percentage terms among those Dalmatians tested which are affected by HD. The virtual explosion in breeding over the past few years will, of course, increase this percentage but for the time being the view taken, as in the UK, is that breeders must remain vigilant to avoid any increase in the problem.

Mr Fitzsimmons said: "Dysplasia is out there. The genes that cause it are in our gene pool, although not widespread. We must guard against it as we must guard against our more serious plagues of the moment. Let's not make Dysplasia a bigger problem than it now is."

PYOMETRA
Pyometra is a collection of pus in the uterus of unspayed and often elderly bitches. The pyometra may be 'open', when pus discharges through the vulva, or 'closed', when the pus is contained within the bitch's uterus. First signs of an impending pyometra are often a greatly increased thirst and frequent licking of the vulva, together with listlessness, a raised temperature and vomiting. If veterinary help is obtained in the very early stages the pyometra can very occasionally be averted with antibiotics, but more usually the only cure is an ovario-hysterectomy. Bitches usually respond well once the source of infection has been removed.

NEUTERING
First of all, forget the myths which exist regarding the neutering of both dogs and bitches. Neutering does not make Dalmatians fat, woolly-haired or less affectionate. By the same token, castration will not transform a fighting dog into a good-tempered animal, nor does a litter of puppies cure nervousness in a bitch. The puppies merely inherit the temperament problems of their parents.

As far as dogs are concerned, we have all witnessed the rapidly disappearing hindquarters of an entire male dog following the scent of an in-season bitch. Such bitches have to be exercised, and whether or not this is done at anti-social hours, they still leave their scent. Apart from removing the sexual interest, castration also discourages the urge to wander off, though a Dalmatian's curiosity is not solely sex-orientated by any means.

A bitch will be attractive to a dog from about the fifth day of her season and, from the tenth day onwards, will definitely be on the look-out for a male admirer. An owner will find great difficulty in exercising the bitch at this time, keeping her happy and at the same time out of the way of male dogs. Unless heavy precautions are taken, the bitch will find a way of passing a message down the grapevine and in no time an unwanted queue will be forming at the gate. The bitch is distressed if a false pregnancy ensues and, in later life, there is always the danger of a pyometra.

For the dog it is a small operation and can be carried out at any time from nine months onwards, or as soon as maturity is complete. Only a day or so will be needed for recuperation, and ten days later the stitches can come out.

Bitches should be spayed only after their first season, which normally occurs when they are six to eight months old. Again, they recover almost immediately and will alarm you by charging off after a rabbit, stitches or no stitches. The latter can be taken out after ten to 14 days.

I must add that spaying does not stop the various signs of coming into season temperamentally, nor does castration necessarily stop a dog instinctively mounting a bitch. I have a dear neutered 12-year-old dog, whose life is made hideous by his great-grand-daughter who delights to torment him at such times. I now keep them separated, not only for his peace of mind but my own as well. Provided you have no plans to breed a litter of puppies, then there is every advantage in giving neutering serious consideration.

BREAKDOWN OF THE IMMUNE SYSTEM

As with human disease, we are beginning to hear more and more of problems being caused by the breakdown of the immune system. Those who have turned to alternative medicine may already have come across Peruvian Pine, and might like to investigate this further. The official name is Uncaria Tomentosa. It is formed from the inner bark of the vine with thorns that resemble the claws of a cat, hence it is also known as Cat's Claw.

At present, this substance is available only through herbal specialists and veterinary practices, but the catalogue of help it can give is very widespread.

ECLAMPSIA

This is dealt with in greater detail in Chapter Twelve. Briefly, it is a condition caused in a bitch due to excessive loss of calcium when feeding a litter. It causes great distress to the bitch, amounting in extreme cases almost to insanity, and it is necessary to rectify the matter immediately.

I have found the use of Collo Cal D to be extremely helpful, and this can be given right through pregnancy and on until the puppies are fully weaned. Failing that, in severe cases, your vet will need to give an immediate injection of calcium.

OSTEOARTHRITIS

Stiffening joints and lameness are more common in the older dog but can appear at any age. Osteoarthritis occurs when the normal 'healthy' cartilage is eroded and the synovial fluid which lubricates the joint thins out, resulting in a loss of mobility. Movement is also restricted by swelling of the joints. These factors combine to cause the dog discomfort and pain.

A warm, comfortable bed and keeping the dog as dry as possible helps with minor cases, but eventually treatment will be necessary. Conventional treatment needs to be administered continuously and can only reduce the swelling and pain of affected joints. However, a revolutionary advance has been made with the use of Cartrophen Vet in the treatment for osteoarthritis and musculoskeletal disease in dogs, which relieves pain and lameness and treats the underlying disease processes, not just the symptoms.

Treatment is similar to vaccination, with a course of four weekly doses. This is followed by booster applications at intervals of about one year, although this varies between individual cases. Most dogs are very quick to respond to the initial course with an increase in activity and general well-being.

PANCREATITIS

Dr Margaret Topping was born in Wales and, with her husband, emigrated to New Zealand where she lived until her tragic death in a car accident in 1983. She was a true and knowledgeable friend to the Dalmatian world, and her contribution to our understanding of pancreatitis in the Dalmatian is reproduced overleaf.

LIVING WITH PANCREATITIS
by **G. Margaret Topping**

"The pancreas is a V-shaped gland which lies in the first loop of the small intestine as it leaves the stomach and adjacent to the liver. It has two or three ducts (or tubes) which open into the duodenum, beside the bile duct.

It has two main functions:

1) It produces digestive enzymes which are passed into the small intestine and which digest and break down protein and fat to a form which can be absorbed by the lining of the digestive tract lower down.

2) The pancreas also contains small islands of cells which produce insulin, which is essential for carbohydrate metabolism. Lack of insulin leads to diabetes.

The underlying causes of pancreatic disease in the majority of cases are unknown. In a few cases Arecoline dosing is blamed, in others damage follows an accident. However it is brought about, damage to the glands causes enzymes to leak out and 'digest' the surrounding tissues – causing varying amounts of cell destruction in the gland itself, the liver, the small intestine and their supporting tissues.

This is the acute stage of the disease and it may last 36-48 hours or so. The dog is in severe pain and characteristically will not lie down. If he does, he supports himself so that his abdomen does not touch the ground. In severe cases, shock is intense. In others, the acute stage passes and is put down to a 'tummy bug' or is hardly noticed at all.

What happens next varies from case to case. Some appear to heal sufficiently for normal function to return. In others, a mild chronic state exists, with or without periodic relapses, and is controlled by diet and enzyme therapy. In more severe cases, usually seen in the older dog, treatment is more difficult and needs to be continued for life.

The result of damage to the pancreas is a reduction in the digestive enzymes, so that although food is eaten it is not digested and cannot be assimilated. Weight loss and eventual starvation occur. Because of failure of fat digestion the stools are often bulky, offensive and greyish.

At this stage, I will relate 'Smudge's' case history as we experienced it. He is now nearly 11 years old. The first sign of trouble was the development of acute abdominal pain, lasting about 36 hours, but which was intermittent in character. He was very miserable, shivering, and I thought might have a gastric torsion (bloat) but he was not vomiting and nothing was found of note when we visited our vet – I think it was during an intermission in the pain. We were very thankful when he returned to normal in a day or two.

The next thing which attracted our attention was completely out of character. He began putting his feet up on the bench and stealing food. Now, no-one has stolen anything in our kitchen since 'Nellie' left us. Smudge came in for some severe words! The thieving continued, so I decided he was hungry and increased the amount of his food. This made no difference, things like loaves of bread and even topside steak disappeared if within reach. But, in spite of increased amounts of his usual mixed diet and adding extra biscuit during the day, he became more and more ravenous and lethargic. He lay on the mat under the kitchen table most of the day and we noticed a steady loss of weight. First his ribs showed, then his face fell in and his spine showed up sharply along his back.

The vet took blood samples which were sent to the laboratory and full blood counts, blood urea, blood sugar and serum amylase levels were requested. A urine sample was also sent. A provisional diagnosis of pancreatitis was made and this was confirmed by the lab results a day or two later – both the serum amylase and the blood sugar readings were markedly increased.

Treatment was started at once and consisted of frequent small, easily digestible meals, with the addition of artificial enzymes every time the dog was fed. We experimented with the diet but, a fortnight before Christmas, things were desperate and it appeared we would have to put Smudge down. However, we had a great deal of help from Joyce and David Renaud, who had experienced pancreatitis in one of their Dobermans, and with their help we made radical changes and drew up the following diet sheet to which we adhered strictly.

Breakfast
8oz cooked fish or finely chopped lean raw beef; 4oz (three heaped tablespoonfuls) of cooked rice; One tablespoonful cottage cheese (plain) moistened with a little fish stock or vegetable water; Two Cotazyme-B tablets (another excellent preparation is Combizym Compositum).

Lunch
A dish of porridge made with water moistened with reconstituted Anchor skimmed milk powder; Two slices white toast (spread with Marmite some days); One Cotazyme-B tablet.

Dinner
8oz finely chopped lean raw beef; 4oz cooked macaroni; One tablespoonful cottage cheese; Two Cotazyme-B tablets, moistened as before.
I also give at this meal two garlic and kelp tablets, two vetzymes plus a water-soluble vitamin capsule (Pluravite) twice a week – or three Vi-Sorbits a day. In addition, as we have had severe coat problems, he is now having one dessertspoonful of coconut oil a

day. This can be replaced by corn oil. This meal is followed by a drink of reconstituted skimmed milk.

Supper
3-4 tablespoonfuls of baby rice mixed with reconstituted skimmed milk; One Cotazyme-B tablet.
In other words, a diet of low fat (four per cent maximum), low-fibre, high-protein, easily digestible carbohydrate in frequent, low-volume feeds.

Within ten days of starting this routine a weight gain was obvious, and it continued until Smudge looked reasonably covered, but not fat. As well as gaining sufficient weight, he also became less lethargic and once again began to quarter the slopes of Mangere Mountain looking for rabbits. He is a happy old dog, and all the hard work in keeping him in good health has been worthwhile. He is still on the same diet. If he does catch a rabbit or scavenge any tasty morsel, he will pay for it, so he has an extra pill or two when he gets home.

Finally, a few points. If your dog is eating well and yet losing weight steadily, do not hesitate to ask your vet to check for this condition. Remember that a dog, once diagnosed as a case of pancreatitis, must never again be purged with Arecoline. Droncit does not affect the gland and can be used quite safely.

Until you have stabilised the dog on a diet, it will be difficult, depressing and worrying. Resist the temptation to 'put him out of his misery'. That step is rarely necessary if you are prepared to make a real effort. If you do succeed, you will need to be vigilant and watch in case he relapses. Keeping him fairly slim will be to his advantage."

6 THE BREED STANDARDS

You may well ask what is a Standard? Why do we have them and how do we work to them? Conversely, I would enquire as to why you want a pedigree dog? Presumably, because you admire its appearance and find its temperament appealing.

But, having chosen a Dalmatian, what if you found that your puppy grew sizes bigger like a Great Dane, or smaller like a Fox Terrier? Suppose the overall shape was more that of a Bedlington or Whippet, and blotches of varying colours replaced those unique spots? How would you feel then?

In the UK 186 breeds are registered; in the USA 134; and, under the FCI (the Fédération Cynologique Internationale), 342 breeds (of which ten are provisional). This vast number of breeds are all different, all easily-recognisable, with their own special features and characteristics. It goes without saying that in each person's eyes his or her own dog is glorious, but unless breeders have an established pattern of perfection before them, differences will creep in and the dogs will become virtually unrecognisable. Eliminating genetic faults is of equal importance, together with overcoming any physical defects – particularly those which cause pain.

Every breeder should read the Standard point by point, drawing in imagination the picture of a perfect Dalmatian. The Standard should be what they are striving for in their breeding programmes, and should be behind every choice of breeding stock.

Judges, carrying out the same exercise, read the Standard, seeing in their mind's eye the perfect animal. When they view the dogs in the ring, they judge them against that Standard and, therefore, the Dalmatian that goes up at the end of the day is not necessarily the one that looks the best in the ring; it is the best set against the Standard.

This also answers the age-old question on how a judge can arrive at a decision when adjudicating between a Rottweiler and a Chihuahua. Unless the judge is to make a complete fool of himself, I would suggest only by going back to the Standard in each and every case.

Those who hold the Dalmatian dear long ago concluded that only by closely following the Standard could we retain those characteristics which, apart from keeping our breed different from all others, render some individual dogs paragons among their peers. The ultimate compliment was paid to the Dalmatian recently when an eminent author wrote: "It is almost impossible to mongrelise your breed – you see any signs immediately."

The perfect dog has yet to be born, but photographs in this book picture Dalmatians which invite close comparison with the Standard. Bear in mind, however, that it is generally accepted that there is no dog more difficult to breed than a good Dalmatian. We ask for correct structure, size, movement, pigmentation and temperament and, finally, we are satisfied only with beautifully-placed spots. We demand the impossible and achieve it rarely.

Read the Standards with care and common sense, always bearing in mind the past, present and future use of the dog. You cannot take one aspect in isolation from the rest; judges only display their ignorance when they pick out a single fault and weigh it with undue severity against otherwise overall excellence.

MAKE AND SHAPE

Encompassing, as it does, the complete dog, the phrase 'good make and shape' should be used only with the greatest discretion. Equally you could say 'well-balanced' – the one indicates the other.

Because this is a structural judgement, a beautiful head is a prerequisite. It includes correct placement of the ears and eyes; proper definition of stop; a length of muzzle complementing that of the forehead, which should also have sufficient breadth between the ears; no throatiness or wrinkle; and a correct 'bite'. The head should sit proudly on an elegant, slightly-arched neck which, in turn, meets a well laid shoulder.

We know that the spine controls movement, so the back must be neither too long nor too short, but of the correct length, thus betraying no inherent weakness. It must be level from behind the shoulder – in dog parlance exhibiting a 'straight topline'.

The Standard calls for the brisket to reach the point of the elbow and for there to be sensible space between the two front legs. In both instances, common sense dictates this is necessary to allow space for the heart to operate adequately, with plenty of room for puppies in a brood bitch.

The correct lay of shoulder ensures that the front legs can swing forward without hindrance to 'take up the ground'; equally, a good bend of stifle, second thigh and strong pastern, will ensure the hind legs provide the necessary driving power to send the Dalmatian forward with a long, powerful, sweeping step carried by round, tight feet, protected by their thick, tough pads.

A correctly-set tail will flow straight out as an integral part of the spine, with a slight upward curve at the end. A tail set on too high or too low will tend to come over the top of the dog's back, which is unattractive and considered to be a serious fault. At this juncture, should we question why this high tail has materialised? Historical illustrations of Dalmatian-type hounds before they were brought to England, picture, almost without exception, an animal with a straight or slightly curving tail. It was not until the coaching pictures of the 18th century that the high tail was seen and, again employing common sense, can we suggest a reason for this?

The coaching fraternity was then on the lookout for a dog possessing feet and legs sufficiently strong to follow the coaches for a distance of up to 30 miles without breaking down. The Dalmatian was the first and only dog to match this requirement, but the coaches themselves had not been built with dogs in mind. Dalmatians are far from stupid, and would quickly have found they needed to anticipate the height of the axle in order to run comfortably and avoid injury. It is not beyond reason to suppose their tails may well have been used to gauge this distance, adopting a high stance as a result.

From the owners' point of view, this would have been an advantage, not only in protecting their coach dogs from injury, but also enhancing the smartness of the equipage. They would have appreciated a coach dog with a long, straight tail no more than an undocked carriage horse; had the Dalmatian not chosen to tuck it up out of the way, is it possible that ours would have ended up as a docked breed?

The scarcity of pictures, or any mention in period novels and books of Dalmatians actually following carriages, indicates that it was by no means a universally adopted practice and, with the advent of the motor-car, it ceased almost entirely. Thus, to our benefit, the high tail so popular at that time was never deeply imprinted on the breed and, with careful breeding and perseverance, it can be eradicated from lines where it still exists. Breeders should not forget, however, that this is a strong genetic fault, and one to avoid in their breeding programmes.

PIGMENTATION

The Dalmatian is a pigmented breed and, as such, the colour is all-important. The white should be dazzling, the best showing a glint of silver in the sunshine. The black should be an intense, shining black with no hint of bronzing or greyness. The liver colour should be a deep, medium-rich liver brown, not wishy-washy, and not so dark that it is difficult to distinguish between that and a poor black. There is no more experienced Dalmatian judge than Mrs Phyllis Piper, and her dictum has always

been: "When looking across a show ring, you must be able to distinguish between a liver and a black immediately, without difficulty or hesitation."

Eye rims and noses can be affected by incomplete pigmentation and, although this is a cosmetic point, it does spoil the overall look of the head. However, both these areas do continue to colour up over the years and an experienced breeder can usually tell if this will happen or not. Certainly, my own first dog was penalised in the ring for an incomplete nose, which finally went over totally at the age of seven. Pigmentation will continue to improve in a maturing puppy, but the reverse can happen if the youngster is badly or inadequately fed.

Into this category comes eye colour and, although this too might be called cosmetic, it certainly does make a great difference to the beautiful, typical expression we all admire. In a black spotted dog, a really dark brown/black eye is preferred and, in the liver, an eye the colour of sweet sherry. The American Standard admits one or two blue eyes, and here we beg to differ strongly. It is not that blue is unattractive, merely that it destroys this typical melting expression. The coldness of a blue eye does not sit well in a Dalmatian head.

MARKINGS

Not content with achieving perfect make and shape and beautiful pigmentation, a spotted dog must have attractive markings to be considered a really good specimen. Pity the poor breeder who must wait until the puppies are ten days old or so before the spots start coming through. Too many, too few, wrongly-placed with unsightly spaces – all these can turn a potential champion into a lovely pet by a fluke of fate.

It is no matter to the Dalmatian, who will

be both valued and loved, but there are no bounds to the excitement of a breeder who sees a potentially promising puppy also exhibiting good spotting. However, there is yet another trick up the sleeve of fate. Secondary spotting can come along at any time up to six or eight months of age, or even later, and put a whole range of tick marks right where they are least required.

TEMPERAMENT

The final agony to the breeder is to find that the Dalmatian, perfect in all other respects, is either shy, aggressive, or simply does not enjoy being exhibited. The first two are by far the most serious. Some breeders shut their eyes to poor temperament because of the beauty of the Dalmatian concerned, but they do the breed and their own line a total disservice. An aggressive or nervous stud dog spreads those genes right through any litters he sires. The same applies to a bitch and, in addition, she will be passing those same flaws through to the puppies as she rears the litter.

As for a dog unhappy in the show ring, this is of less moment, disappointing though it is to the breeder or owner who will not have the fun of exhibiting a lovely Dalmatian and will deprive breed lovers of seeing it in the ring. However, there is no sight more unhappy than that of a miserable Dalmatian being forced to appear in the ring against its will.

BREED STANDARDS

There are many Breed Standards, but I am going to concentrate on three: the Kennel Club Standard for the UK which was last published in 1994; the American Kennel Club Standard of 1992 (AKC); and the Fédération Cynologique Internationale of 1994 (FCI).

THE FIRST STANDARD, 1882

In addition to the three mentioned above, I thought the original Standard, which was produced in 1882 by Mr Vero Shaw, BA, might be of interest. I am indebted to the Kennel Club Library for finding this for me in *The Illustrated Book of the Dog*, and I quote from it:

The **Head** of the Dalmatian should be wide and flat, blunt at the muzzle, and tight-lipped; nose black.

Ears rather small, V-shaped, and very fine. If these are well spotted, great beauty is added to the dog's appearance.

Eyes dark, and inclined to be small.

Neck arched and light, tapering on to powerful and sloping shoulders.

Chest deep, and rather broad.

Body round in ribs, and well ribbed up behind.

Fore legs straight and very muscular; plenty of bone is essential in this breed, so as to enable a dog to stand the wear and tear he has to encounter on the hard roads he is compelled to traverse.

Feet round, with the toes arched and well split up; pads round, firm, and elastic.

Hind legs muscular, with clean hocks placed near the ground, as in the Bull-dog.

Tail tapering from the root, and carried as a Pointer's: this must be well spotted.

Colour and Markings: Well spotted all over with either black or liver-coloured spots, or both. These should not intermingle, and should be of the size of a sixpence to a halfpenny.

Coat is short, close, and fine.

General appearance is that of a strong muscular dog, capable of enduring considerable fatigue, and possessing a fair amount of speed.

The scale of points by which these dogs should be judged is as follows:

General appearance	10
Colour, markings, and coat	25
Neck, chest, and body	5
Head, including ears and eyes	5
Legs, feet, and tail	5
Total	**50**

In 1994, the UK Kennel Club issued its current Standard which is reproduced below, and you will be interested to note how few changes have been made in the intervening years.

The Standard is preceded by three drawings which I hope will add to your interest. Firstly, an outline drawing of a well-bred Dalmatian with the major points labelled. Secondly, with the skin removed, showing the important muscles below. Thirdly, the skeleton underneath which supports the muscles.

Unless the dog has the correct bone structure covered with the appropriate muscles, it will not look right and, even more important, it will not be able to move correctly and sustain its movement, as required in the Standard.

STRUCTURE OF THE DALMATIAN
Drawings Peter Aldenhoven.

Points of Anatomy

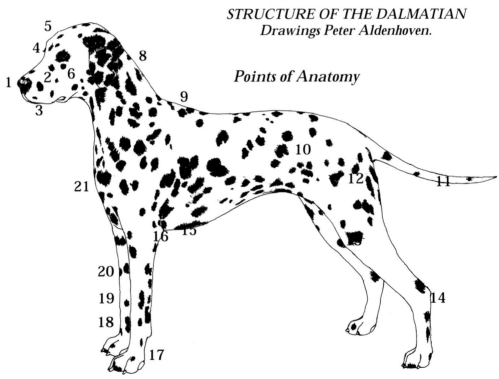

1. Nose	8. Arch	15. Brisket
2. Muzzle	9. Withers	16. Elbow
3. Lips	10. Loin	17. Foot
4. Stop	11. Tail.	18. Pastern
5. Forehead	12. Rump	19. Knee
6. Cheek	13. Stifle	20. Forearm
7. Ear	14. Hock	21. Chest

The muscular system.

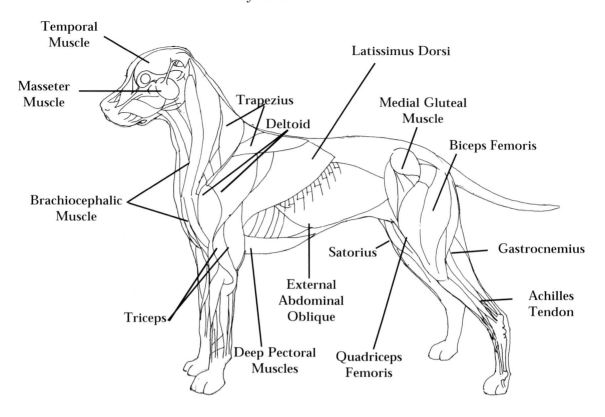

Temporal Muscle

Masseter Muscle

Brachiocephalic Muscle

Triceps

Trapezius

Deltoid

Latissimus Dorsi

Medial Gluteal Muscle

Biceps Femoris

Satorius

External Abdominal Oblique

Deep Pectoral Muscles

Quadriceps Femoris

Gastrocnemius

Achilles Tendon

The skeletal system.

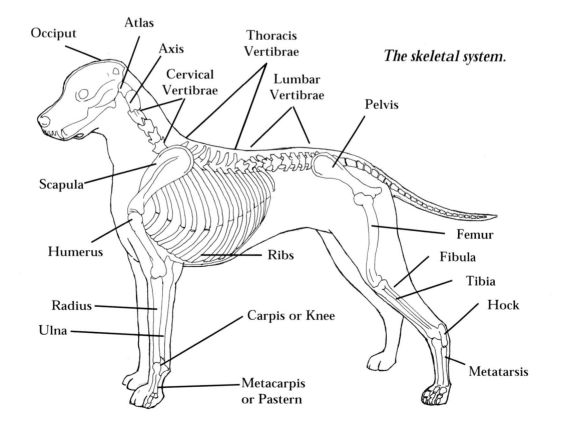

Occiput

Atlas

Axis

Cervical Vertibrae

Thoracis Vertibrae

Lumbar Vertibrae

Pelvis

Scapula

Humerus

Radius

Ulna

Ribs

Carpis or Knee

Metacarpis or Pastern

Femur

Fibula

Tibia

Hock

Metatarsis

UK KENNEL CLUB STANDARD 1994

General Appearance: A distinctively spotted dog, balanced, strong, muscular, active dog. Symmetrical in outline, free from coarseness and lumber.

Characteristics: A carriage dog of good demeanour, capable of great endurance and a fair turn of speed.

Temperament: Outgoing and friendly, not shy or hesitant, free from nervousness and aggression.

Head and Skull: Of fair length, skull flat, reasonably broad between ears, moderately well defined in front of ears. Moderate amount of stop. Entirely free from wrinkle. Muzzle long, powerful never snipey; lips clean, fitting jaw moderately closely. Nose in black spotted variety always black, in liver spotted variety always brown.

Eyes: Set moderately well apart, medium size, round, bright and sparkling, with intelligent expression. Colour, dark in black spotted, amber in liver spotted. Eye rims preferably completely black in black spotted, and liver brown in liver spotted.

Ears: Set on rather high, moderate size, rather wide at base, gradually tapering to rounded point. Fine in texture, carried close to head. Marking well broken up, preferably spotted.

Mouth: Jaws strong, with a perfect, regular and complete scissor bite, i.e. the upper teeth closely overlapping the lower teeth and set square to the jaws.

Neck: Fairly long, nicely arched, light and tapering. Entirely free from throatiness.

Forequarters: Shoulder moderately oblique, clean and muscular. Elbow close to body. Forelegs perfectly straight with strong round bone down to feet, with slight spring at pastern joint.

Body: Chest not too wide but deep and capacious with plenty of lung and heart room. Ribs well sprung, well defined withers, powerful level back, loin strong,

clean muscular and slightly arched.

Hindquarters: Rounded, muscles clean with well developed second thigh, good turn of stifle, hock well defined.

Feet: Round, compact, with well arched toes, cat-like, round, tough, elastic pads. Nails black or white in black spotted variety; in liver spotted, brown or white.

Tail: Length reaching approximately to hock. Strong at insertion gradually tapering toward end, never inserted too low or too high, free from coarseness and carried with a slight upward curve, never curled. Preferably spotted.

Gait/Movement: Great freedom of movement. Smooth, powerful, rhythmic action with long stride. Viewed from behind, legs move in parallel, hindlegs tracking the fore. A short stride and paddling action incorrect.

Coat: Short, hard, dense; sleek and glossy in appearance.

Colour: Ground colour pure white. Black spotted, dense black spots and liver spotted, liver brown spots; not running together but round and well defined. In size, one pence to fifty pence piece. Spots as well distributed as possible. Spots on extremities smaller than those on body. Patches, tri-colour and lemon spots highly undesirable. Bronzing on spots undesirable in adults.

Size: Overall balance of prime importance. Ideal height: Dogs 58.4-61cms (23-24ins.) Bitches, 55.9-58.4cms (22-23ins.)

Faults: Any departure from the foregoing points should be considered a fault and the seriousness with which the fault should be regarded should be in exact proportion to its degree. **Note**: Male animals should have two apparently normal testicles fully descended into the scrotum.

We now turn to the AKC and the FCI Standards, both of which are set out in full below. You will note that they continue

Ch. Flutist of Frohocks: Winner of 20CCs, 14 RCCs, BIS Birmingham, Ch. Show 1991, BIS Leicester Ch. Show 1991, BIS BDC Ch. Show 1991, BOB and Utility Group Blackpool Ch. Show 1993, BOB, Utility Group and RBIS Bath Ch. Show 1995. The Dalmatian's expression should be alert and intelligent.

along much the same lines, the exception being the eye colour clause in the AKC Standard and the fact that both the AKC and FCI include disqualification clauses for some faults. Under the UK Standard, the identification and degree of the fault is left to the discretion of the judge.

Apart from the permitted blue eye in the AKC Standard, a major difference lies in the rigid ruling on size (24ins maximum at the shoulder), whereas in the UK this is expressed only as a strong suggestion. This allows for an otherwise excellent animal not to be eliminated by reason of being slightly over the maximum permitted height.

AKC STANDARD 1992

General Appearance: The Dalmatian is a distinctively spotted dog; poised and alert; strong, muscular and active; free of shyness; intelligent in expression; symmetrical in outline; and without exaggeration or coarseness. The Dalmatian is capable of great endurance, combined with fair amount of speed. Deviations from the described ideal should be penalized in direct proportion to the degree of the deviation.

Size, Proportion, Substance: Desirable height at the withers is between 19 and 23 inches. Undersize or oversize is a fault. Any dog or bitch over 24 inches at the withers is disqualified. The overall length of the body from the forechest to the buttocks is approximately equal to the height at the withers. The Dalmatian has good substance and is strong and sturdy in bone, but never coarse.

Head: The head is in balance with the overall dog. It is of fair length and is free of loose skin. The Dalmatian's expression is alert and intelligent, indicating a stable and outgoing temperament. The **eyes** are set moderately well apart, are medium sized and somewhat rounded in appearance, and are set well into the skull. Eye color is brown or blue, or any combination thereof; the darker the better and usually darker in black-spotted than in liver-spotted dogs. Abnormal position of the eyelids or eyelashes (ectropion, entropion, trichiasis) is a major fault. Incomplete pigmentation of the eye rims is a major fault. The **ears** are of moderate size, proportionately wide at the base and gradually tapering to a rounded tip. They are set rather high, and are carried close to the head, and are thin and fine in texture. When the Dalmatian is alert, the top of the ear is level with the top of the skull and the tip of the ear reaches to the bottom line of the cheek. The top of the skull is flat with a slight vertical furrow and is approximately as wide as it is long. The **stop** is moderately well defined. The

cheeks blend smoothly into a powerful **muzzle**, the top of which is level and parallel to the top of the skull. The muzzle and the top of the skull are about equal in length. The **nose** is completely pigmented on the leather, black in black-spotted dogs and brown in liver-spotted dogs. Incomplete nose pigmentation is a major fault. The **lips** are clean and close fitting. The teeth meet in a **scissors bite.** Overshot or undershot bites are disqualifications. **Neck, Topline, Body**: The **neck** is nicely arched, fairly long, free from throatiness, and blends smoothly into the shoulders. The **topline** is smooth. The **chest** is deep, capacious and of moderate width, having good spring of rib without being barrel shaped. The brisket reaches to the elbow. The underline of the rib cage curves gradually into a moderate tuck-up. The

TOPLINE AND LAY OF SHOULDER
Drawings Julia Swinburn.

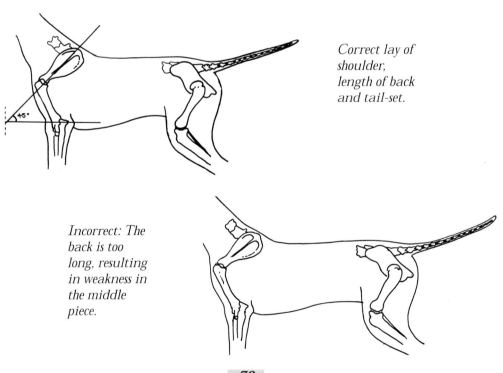

Correct lay of shoulder, length of back and tail-set.

Incorrect: The back is too long, resulting in weakness in the middle piece.

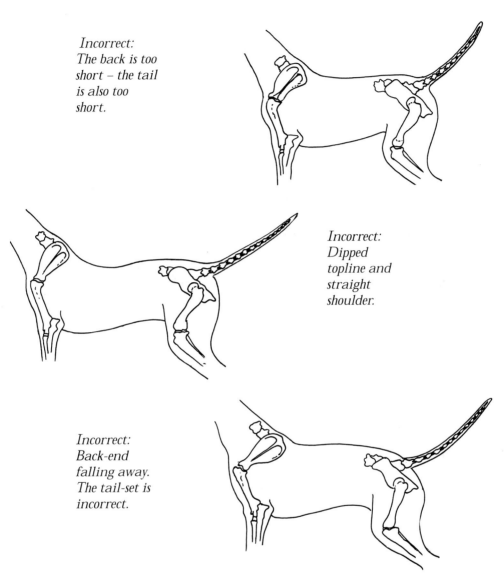

*Incorrect:
The back is too
short – the tail
is also too
short.*

*Incorrect:
Dipped
topline and
straight
shoulder.*

*Incorrect:
Back-end
falling away.
The tail-set is
incorrect.*

back is level and strong. The **loin** is short, muscular and slightly arched. The flanks narrow through the loin. The **croup** is nearly level with the back. The **tail** is a natural extension of the topline. It is not inserted too low down. It is strong at the insertion and tapers to the tip, which reaches to the hock. It is never docked. The tail is carried with a slight upward curve but should never curl over the back. Ring tails and low-set tails are faults.

Forequarters: The **shoulders** are smoothly muscled and well laid back. The **upper arm** is approximately equal in length to the shoulder blade and joins it at an angle sufficient to insure that the foot falls under the shoulder. The **elbows** are close to the

TAILS

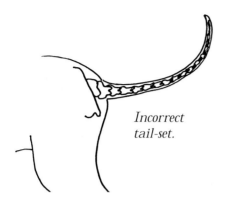

Incorrect tail-set.

Incorrect: The tail is set too high.

body. The **legs** are straight, strong and sturdy in bone. There is a slight angle at the **pastern** denoting flexibility.

Hindquarters: The **hindquarters** are powerful, having smooth, yet well defined muscles. The **stifle** is well bent. The **hocks** are well let down. When the Dalmatian is standing, the hind legs, viewed from the rear, are parallel to each other from the point of the hock to the heel of the pad. Cowhocks are a major fault.

Feet: **Feet** are very important. Both front and rear feet are round and compact with thick, elastic pads and well arched toes. Flat feet are a major fault. Toenails are black and/or white in black-spotted dogs and brown and/or white in liver-spotted dogs. Dew-claws may be removed.

Coat: The **coat** is short, dense, fine and close fitting. It is neither woolly nor silky. It is sleek, glossy and healthy in appearance.

Color and Markings: Color and **markings** and their overall appearance are very important points to be evaluated. The ground color is pure white. In black-spotted dogs the spots are dense black. In liver-spotted dogs the spots are liver brown. Any color markings other than black or

liver are disqualified. **Spots** are round and well-defined, the more distinct the better. They vary from the size of a dime to the size of a half-dollar. They are pleasingly and evenly distributed. The less the spots intermingle the better. Spots are usually smaller on the head, legs and tail than on the body. Ears are preferably spotted. **Tri-color** (which occurs rarely in this breed) is a disqualification. It consists of tan markings found on the head, neck, chest, leg or tail of a black- or liver-spotted dog. Bronzing of black spots, and fading and/or darkening of liver spots due to environmental conditions or normal processes of coat change are not tri-coloration. **Patches** are a disqualification. A patch is a solid mass of black or liver hair containing no white hair. It is appreciably larger than a normal sized spot. Patches are a dense, brilliant color with sharply defined, smooth edges. Patches are present at birth. Large color masses formed by intermingled or overlapping spots are not patches. Such masses should indicate individual spots by uneven edges and/or white hair scattered throughout the mass.

Gait: In keeping with the Dalmatian's historical use as a coach dog, gait and endurance are of great importance. Movement is steady and effortless.

FOREQUARTERS
Drawings: Julia Swinburn.

Correct.

Incorrect: Too narrow and toeing in.

Incorrect: Too wide.

HINDQUARTERS

Correct.

Incorrect: Cow-hocked.

Incorrect: Bowing in, weak stifle.

Balanced angulation fore and aft combined with powerful muscles and good condition produce smooth, efficient action. There is a powerful drive from the rear coordinated with extended reach in the front. The topline remains level. Elbows, hocks and feet turn neither in nor out. As the speed of the trot increases, there is a tendency to single track.

Temperament: Temperament is stable and outgoing, yet dignified. Shyness is a major fault.

FEET

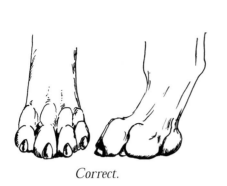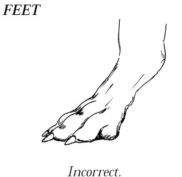

Correct.   *Incorrect.*

MOVEMENT
Drawing: Peter Aldenhoven.

Movement should be steady and effortless, with balanced angulation fore and aft.

SCALE OF POINTS

General Appearance	5
Feet	5
Size, proportion, substance	10
Coat	5
Head	10
Color and markings	25
Neck, topline, body	10
Gait	10
Forequarters	5
Temperament	10
Hindquarters	5
TOTAL	**100**

Disqualifications

Any dog or bitch over 24 inches at the withers.

Overshot or undershot bite.

Any color markings other than black or liver.

Tri-color.

Patches.

Approved July 11, 1989.

FCI STANDARD 1994

FCI classification: Group 6 (Scent hounds and related breeds)
Section 3 (Related breeds) Without working trial.

Brief historical summary: The origin of the Dalmatian is still obscure and rests solely on suppositions. The earliest firm indications are to be found in pictures by Italian painters of the 16th century. From depictions discovered in the tombs of ancient Egyptian pharaohs and corresponding to those in mediaeval paintings, it may be surmised that the Dalmatian has been in existence for some two thousand years. These indications provide serious grounds for concluding that the breed originated in the Mediterranean region. A work of Thomas Bewick, published in 1792, contains a description and a drawing of a Dalmatian, which Bewick refers to as "The Dalmatian or Coach Dog". The first Dalmatian Standard was drawn up in the year 1882 by an Englishman named Vero Shaw. This Standard was then incorporated in an official standard in 1890.

General Appearance: Distinctively spotted, strong, muscular and active dog. Symmetrical in outline, free from coarseness and lumber, capable of great endurance and a fair turn of speed.

Behaviour/Temperament: Outgoing and friendly, not shy nor hesitant, free from nervousness and aggression.

Head and Skull: Of fair length, skull flat, broadest between ears, temporal well defined. Stop well defined. Entirely free from wrinkle. Muzzle long, powerful, never snipy, lips clean, fitting jaw closely. Nose in black spotted variety always black, in liver spotted variety always brown.

Mouth: Jaws strong with a perfect, regular and complete scissor bite.

Eyes: Set moderately well apart, medium size, round, bright and sparkling, with intelligent expression. Colour dark in black spotted, light brown up to amber in liver spotted. Eye rims completely black or very dark coloured in black spotted, and liver brown in liver spotted.

Ears: Set on high, moderate size, rather wide at base, gradually tapering to rounded point; carried close to head; thin and fine in texture, well spotted.

Neck: Moderately long, well arched, light and tapering; entirely free from throatiness.

Body: Chest deep and capacious. Ribs well sprung; well defined withers; powerful level back; loin strongly muscular and slightly arched.

Tail: Reaching approximately to the hock. Strong at the base, gradually tapering towards end, free from coarseness, never inserted too low nor too high. Carried with a slight upward curve, but never curled. Preferably spotted.

Limbs
Forequarters: Shoulders moderately oblique, clean and muscular. Elbows close to body. Forelegs perfectly straight, strong, with good bone. Resilient pasterns.

Hindquarters: Muscles well developed and clean; good turn of stifle; hocks slightly bent; viewed from behind, hind legs parallel.

Feet: Round, compact, with well arched toes, cat-like; pads round, tough and elastic. Nails black or white in black spotted variety, in liver spotted brown or white.

Gait: Great freedom of movement. Smooth, powerful, rhythmic action with long stride; viewed from behind, legs moving parallel, hind legs tracking the fore. A short stride and paddling action incorrect.

Coat
Texture: Short, hard, dense, smooth and glossy.
Colour: Ground colour pure white. Black spotted variety with dense black spots, liver spotted variety with liver brown spots; not running together but round, well defined and well distributed; size 2-3 cm in diameter. Spots on head, tail and extremities smaller.

Size and Weight: Overall balance of prime importance.
Height for Dogs: 56-61 cm (Ideal height 58-59 cm)
Height for Bitches: 54-59 cm (Ideal height 56-57 cm)
Ideal weight for Dogs: about 27 kg
Ideal weight for Bitches: about 24 kg

Faults: Any departure from the foregoing points should be considered a fault and the seriousness with which the fault should be regarded should be in exact proportion to its degree.

Disqualifying Faults: Patches. Monocle. Tri-colours (black and liver-brown spots on the same dog). Lemon (lemon spots and bronzing). Other faults of pigmentation. Blue eye, wall eye. Definitely over- and undershot mouth. Deafness. Ectropion, entropion. Very timid or aggressive behaviour. (N.B. Male animals should have two apparently normal testicles fully descended into the scrotum.)

SUMMARY
To the envy of many, the FCI has now transferred the Dalmatian to Group Six (Scent Hounds and Related Breeds), which has long been considered far more appropriate. Here they would seem to be in their element and have already won well. The only exception to this ruling lies in France, where they remain in Group Nine (Companion Dogs) at the express wish of The Dalmatian Club of France's highly-respected president, Madame Garaix.

Knowing the stringent rules regarding missing dentition which obtain in most European countries, it is surprising to find no mention of this in the FCI Standard.

If you look for a single reason for dog shows, then it must be because they are the means by which the best breeding animals are produced for the future. By passing judgment against inadequate dogs in the show ring, judges take on the responsibility of maintaining and enhancing the quality of breeding stock. Human beings are fallible, but every animal has the opportunity to go before many different judges, and there is no surer way to assess a dog correctly than to see it alongside its contemporaries. Set aside for a moment the winning of prizes and the making up of Champions. When you become involved in the breeding of bloodstock of any kind, then you are constantly looking to produce fine animals of excellent temperament, relating always back to the Standard. You may have to try again and again to achieve the impossible – physical and temperamental perfection in this most difficult of breeds.

7 *THE SHOW SCENE*

Above all else, dog shows are fun. You cross the path of a great many people you would not otherwise have met; you also get to know their dogs, and you all share together in the thrill of a good win. Winning itself is addictive and, if your first dog wins well, the chances are that this is the start of a deeply interesting, enjoyable, exasperating way of life.

You may have bought a puppy with show potential, an 'ugly duckling' may have turned into a swan, or you may just feel you would like to have a go. Most exhibitors start in just that way and, if the puppy wins, they are encouraged to continue. The more serious side comes later, when a fairly superficial interest is superseded by a deep and abiding passion for the whole subject.

You travel enormous distances for the opinion of a knowledgeable judge and, at the same time, have the opportunity to see some of the finest dogs in the country and form your own judgment. If your interest continues you may well breed a litter or two yourself, and the knowledge which began in the show ring could form the basis of an important line of the future.

This is how it should be but, as in all things, there is the reverse side. It is a glorious thrill to come first, but is it important to the exclusion of everything else? Not when disappointment clouds your judgement to the extent that you lose all sense of proportion. Not when a 1st place under an excellent judge means nothing because it did not convert into a CC. Not when one sees the treatment sometimes meted out to a dog which has failed to win. The dog is there for the owner's pleasure, not to win prizes.

There is always going to be disappointment, so keep a smile on your face, congratulate your opponents, reward your dog and wait for the next show. Do not blame the judge. You gave them an entry – if you do not like the judging, do not do so again.

CONSULT YOUR BREEDER
Your puppy is approaching six months of age and, at this stage, you really need an expert opinion on whether he has the finer points which make it worthwhile for you both to embark on a show career.

No-one can be of more help to you here than the breeder, who knows the line and can give an opinion based on knowledge of previous stock. The stud dog owner could also be helpful, having seen litters his dog has produced previously, but if neither are available then consult a knowledgeable friend. Between them all, they will be able to help in making an assessment. They will look at every aspect, including movement, and weigh up the good and bad points. Included among these is the spotting itself. A second, even a third, crop of spots can come through, ruining what was a very well-spotted coat. Although most judges will not put spotting at the top of the list, nevertheless, if your aim is to achieve the heights, then good spotting is an undoubted help. It should not win over a better-constructed, better-moving dog, but if all things are equal, then the better spotting will definitely give an advantage. What is more difficult to pinpoint is whether the puppy has that touch of magic, showmanship, call it what you will – with it you will go far, without it you will struggle.

Many owners prefer the smaller Sanction, Limited and Open shows, and you may be told the puppy will give you a lot of fun at these. If you are ambitious, and have your sights set on the more important Championship shows, you will want to get some indication as to whether the puppy is of the calibre to compete at that level.

Even at this age, it is often difficult to give more than an educated guess, but I hope your advisers will be honest and kind enough to give you a straight answer, and that you yourself will not be too disappointed if they discourage you from going ahead. Whatever happens this is the same lovely animal you took on at the age of eight weeks, and it will give you no pleasure to see it fail in the show ring. There are many worlds this dog can take you into outside the show scene, not least as a most loving companion.

SHOWS AND CLASS CLASSIFICATION
All countries have their own licensing method and organise their shows accordingly. Governing bodies have their own rules and qualifications, but I think it is probably true that, if the same set of excellent dogs was shown in all the countries under all the various systems, the same dogs would still stand a good chance of being the winners on each occasion.

CHOOSING YOUR FIRST SHOWS
If you are ambitious, your eyes may already be turning to major shows but, in the beginning, smaller shows will act as a learning exercise for both you and the puppy. A small, friendly Open show with a kindly judge, plus your breeder and one or two friends present, is the ideal.

A puppy between six and 12 months is still growing and needs plenty of play time and, above all, rest. Shows tend to upset this routine, so withstand temptation and, however keen you become, avoid over-showing the young dog. There will be plenty of time for serious campaigning at a later stage.

If the puppy does well and you enjoy the smaller shows, you may like to try your luck at a Championship show. Once again, the choice of judge is all-important and travelling vast distances becomes part of your way of life. Unlike Open shows, your entry will be acknowledged and you will receive a ticket which allows you in and acts as a removal pass at the end.

BAIT
There is a certain mystique about bait in the ring, some owners making a great secret of how their particular brand is prepared. I was told the following, and it has always served me well.

Buy the best liver you can afford, bring it to the boil in plenty of water, and simmer very gently for 30 minutes. Leave it in the saucepan until the water has gone quite cold. Tip the water away (this is much too rich for the stock pot) and wash all the residue off the liver. Cut it into thin slices and lay these on a baking tray. Pre-heat a moderate oven (160 degrees Centigrade), and put the liver in for 15 minutes. Take it out and leave on a high surface until it is quite cold. Be sure not to leave it within the dog's reach or you will find the entire lot gone. Once the liver is cool, it can be put into a polythene bag and packed in an inaccessible part of the show bag. If you have any left over, it freezes extremely well and can be taken out for the next show.

PACKING THE SHOW BAG

It is often quite a long walk from the car to the benches and you really need the equivalent of a shopping trolley on wheels, preferably with a handle that folds down. This enables you to carry all your gear with minimum effort, without having to put it down in the mud, and leaves a hand free to control an enthusiastic puppy. There is an added advantage, in that you can stand it in front of the bench giving a measure of protection to the occupant. Choose a model with large-size wheels, as these are very helpful when manipulating steps. The bag itself should be waterproof and roomy, and an extra front pocket is very useful. Make a list of what goes in the show bag, otherwise, like me, you will leave something behind. For a Championship show only, you need a leather collar and benching chain, a blanket or mattress, and many people take a newspaper to put under this as a guard against infection.

You will require a show collar and lead, some bait, a small thermos of warm milk and water for the puppy, its normal meal, a bottle of water in case the water on the show ground is polluted, a grooming bag containing a clean rubber grooming glove and a soft finishing brush, a pair of nail clippers, a file, a silk scarf, disinfectant, wound powder and a small aerosol of dry shampoo. A couple of clean towels, a damp sponge and a chamois leather in a waterproof bag complete your requirements for the dog, other than a dog coat. This can be useful on the bench if it is cold and draughty, and is sometimes needed if you come out of an overheated hall straight into a driving wind.

For yourself, a hot drink and some sandwiches, the show schedule and your entrance ticket, a biro pen, ring clip and aspirin tablets, plus some spare plastic bags and an extra pair of shoes in case you arrive covered in mud. This is a basic list of what you may need and doubtless you will add to it. Above all else, do not forget your entrance ticket; everything else can be bought or borrowed on the day.

OFF TO YOUR FIRST SHOW

Preparing your puppy for the ring is covered in Chapter Three, but do this in good time, partly so that you all get an early night before the show. Adult dogs can manage their breakfast and then sleep happily in the car but, with a puppy, you may prefer to give half the breakfast at home and the other half on arrival. Have a comfortable bed in the car for the dog – I find a large bean bag absorbs most of the bumps.

If you are off to an Open show, aim to reach the ground an hour before you are due in the ring. If the show is indoors, you may either leave your dog in the car until such time as he is needed, or if it is too hot or too cold the puppy can be brought in. If this is the case, some people like to have a crate in which the puppy can sit well out of the way and be able to rest in peace.

If it is a Championship show, again give yourself plenty of time; you may like to leave the dog in the car while you take your

Ch. Spring Classic by Apalossa: Winner of 29 CCs (24 with BOB), 11 RCCs, BPIS BDC Ch. Show 1983, BIS BDC Open Show 1984, BIS Joint Dal Clubs Ch Show and DCS Ch. Show 1984, BIS DCS Ch. Show and BDC Ch. Show 1985, BIS Joint Dal Clubs Ch. Show 1986. Top stud dog 1988-1990. BOB and Utility Group Three Counties Ch. Show 1985. BOB Crufts 1988, Best Veteran and RCC Crufts 1992, Best Veteran in Show Joint Dal Clubs Ch. Show 1992.
Photo: Fall.

Ch. Peroca Pride of Elaridge: The well-trained show dog learns to show himself off to advantage.

show bag in and sort out the bench. You can then take the puppy for a walk, with time to be clean, before being put on the bench. Keep your plastic bags with you at all times, as any mistake on a show ground must be cleared away and put in one of the bins.

Some puppies jump on to the bench without a problem, particularly if there is the prospect of a nice breakfast or a biscuit waiting at the back. Others draw back, in which case make as little fuss as possible,

but simply lift them in bodily. Produce a warm drink or a small meal immediately, and then sit down in front of the puppy on the bench and let him settle down. Make sure the benching chain is clipped on at the correct length. It should be short enough to prevent the animal slipping off the bench, but long enough to be comfortable. Many people never leave their dogs unattended on the bench, and certainly a young puppy attending a show for the first time should not be left under any circumstances. If you are there on your own and need to leave your puppy for a short time, enlist the help of somebody sitting nearby.

Once the puppy has become accustomed to the bench, it will gradually gain sufficient confidence to curl up and go to sleep if you must leave for a short while. Although you should never leave the bench unattended for any length of time, it is useful to be able to do so in an emergency. However, you must check back regularly to ensure your dog is neither in trouble nor causing it.

However friendly your own dog is, I am afraid you will find some on the show ground who can be uncertain. It is essential for your puppy's temperament that you do not allow it to fall foul of another in case the worst happens and an injury results. Keep the dog closely to heel and well away from others unless they have proved to be completely friendly. In particular, do not approach benched dogs too closely and, under no circumstances, allow your dog to put its head into the bench when another dog is in possession. Some are very territorial about their benches, and yours might get a poor reception.

It is just as important to keep your dog from annoying others in the ring. A dog who is permitted to interfere with another at a critical stage of the judging is not lightly forgiven by other exhibitors. Equally, the dog must be prevented from annoying onlookers and one develops a sixth sense in avoiding such hazards. One WELKS (West of England Ladies' Kennel Show) stands out in my memory. As a complete novice, I stood in the ring listening as a well-dressed Italian expressed himself volubly about the dogs being exhibited. My puppy watched him intently and seconds later the Italian gazed down at his formerly-immaculate trouser leg. I will never forget his glazed expression, nor the comment from the elderly gentleman sitting alongside: "Well, guv'nor, there's no need for such a fuss. It isn't as though you've got turn-ups!"

Your own show clothes should be chosen carefully. You need two pockets, and preferably these should be just above nose height of the dog. Choose something simple, uncrushable and of a colour that will complement your dog. White will make your Dalmatian look dirty, and a fussy pattern does anything but enhance the spots. Flat shoes with rubber soles are best, and trainers are fine as long as they are clean. Men should avoid a pocket full of loose change.

If Dalmatians are first in the ring then it is not difficult to gauge when you will be expected but, particularly at Open shows, you may find there are other breeds before you. Enquire at the show secretary's desk about the approximate starting time, and after that it is up to you to keep an eye on the ring in question. Providing weather permits, leave the puppy in the car until the last minute. Puppies quickly tire with all the excitement and are much better off resting.

Once the ring is ready for you, make sure you are wearing your ring clip; at a Championship show your card number is waiting for you on the bench, and at an Open show you receive this in the ring from the Steward. Have your liver tidbits in your pocket and take a couple of deep breaths. Do not worry if the puppy is bouncing up and down; for him it will be a great excitement, and no-one will be too concerned about the behaviour of a young puppy at his first show.

Station yourself towards the end of the exhibitors, so that you have a chance to watch what goes on. Do not be distracted by another exhibitor or anyone outside the ring but concentrate totally on the puppy, keeping one eye on the judge. Remember that no-one is looking at you, so forget about yourself completely and put every effort into making your Dalmatian appear to his very best advantage. Handling a dog in the ring is something you learn with time, partly through experience and partly through watching others. Here are a few tips which I hope may be helpful.

When showing out of doors, the ground is not always even or on a level. Stand with your dog's head at the highest point, and make sure he has not got a foot in a hole. Out in the open, if the sun is really hot, it is permissible to take a wet towel to the side of the ring and put it over your dog's back while you are waiting to be judged. At the same time, place yourself between the sun and the dog to give maximum shade and also to avoid him squinting into the sun. Equally, if you are standing in a biting cold wind, keep a dog coat at the ringside and slip it over your puppy's back if you have a long wait.

Whether inside or out, turn the dog in a circle if he is standing awkwardly and encourage your puppy to straighten up. Do not be tempted to move one of the dog's feet with your own and, while continuing to concentrate, keep one ear and eye on the judge at all times. Teach the dog beforehand to move and stand on a loose lead.

Judges who are well-experienced in the breed can see the make and shape of your puppy even when he is dancing on three legs, and can make an assessment if he stands still only for a few seconds. You gain nothing if you reprimand the puppy for jumping up and are left exhibiting a shrinking heap with his tail between his legs.

Normally, you will be asked to run round the ring with the other exhibitors. The judge will then beckon each to the centre individually. When it comes to your turn, stand the puppy up as well as you are able, and try not to be too anxious. When the judge has examined the puppy he will ask you to move your Dalmatian either in a triangle or straight up and down. You may then be asked to move again, this time with the judge moving away to the side, to assess the puppy's topline and side movement. At all times, take care not to run between the judge and your dog. As you finish showing, stand the dog again quickly for the judge and when he signals he has finished with you, take your place at the end of the line.

When all the dogs have been seen, the judge will pull out his winners, or, if it is a huge class, a dozen or so for further consideration. If you are lucky enough to be among them, you can be pleased to have been 'pulled out' even if you go no further. In the UK, if you are among the first three, remain in the ring so the judge may write his report. On the continent, every dog receives a written report as the judging continues. In the US, no written report is made, though a judge is sometimes asked to address a few words to the exhibitors if the show is followed by a social function.

Irrespective of whether or not you win, if you are pulled out into the centre as one of the last five, do remember to congratulate those on either side of you. Win or lose, a smile is appreciated, and it is also a pleasant gesture to go back at the end of the classes and thank the judge. Once the show is finished, take time for a walk. It may be many hours before you get home, and a small meal will make the dog settle for the journey. Otherwise, a warm drink is always appreciated. The important thing is to try and make a day at a show as pleasant as possible for your dog.

Winning is a heady business, but showing disrupts the puppy's routine and development, both physically and mentally,

Ch. Hollycombe Polaire of Courbette: 16 CCs and 9 Reserve CCs, BCC Crufts 1987, BIS NOEDC Ch. Show 1989, Top winning Dalmatian 1989.

Photo: Anne Roslin-Wiliams.

so, however well your Dalmatian does, avoid too many shows too close together. Always make the day fun, always make it finish well and, if you are disappointed, never let the puppy feel that he has been the cause. However badly the puppy may have behaved, there should only be generous praise. Shoulder the blame yourself and give the dog a little extra training.

It is just possible that your puppy will actually hate dog shows. This may manifest itself in extreme nervousness or even bad temper. Either way, instead of the happy extrovert character you have at home, you may be disappointed at the shivering puppy with his tail tucked between his legs refusing to be handled by the judge. This problem can be overcome with much training and care, but in some cases it is hopeless. Once you have arrived at that conclusion, take the dog out of the ring and forget about dog shows. You may be disappointed, but there is no joy in putting an animal through the agony that is obviously experienced. It may even be that you will have a better result elsewhere, for instance in the Agility ring.

To sum up, I think I can do no better than quote the last paragraph of the British Dalmatian Club Code of Conduct:

"In the show ring, present your dog and yourself in immaculate condition. Watch to see what the judge will require and ensure that neither you nor your dog interferes with any other. Treat your dog calmly and kindly – he is there only to please you, not to obtain prizes. Do not allow disappointment to mar your behaviour either to your dog or to other exhibitors, and certainly not the judge. Malicious comments regarding the judging, other exhibitors or their dogs, are totally unacceptable either in the ring or outside it."

JUDGING THE DALMATIAN

The Dalmatian is not only a difficult dog to breed; in the ring, it presents considerable problems to a judge. For this reason, we have tended to rely more on specialist breed judges, thinking, perhaps wrongly, that all-rounders may not have the necessary in-depth knowledge of the breed.

Bone structure must be correct, thereby leading to good movement. The overall condition of the dog must be taken into consideration. So far, so good. This is a breed that carries unique markings, so these must come into consideration. The arrangement, size and colour each carry their own importance and must be treated accordingly. Additionally, the spots themselves can be very misleading, hiding a fault as they sometimes do, or pinpointing a virtue out of its true proportion. Nevertheless, the informed views of the top all-rounders are essential for the well-being of the Dalmatian breed, and it is to our own detriment if we forego a chance to avail ourselves of this knowledge.

"Any judge, at whatever level, should read the Standard every night for a week before an appointment." This advice was given to me years ago by one of our leading judges, and I have seen no reason to ignore it. It is only by having a picture of the 'Standard' Dalmatian in the mind that one can approach judging this breed. The much-quoted 'eye for a dog', though invaluable, is not sufficient.

It is easy for a judge to forget what a bewildering place the show ring is to a novice exhibitor. Apart from the manifold problems of controlling an unruly puppy, the language itself can present difficulties. "Move your dog", I was told at my first show and I carefully took several steps towards my neighbour in the line-up. I had read all the books, but in sheer fright one tends to become brain-dead. The steward was appalled, but the judge was kindness itself.

As a judge, you are there to judge the dog, not the behaviour of the dog, and certainly not the exhibitor. The judge should remember that it is all too obvious to onlookers when a glance up at the face of the handler settles a decision. It does not occur often, indeed not nearly as often as people would have you believe, but equally when it does happen it is not forgotten.

Each UK judge receives an invitation from both dog papers to complete a write-up on their entry and send it in for publication. I believe that this is part and parcel of the judging appointment, and that exhibitors are entitled to a written report. Some judges ignore the request altogether and one reaches the conclusion that they may be anxious to avoid explaining their decisions.

I do not accept the argument that only those whose dogs are placed wish to read a critique. Everyone present at a show will want to read the thoughts of the judge in question, particularly if there are some general comments. How can we all learn if judges, having given a silent opinion on the dogs by their placings, decline to elaborate? It is also deeply disappointing for those who, for one reason or another, are no longer able to get to shows. They may not have stock in the ring, but they still retain a deep interest in the breed and find it immensely disappointing when show reports are conspicuous by their absence.

8 *THE VERSATILE DALMATIAN*

If the small but vociferous anti-dog campaign were to succeed, and in one moment all dogs disappeared from the face of the earth, what difference would it make? Farmers would have difficulty running sheep over impassable country; the police would miss them badly for their tracking prowess, as well as sniffing out bombs and drugs. How many lives would be lost on mountains, under avalanches or in wrecked buildings? The blind and profoundly deaf would lose their independence. Doctors and nurses have come to value their help with people sick either in body or mind. Children would lose out badly, and those of us who rely so heavily on canine companionship would find life a desolate place. There is no other domestic animal whose achievements can compare with those of a dog – and how impressive it is to find that in every aspect, somewhere in the world, a Dalmatian has been playing its part.

COMPANION DOG
I borrowed my first Dalmatian for a week and, when her owner collected her, I was quite unprepared for the sharp sense of loss. I had become accustomed to her warm presence under my desk; to a determined paw on my knee signalling lunch time and a walk in Hyde Park; to the sight of her shining face in the driving mirror as we drove around London. I remembered with nostalgia the Spaniel of my youth and it was no great surprise when, some three months later, a fat spotted puppy dog marched in through the front door.

Companionship is a very personal thing and those of us who receive it from a Dalmatian are singularly blessed – though, with their strength of character, it is not all roses. They make demands, as is fair in any relationship, but their love is endless; and who is so rich that they can turn down this gift, so freely offered, with so little demanded in return? You will not always find Dalmatians easy, but as Dorothy Allen (Semmering) is fond of saying: "These are people dogs."

GUIDE DOGS FOR THE BLIND
Guide dogs for the blind have been bred and trained in New Zealand for many years, and it is interesting to note that they have all come down from one dog, Paddy Lockett's Ch. Brough of Farley Green. The 'Farley Green' prefix was adopted by Marie Spiers as a compliment to Hazel Godfrey,

85

Guide dog Ch. Brough of Farley Green with Moya Badham.

Guide dog Tom with Anne-Marie Coulton.

who lives in the village of Farley Green, in Surrey. Marie picked out a Stallions bitch puppy during a visit to England, and Dido was duly exported by Hazel in 1973, to become Ch. Stallions Dido. In one of the first attempts from this country, Dido was mated via artificial insemination with James Hally's Ch. Northern Granada of Leagarth. The resulting litter was the beginning of Marie Spiers' well-known line.

Ch. Brough of Farley Green had a successful showing career under the joint ownership of Paddy Lockett and Jo Harris. After his show career, he was placed in a pet home and when his owner, Moya Badham, became blind, he trained and qualified as a guide dog, being then 12 years of age. An exceptional dog, he combined stud work with his guide dog career without any

problem.

Two puppies from different litters qualified as guide dogs, Celaenos Nick bred by Raewyn McLiver and Paddy's own Stedfast Gertrude. Gertrude, in turn, produced three sons accepted for puppy walking; Stedfast Raleigh, Renault and Rocki, who all qualified well.

Ch. Stedfast Out of Sight (litter sister to Celaenos Nick) whelped a dog puppy, Stedfast Tom, who also qualified. Ch. Stedfast Wired for Sound (ex Stedfast Gertrude) was shown successfully, then mated, and produced in turn a fine dog puppy who was also destined as a guide dog. However, he had one foot which turned out and, in the vet's opinion, would have become unsound working on hard pavements. His future lay at the Linton army camp where he was welcomed as a mascot to the fire station, and where he taught children to crawl under smoke, etc.

Ch. Stedfast Out of Sight then whelped her second litter, and from this came Toffee of Stedfast who has now completed her puppy walking and is in training. Celaenos Hestia, bred by Raewyn McLiver, is now nine months old and being puppy walked, and Widget, bred by Paddy Lockett, is five months old and has just been accepted for puppy walking, having become too spotty to show. This is quite late for a youngster to start going into shops, etc., so her progress is being watched with interest.

The puppies are in the charge of their walkers for the first 12 to 15 months, and are assessed once a month by Guide Dog staff. Excursions to town are organised as often as possible, and include shopping in supermarkets and in all public shops. As in many countries, dogs are not normally welcome in shopping areas, so the puppies wear little red coats with 'Guide Dog Pup in Training' written on them. They then pass without comment.

Puppy walkers find their main problem is aggression shown by other dogs towards the guide dogs, who must of course ignore any sort of dog distraction. At home they live a totally normal life, but there are strict rules regarding tidbits. Once again, they must not become food-distracted.

THERAPY DOGS
In 1983, Lesley Scott-Ordish had the brilliant idea of organising PAT dogs (Pets as Therapy). Therapy dogs operate nowadays in hospitals, residential and private homes, having first passed a behaviour and temperament test. Dalmatians played their part in this almost from the beginning, and organisers and patients have owners as well as dogs to thank for the time they give up to this.

Lately, doctors have begun to discover the benefits of using dogs in the treatment of children as well as adults, particularly with those who are mentally troubled. In hospitals and nursing homes, where dogs were previously forbidden, they are now welcome and rightly so. Dalmatians, because of their great affinity with people, are well-suited to this work and, of course, their short, dirt-free coats make them even more welcome.

WORKING WITH CHILDREN
Dalmatians create a fascination in children. Whether this is because of the spots, or the short, sleek coat, or merely because the youngsters sense a friend, the feeling of kinship certainly exists. Dalmatians are greatly in demand at schools and, in many countries, the USA in particular, they are responsible for teaching the children fire drill.

Lupin is one such working dog. He is the constant companion of his owner, Mary, who teaches eight and nine-year-olds in a school for deprived children in a poor area of London. Lupin attends full-time school and his effect on these children is extraordinary. Those who cannot be persuaded to write will produce a story about Lupin. Those who cannot draw will try their hardest to produce a portrait. Many find physical exercise lessons difficult, but, if Lupin is there to watch, they will do their best. Everyone is punctual for assembly because Lupin is there to lead them in and, for those who retire unhappily to the quiet room, Lupin will go along to offer a sympathetic paw.

The sketch is by Alice Leader, aged eight, who lay flat on the floor with her nose nearly touching the dog as she drew this picture. Lupin is welcomed each morning by 23 separate sets of patting hands; takes an active part in all the lessons; goes for 23 separate walks and generally does a first-rate public relations job. Those children will surely carry the memory of that kindly Dalmatian with them for the rest of their lives.

ASSISTANCE DOGS

Dogs trained to assist the disabled are well established nowadays, and Dalmatians are especially well-suited to the role. Such dogs are represented in the USA by Touchstone's Topaz, who not only acts as Melissa Ericksen's Assistance Dog, but also completes Obedience trials for her in the ring at top level.

Melissa is confined to an electric wheelchair and, in her 'Assistance' capacity, Topaz is permitted to travel with her mistress by public transport, both on land and in the air, normally having her own seat. She impresses staff everywhere with her good behaviour and impeccable manners, and is on 24-hour call to fetch and carry, as well as carrying out innumerable tasks. Responding to something like 70 commands, she must make all the difference in the world to her owner. As far as Obedience is concerned, apart from certain problems caused by the wheelchair, this pair are well on the way to their CD title, if they have not already achieved it, and will doubtless be continuing on to greater things.

Two UK organisations in this field are Dogs for the Disabled, which trains dogs on a highly personal basis to fulfil the requirements of a particular patient, and Support Dogs, which sends trainers into homes to teach both owner and dog the necessary skills.

FIRE HOUSE DOGS

Throughout the USA, Dalmatians have been used as fire house mascots for many years. They were originally adopted, back in the days of horse-drawn appliances, because of their great affinity with the horses and their devotion to guarding the fire fighters and stations. Over the years, children have grown up associating Dalmatians with Fire Departments. Although the horses have long since gone, some US fire houses still keep a Dalmatian for use on ceremonial occasions, when he rides alongside the firefighters, his handsome looks complementing the smart uniforms and appliances.

FIRE DOG KITT

Barbara McCumisky has had a long association with the Metropolitan Fire Brigade in Melbourne, Australia. She bred her first Dalmatian litter in 1985 and kept a dog puppy, Fire Chaser Phoenix, pet name Kitt. Kitt indicated at an early age that he much preferred Obedience work to showing, and went on to compete in Trials, winning several trophies and ribbons. When introduced to the fire brigade, he was not at all troubled by the sirens and soon began to recognise fire fighters as special friends.

Barbara was Curator of the Melbourne Fire Museum from 1986 to 1994 and, in 1986, the Museum suggested that Kitt should ride on one of their pumpers in a pre-Christmas street procession. Although only 18 months old, he behaved like a seasoned professional and, after participating in several more displays, was appointed official mascot for the MFM in 1987.

As mascot, Kitt attended a number of ceremonies including official openings and the Victoria state governor's visit to the Eastern Hill Fire HQ. On all occasions, he featured on the TV news and in local newspapers. Later he rode on the pumper in Melbourne's famous Moomba procession, and on the Leyland Ladder in a Fire Brigade parade at the Royal

Fire Dog Kitt demonstrating "Get down low and go, go, go".

Melbourne Show. In 1989 Station Officer John Laverick of the MFB's Fire Prevention Department asked if Kitt could be trained to demonstrate fire safety, and take part in future projects for fire training for children.

Although by then nearly four years old, Kitt responded enthusiastically to the training and before long was 'dropping, rolling and crawling', and later added 'stop, drop and roll' and 'stay, low and go' to his repertoire. A new sequence was added when Kitt woke a sleeping person by pulling the sheet off and then crawling with the person to safety. From then on, Kitt demonstrated to groups of kindergarten children and various schools in the area, all of whom gave maximum attention to a dog demonstrating the lessons.

In 1990 Kitt was offered the leading role in a video planned to train pre-school and very young schoolchildren in fire safety. For this he had to perform in a room filled with smoke and, as always, was more than up to the challenge. So successful was Kitt as a promoter of the fire safety message that this same video is still being used in the Juvenile Fire Awareness and Intervention Programme.

As a reward, Kitt was invited to be official mascot for Fire Awareness Week 1990, and appeared on a national TV programme. At the same time, he was presented with the official Fire Brigade badge which was attached to his collar. He was accorded the title MFB Fire Dog Kitt 1, thus becoming the first officially-recognised canine fire safety educator in Australia.

In 1992, Kitt 1 was mated to Rondaglen Buttonsn Bows and, from that litter, Barbara kept a dog registered as Fire Chaser Denis. Denis later graduated officially as MFB Fire Dog Kitt 2, and was presented with the traditional collar along with his own turnout coat and miniature helmet. Sadly, in the meantime, Kitt 1's career was to be cut short by illness. He never recovered completely from an operation to remove a testicular tumour, although in 1993 he experienced two highlights in his career. He featured in the national TV programme Doctor Harry

Copper's *Talk to the Animals*, and he was later invited to Sydney to take part in the NSW Fire Brigade Triple O Spectacular, before a crowd of 40,000. His health then deteriorated, and in February 1994 he retired. His legend now continues through his son.

OBEDIENCE
The Dalmatian is an intelligent breed and does well in Obedience. Dalmatian owners in the USA have taken Obedience seriously for some years, and a growing interest is now also appearing in the UK.

Invariably, owners of new puppies are advised 'go to classes'. One series is usually enough; the puppy has learnt the basic obedience, no Dalmatian enjoys repetitive exercises, and nothing is more contagious than the boredom of a bored Dalmatian.

It was left to the late James Halley of the famous Leagarth prefix to prove wrong those who doubted the Dalmatian's aptitude for Obedience.

Mr and Mrs Simpson campaigned his show dogs, but the Obedience work he handled himself. Camerton Penny Black qualified in Championship Test "C", where a dog must have scored a minimum of 290 points out of 300 on three different occasions under three different judges at Open Shows. She was then the only Dalmatian ever to have qualified to compete in Champion Test "C" Obedience. At her last show, Penny scored 298.5 points out of 300, finishing second in a class of 31. She was beaten only by an Obedience Champion, and beat another Ob. Ch. into third place after a run-off. In great jubilation Mr Halley wrote: "Who said Dalmatians can't do the top tests in Obedience?"

Penny, mated to Mrs Eady's Ch. Greenmount Grindlewald, produced Fetlar St Clare. Having won the Reserve CC at

Belfast, Fetlar distinguished herself by winning Test "A" and Test "B" Obedience on the same day. Unfortunately her dual-purpose career came to an end when she was tragically killed in a car accident.

This all took place in the 1970s and, since then, I believe I am right in saying that no Dalmatian has ever quite achieved the same heights. Nevertheless, many people do get a lot of enjoyment out of training their Dalmatians to Obedience work and it would be good to see a Champion or two coming through.

Details of local Obedience classes and clubs are available in the UK from the KC, and local vets and canine societies will also be helpful. Some trainers show a degree of scepticism in the Dalmatian's power of concentration; the breed's temperament is different from that of the Border Collie, but do not be daunted. There are many more trainers now with the experience and open-minded approach needed to teach a variety of breeds. As always, the key is to make the occasion fun for dog and human alike.

To keep the attention of a young Dalmatian you may need to employ a favourite toy or small tidbit. Short, intensive sessions give better results than repetition and, if the youngster begins to tire or lose interest, stop and have a break for play. It is also useful to have a release command in order to recover the toy and get back to work. Saying "That'll do" avoids the training session turning into a tug of war.

The Dalmatian has a retentive memory and, once an exercise is established, is usually able to go through it with ease, even after a considerable gap in training. As we all know, Dalmatians are not dogs who obey slavishly, and regular practice is always important; the handler must be able to identify the moment when the dog 'switches off' and commands seem to fall on deaf ears.

As far as competition work is concerned, an entry at one of the many small local Exemption shows is a good start. Dalmatians make all-too-rare appearances in Obedience rings, and judges are usually pleased to see them and will offer helpful tips. You may be lucky and find a local club which also organises Working and Gun Dog Trials. These give scope for Dalmatian training and competition, and can be an enjoyable step on from basic Obedience. The breed is quite capable of retrieving objects by scent, and those who like swimming will happily retrieve a training dummy from water.

Meanwhile, Obedience is playing an ever-increasing role on the US show scene. Many Dalmatians successfully complete their Companion Dog (CD) and Companion Dog Excellent (CDX); some achieve Utility Dog (UD) and Utility Dog Excellent (UDX); one or two have now become Obedience Trial Champions (OTCH). From the number of Dalmatians taking part in this sport, it can certainly be presumed that before long there will be many more members of our breed winning these awards.

AGILITY

Interest in Agility started to surface in our breed towards the end of 1988, and this sport is now enjoying increasing popularity. Owners of the few Dalmatians who took part initially were so enthusiastic that gradually others joined them and found, somewhat to their surprise, that Dalmatians not only liked Agility, but were very good at it.

Dalmatians can combine Agility quite happily with a show career or Obedience, and their natural athleticism and enthusiasm ensure that it is great fun for dog and handler alike. The set course of a variety of obstacles provides a test of control and communication, with the aim of achieving maximum empathy between dog and handler. The dog must complete the course free of collar and lead or any other physical control and, in most competition classes, the winners will be those who have completed the course in the fastest time without error.

When training starts, differing personalities soon become apparent. One dog will think only of abandoning the ring for a hunting session, while another needs encouragement to move smoothly through the course alongside or ahead of its handler. The key, as always, is perseverance.

As is usually the case with Dalmatians, training should be a little and often. Classes do not start until the dog is one year old (it is too strenuous for baby bones) but you can make a start at home with the four basic words of command.

"DOWN": This can be taught from puppyhood and is a valuable lesson whether you continue with Agility or not.
"HEEL": Another valuable asset. For Agility the dog is kept at heel beside you rather than behind and normally runs about two feet from you.
"BACK": Used for getting the dog to turn left. Have the dog on a short lead and walk on. Give the command "Back" and turn left, right into the dog. Repeat until he himself turns on command.
"THIS WAY": Used to make the dog turn right. Again, have the dog on a short lead and walk on. Give the command "This way" and turn right immediately, keeping the dog close to you. Repeat until the dog turns right on command.

No dog may take part in competition work under the age of 18 months and,

Dalleaf Angelica (Hannah) in action over the hurdles.

from a safety aspect, an experienced trainer is always on duty at all times. Training classes are now available in most areas and provide wonderful opportunities for socialisation, quite apart from Agility training. Information on these can be obtained from the KC or the main Agility club, and often from local Obedience organisations.

Those who take part in this sport always emphasise the tremendous rapport that is established between the Dalmatian and its owner as training continues. Results obviously vary a lot but, to everybody's great delight, we are beginning to get increasingly good results. Though no Dalmatian club team has yet appeared at Crufts, with the numbers now taking part the chances are definitely improving.

Individual Dalmatians are also beginning to reach the limelight, beginning back in 1988 when 'Monty', escorted by Rachel Callow, appeared on ITV's Telethon. More recently, a great triumph was scored when Dalleaf Angelica (Hannah), owned by Jill Haines and bred by Stevie Baker, qualified for the Final in the ABC (Any Breed but Collies) Agility Class, which took place at the 1995 Christmas Horse of the Year Show at Olympia. Despite the awe-inspiring arena, Hannah, in typical Dalmatian style, began by putting her paws up on the barrier and greeting the crowd. Totally unfazed, she went on to complete a splendid clear round in record time. Then, true to her Dalmatian background, she could not decide to stay down at the table and lost a few precious seconds which gave her a 4th place. It was a marvellous result nevertheless, and Hannah was a very worthy winner of the prize presented by HRH The Duke of Kent.

In the USA, Agility followed swiftly on Obedience, and made its first appearance at a titled show in 1990. In 1994, the AKC authorised six titling shows and, by 1995, this number had risen to 156. This figure may well have doubled in 1996.

ROAD TRIALS

Road trials are popular in the USA, and their origins go back over a long period. The first were held at Wissahickon, Pennsylvania in 1906, when the dogs were judged 75 per cent on their ability to run under a carriage and 25 per cent on their show qualities. The entry on that occasion was limited to seven dogs and the Winner's' ribbon awarded to William Anson's 'Ponto'. Road Trials became a great favourite in the Dalmatian world, and the DCA organised Trials in almost every section of the country. Handlers were permitted to enter one or more dogs, to be run singly or as a group (not to exceed six).

The dogs were judged on their running, conduct and obedience, plus their ability to keep up with the horses. The dogs were not penalised for leaving their handlers, but had to remain within calling distance. They were not permitted to chase other animals, wild or domestic, and were not to be excessively noisy, though a warning bark was desirable. Handlers rode at a reasonable cross-country hacking pace, walking where necessary, trotting a good third of the time, cantering where the trail permitted and showing a good hunting pace at least once across an open field or stretch of trail, to allow the dogs to show their range and speed. Nowadays, Dalmatians may earn the title of Road Dog (RD) and Road Dog Excellent (RDX); the Road Trials are held in conjunction with the DCA national Specialty as well as some other regional clubs.

TRACKING, SEARCH AND RESCUE DOGS

Dalmatians have proved their worth in this capacity in the USA, as in so many countries, and have also been used as hunting dogs. During World Wars I and II, and also the Vietnam War, Dalmatians were used as guard dogs at some Army camps.

KENNEL CLUB JUNIOR ORGANISATION (KCJO)

National kennel clubs are working hard to promote the development of junior organisations. In the UK, the KC added the triathlon to the range of KCJO activities, and this has proved to be a great success. The triathlon brings together the three disciplines – showing, agility and obedience – and all dogs must be handled by KCJO members. Regional rounds are followed by a final at Crufts, and in 1996

the Dalmatian fraternity were delighted when Benson, handled by Justin Graham-Weall, finished in the last three.

ADVERTISING AND FILMING

The economy of most countries is based on advertising and it forms an important part in all our lives. Dalmatians are attractive and unusual in appearance and are therefore popular as models, but it is difficult to know how far this should go.

Everyone has to form his or her own judgement, but I think we can agree that the dignity of the Dalmatian must be protected, and a dog should not be demeaned by taking part in something which is inappropriate. The welfare of the dog during the filming process must be the first consideration and anything which falls short of this should be dismissed out of hand.

One side-effect of advertising or filming must not be forgotten. The more attractive the picture, the greater number of people will admire the dogs. From there it is but a short step to deciding they might want a puppy. Any sudden increase in demand will not always be satisfied through the normal breed channels, thus leaving the door open for questionable breeders producing poor Dalmatians, badly-reared and of unsound temperament. Large sums of money are paid for animals taking part in advertising and filming – please bear in mind some of these resultant ills. There is no joy attached to re-homing a seven-month puppy in its fourth home.

For those whose vision of the Dalmatian is built up from seeing them on the screen, I can only beg them to look again more deeply into the characteristics and general requirements of this far-from-easy breed.

GENETICS FOR THE DALMATIAN BREEDER

9

by Professor David T. Parkin BSc. Phd.

Dept. of Genetics, Nottingham University

I t is a commonplace observation that individuals vary in their appearance, but equally familiar to us all is the fact that relatives tend to resemble one another. The analysis of such difference and resemblance lies in the field of genetics, the scientific study of inheritance. In general, the appearance of an individual depends upon two factors: inheritance and environmental effects, and separating them is very important. Environmental effects are not restricted to physical factors like temperature, but may include biological factors such as diet and nutrition, crowding and socialisation.

Before approaching the tricky problems of separating these effects, it is necessary to gain a firm grasp of the principles of inheritance, and the first part of this chapter deals with this. Throughout, I shall use 'male' and 'female' to denote 'dog' and 'bitch', and the word 'dog' to mean an animal of either sex. I shall assume that a breeder is male, using 'he' rather than 'he or she'; I apologise for this, but paper is expensive, and trees should be conserved wherever possible.

THE PHYSICAL BASIS OF INHERITANCE

The laws of inheritance were discovered by Gregor Mendel during the 18th century, and have been honed and refined extensively over the last hundred years. It is now known that genetic information is passed from parents to their offspring via genes which are parts of extremely long molecules called chromosomes. These molecules are made from a substance called deoxyribonucleic acid (or DNA) which itself consists of a series of small sub-units called 'bases', of which there are four types. We will return to these later, but, for the present, it is important to appreciate that chromosomes are found in the nucleus, which is a small structure contained in almost every cell in an animal's body.

The number of chromosomes in a cell is almost always constant for a particular species. In the dog, there are 78 which comprise 38 pairs plus two extra ones called X and Y. Under a microscope, skilled scientists can identify the 38 pairs from their size and shape, and also using complicated stains that reveal different patterns of light and dark bands. Members of a pair are called 'homologous' because their structure is identical. The X and Y

1

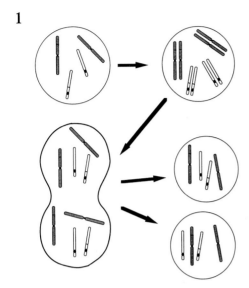

The process of mitosis. Note that each chromosome is replicated, and that one copy migrates to each end of the nucleus which then divides. The resulting nuclei each has a complete set of chromosomes, exactly as in the ancestral cell. The chromosomes are coloured grey and white, and one of each pair is marked with a bar for clarity.

chromosomes can also be distinguished using size and staining reactions: a male has one X and one Y chromosome; a female has two X chromosomes.

When an individual grows, the cells in its body enlarge and then divide. Since many of the chemicals required to sustain life are produced from the information in the genes, it is essential that every new cell obtains its full complement of chromosomes. Thus, every chromosome must be replicated so that there is a full set for each of the two daughter cells. This takes place during cell division when the nucleus undergoes a series of changes, called *mitosis* (MY-TOE-SIS). Figure. 1 (above) shows this in diagrammatic form:

to make the image more simple, I have reduced the number of chromosomes to four – two homologous pairs. There is a pair shaded grey and an unshaded pair, and to make it easier to follow individual chromosomes, I have marked one of each homologous pair with a black bar. Firstly, every chromosome is replicated, so that there are now twice as many within the nucleus. The chromosomes then begin a migration within the nucleus so that one copy of each chromosome moves to one end, and the other copy to the other end, to give two groups of four chromosomes with one of each of the four in both groups. The nucleus now divides, to give each 'daughter cell' one copy of every chromosome. This seemingly complex exercise is essential if every cell is to have a full complement of chromosomes (and hence genes) within its nucleus. In the case of a growing dog, the 78 individual chromosomes would behave in just this way: replicate themselves, and then migrate to opposite ends of the dividing nucleus.

When an egg is fertilised by a sperm, the nuclei merge together. If a cell contains 78 chromosomes, and two sex-cells (or gametes) unite, the number of chromosomes in the resulting progeny would double, and double again next time, and again until the nuclei became very crowded indeed. In order that this does not happen, when a gamete is produced, the chromosomes undergo an even more complex series of manoeuvres called *meiosis* (MY-OH-SIS). Figure 2 (page 96) attempts to show this, again simplifying the situation to two pairs of chromosomes. Instead of dividing once to give two daughter cells, the nucleus divides twice to give four daughter cells, each with half of the chromosomes in the nucleus – 39 in the case of a dog. This partitioning of chromosomes among the daughter nuclei is

2

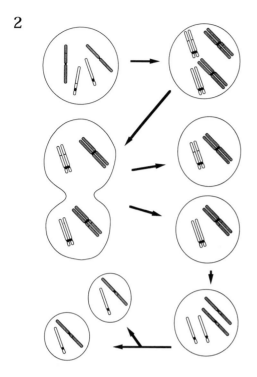

The process of meiosis. Note that the chromosomes are replicated, but remain attached at one point as doublets. One of each pair moves to each end of the nucleus which divides to give two daughter nuclei each having precisely half the complement. The doublets now separate, and again one copy of each moves to either end. The nucleus divides for a second time so that the resulting cells have exactly half the number of chromosomes in the original.

even more precise than in normal cell growth.

First of all, when the chromosomes replicate, the new copy remains attached to the old so that in Fig. 2 there are four double chromosomes ('doublets'). One doublet from each chromosome pair moves

to either end of the nucleus which now divides to give two daughter cells. The doublets then come apart, to give four individual chromosomes, but notice that the two pairs of chromosomes are identical copies from the original cell (either both have a black bar, or neither do). One of each pair now migrate to opposite ends of the new nucleus, which divides again. Now there would be four daughter cells, each of which contains half the number of chromosomes in a typical cell, and one copy of each chromosome pair, although for clarity I only show the second division of one cell.

The upshot of this rigmarole is that each egg or sperm contains exactly one half of the normal complement of chromosomes, together with an X or a Y, a total of 39 in a dog. These consist of one copy of each homologous pair. Whether the chromosome transmitted to a progeny came from the grandfather or the grandmother is a matter of chance. On the average, half the chromosomes in an egg or sperm come from the grandfather and the rest from the grandmother. When the egg and sperm unite, the total is brought back to 78 so that the newly fertilised cell (or *zygote*) contains the full set of chromosomes. This means that, in any individual, one member of each chromosome pair is inherited from the father, and the other from the mother, and approximately one quarter from each of the four grandparents.

GENES
Situated along the chromosomes are regions called genes, and these are responsible for determining the nature of inherited characters. A good example is the colour of the spots on a Dalmatian which can be liver or black. Liver-spotted dogs breed true; in other words, if a liver-spotted

3

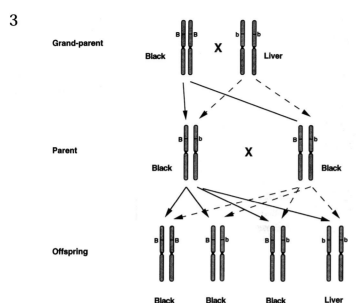

Diagrammatic representation of the segregation of chromosomes carrying the spot-colour gene during fertilisation. One grand-parent is homozygous for the B (black) allele, and the other for recessive b (liver). Their offspring receive a B allele from one (solid line) and a b allele (broken line) from the other. If two of these are mated together, either a B or a b allele can be passed on to the next generation. Four possible progeny can be produced, representing three genotypes and two phenotypes.

male is mated with a liver-spotted female, all of the progeny will have liver spots. However, if a black-spotted animal (of either sex) is mated with a liver-spotted individual, in many litters the puppies will all have black spots. Should two of these black-spotted puppies then be crossed, liver-spotted animals may appear among their progeny. The character of liver-spotting disappears in the first generation, to re-emerge in a subsequent generation.

The explanation for this is fairly simple. At a point on one chromosome there is a gene for spot-colour; the position of the gene is called its *locus*. In fact, this particular gene determines not just spot colour in Dalmatians, but the ability of a dog of any breed to produce black pigment. There are two types of gene that differ very slightly in their structure. One copy (or *allele*) allows the animal to produce black pigment; the other allele

does not, and liver (or 'chocolate' or 'tan' or 'red') pigment is produced instead. Even 'white' dogs such as Samoyeds or West Highland Whites possess the black allele, for black pigment can be seen in the nose.

Since there are two pairs of chromosomes, there will be two copies of each gene in every dog. An individual from a line of pure-breeding liver-spotted Dalmatians will have two copies of the liver allele, whereas one from a pure-breeding line of black-spotted has two copies of the black allele. When a puppy is made, each parent gives one copy of each pair of chromosomes, in other words one copy of each of its genes. So, as shown in Fig. 3, a cross between a liver and a pure black will produce puppies with a black allele from one parent, and a liver allele from the other. They are black-spotted.

This situation introduces a series of important terms. An individual that has two copies of the same allele is said to be *'homozygous'* for that allele; if the alleles differ, it is said to be *'heterozygous'*. So, a liver-spotted dog is homozygous for the liver allele, but a puppy produced by crossing liver- and black-spotted animals will be heterozygous for the black and liver alleles. The heterozygous puppy has black spots, so the black allele is said to be *'dominant'* over the liver allele – which in turn is described as *'recessive'*. Finally (for now), the genetic composition of the animal is called its *'genotype'*, but its appearance is its *'phenotype'*. The homozygous dog with two black alleles and the heterozygous dog with one black allele and one liver have different genotypes, but the same phenotype.

The black allele is conventionally called *B* as a capital letter because it is dominant; the liver allele is called *b* in lower case because it is recessive. So, a liver dog will be denoted as *bb*. We can illustrate the inheritance of spot colour as follows (see also Figure 3, page 97):

Parental genotype	**BB**	x	**bb**
Parental phenotype	Black		Liver
Egg or Sperm	**B**		**b**
Progeny genotype		**Bb**	
Progeny phenotype		Black	

Note again that, although the spot colour (or phenotype) of the puppies is the same as one of their parents, their genetic make-up (or genotype) is different. This means that they can produce two different kinds of gametes or sex cells – one with a *B* allele and the other with a *b* allele. This is shown in the lower part of Fig. 3. Fertilisation is accompanied by the random union of gametes, so that there are four possible combinations: *B* (father) + *B* (mother); *B* (father) + *b* (mother); *b* (father) + *B* (mother); *b* (father) + *b* (mother). The solid arrows show the transmission of alleles from one parent, and the broken arrows from the other: the resulting progeny will occur in equal proportions. You will see that genetically there are three kinds of progeny: *BB*, *Bb* and *bb*, which occur in the ratio of 1 *BB* to 2 *Bb* to 1 *bb*. There are twice as many heterozygous offspring because these can be formed either by a *B* from the father and a *b* from the mother, or the other way round. There are only two possible phenotypes, however, black or liver, which occur in the ratio of 3 black to 1 liver.

A heterozygote has two different alleles, and it is important to appreciate that whichever is present in an individual egg or sperm is a matter of chance. On average, half of the gametes will contain one allele and half will contain the other. However, just as with tossing a coin, so with breeding puppies; expectation and reality need not be identical. If a sufficiently large number of puppies is raised, the ratios will be very close, but smaller numbers can give chance deviation from these expectation. The statistics of genetic ratios is well studied, but is beyond the scope of this Chapter. Interested readers should look in a more specialist textbook such as *Genetics of the Dog* by Willis.

Nevertheless, using a diagram such as Fig. 3, it is possible to show that *backcrossing* a heterozygous *Bb* dog to a *bb* mate will produce equal numbers of *Bb* (black) and *bb* (liver) puppies. The other backcross of *Bb* to *BB* will produce equal numbers of *BB* and *Bb* puppies, but these will all be black-spotted. In general, a 'global' table of all possible crosses can be produced showing the outcome of all possible crosses of spotting genotypes:

One parent	Other parent	BB - Black	% of puppies of each type		
			BB - Black	Bb - Black	bb - Liver
BB - Black	BB - Black	100	0	0	
BB - Black	Bb - Black	50	50	0	
BB - Black	bb - Liver	0	100	0	
Bb - Black	Bb - Black	25	50	25	
Bb - Black	bb - Liver	0	50	50	
bb - Liver	bb - Liver	0	0	100	

Again, remember that these are ratios of *expected* proportions.

SEX DETERMINATION

We have already seen that a male dog has 38 pairs of normal chromosomes (autosomes) plus X and Y sex-chromosomes, whereas a female has two X chromosomes. This means that a female can only pass on an X to her offspring, whereas a male can transmit either X or Y to each of his progeny (see Figure 4, below). If the sperm contains an X chromosome, then the puppy will be

4

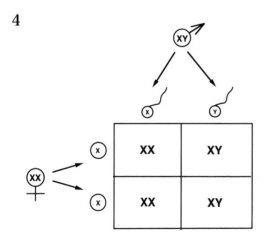

The determination of sex by the transmission of X and Y chromosomes. Males are XY and females are XX. Thus, fathers transmit either X or Y in their sperm, and the sex of the progeny is determined by this.

female, if a Y then a male. Just as with the spot-colour alleles in the previous section, whether a male transmits an X or Y chromosome into his sperm is a matter of chance. The probability is very close to 50 per cent, which is why litters tend to have approximately equal numbers of dogs and bitches.

Thus the sex of a puppy is determined by the father; for a female to have an influence upon the sex of a puppy would imply that she had some means of differentiating between X and Y bearing sperms in her reproductive tract! While not impossible, there is very little evidence that this occurs. If a female has several litters to the same male that are predominantly of one sex, it is possible that the male has some abnormality causing him to produce an excess of X or Y bearing sperm. If she was mated to a series of different males, it is probably just chance that has caused an unbalanced sex ratio. In either case, large litters and careful statistical analysis are needed before any conclusion can be drawn.

SEX LINKAGE

Some genes are situated on the X chromosome, and so their alleles are transmitted differently with sex. A familiar example is the appearance of tortoiseshell in cats, less common is haemophilia in dogs. This condition causes failure of the blood clotting process, and is usually fatal. It is much commoner in males, and usually

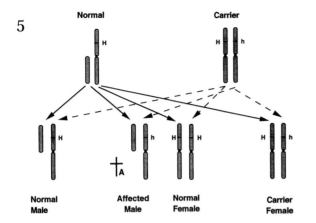

The transmission of a sex-linked condition (haemophilia) from a normal father and carrier mother. Note that the small Y chromosome is transmitted to half of the progeny, and these are male; if they inherit the recessive allele from their mother, they will be haemophilic. Half of the female progeny will be carriers, since they inherit the disease allele from their mothers.

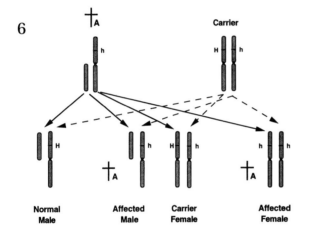

The less common transmission of a sex-linked trait from an affected father to a carrier mother. Again, half of the sons will be affected, but here half of the females will inherit the recessive allele from both parents. They will be homozygous and so will show the condition.

occurs among some but not all male puppies in an affected litter. It has been shown to be due to a gene on the X chromosome which is recessive since heterozygous females are not haemophilic.

The pattern of inheritance is shown in Figures 5 and 6 (above). Because the condition is so debilitating, the majority of cases involve a phenotypically normal female who produces affected sons when mated with a non-haemophilic male. The Y chromosome is very small, and carries very few genes; certainly not one for haemophilia. In Fig. 5, the male has a normal allele (*H*) on his X chromosome,

and the female is a 'carrier' – that is, she is heterozygous (*Hh*) for the haemophilia allele, but because this is recessive she is phenotypically normal with a normal pattern of blood clotting. The male gives an X chromosome carrying the normal allele to half of his offspring and a Y chromosome to the rest with no allele at the haemophilia locus. The female gives half of her offspring a chromosome with a normal (*H*) allele and the rest one with the allele (*h*) for haemophilia. Those progeny that inherit the Y chromosome are male. Those that receive the allele *H* from their mother will be normal, but those that inherit *h* from her will be haemophilic. All of the daughters will be phenotypically normal since they have inherited the *H* allele from their father. However, half will be carriers like their mother since they will inherit the *h* allele from her.

The majority of affected males will die young from severe haemophilia. However, if one does survive to mate with a carrier female, a pedigree like Fig. 6 will result. As with the previous example, half of the sons will be affected since they receive the *h* allele from their mother. Half of the daughters will inherit an *h* allele from each parent and be homozygous *hh* and die early in life. Using a similar diagram, it is possible to show that a mating between an affected male and a normal *HH* female will produce normal males and carrier females.

Fortunately, sex-linked conditions are rare in dogs, but the pattern of inheritance is distinctive, with a trait typically appearing in the male line, but being transmitted by the females.

LINKAGE
There are more genes than chromosomes. This means that many genes occur on the same chromosome, and so potentially may be inherited together. In fact, there is a process called 'recombination' which allows re-arrangement of alleles between chromosomes. When the chromosomes are replicated in the first stages of meiosis (Fig. 2), the paternally-derived and maternal copies come into close proximity. The chromosomes break at the same point, and when they are repaired, the 'wrong' ends become attached. Thus a fragment of a paternal chromosome may be transferred to its maternal counterpart, being replaced by the same piece from the maternal chromosome as shown in Fig. 8.

This process results in a continual mixing or 'recombining' of DNA strands, and hence genes. Thus, a breeding individual may pass on some of its father's chromosomes and some of its mother's to its progeny, but the chromosomes themselves will have new combinations of alleles. From an evolutionary point of view, this is a good thing since it results in the genetic structure of members of a species being continually modified, allowing natural selection to 'test' new combinations of alleles. It is of mixed benefit for a breeder. On the positive side, the re-assortment of paternal and maternal chromosomes, and the recombining of the individual chromosomes themselves, will result in new combinations of characters being continually produced. These the breeder can examine and choose to breed from or discard. The possibility exists for desirable attributes that exist in different animals but are controlled by the same chromosome, to recombine to produce puppies with the characters in combination. The counterside to this, of course, is that some puppies will be produced that possess neither of the attributes!

In general, however, recombination is to be regarded as beneficial, since it is a provider of novel combinations of alleles, with the possibility that superior progeny will be found among the litter.

QUANTITATIVE CHARACTERS
Not all traits are controlled by single genes; indeed many of the more familiar characteristics such as size, shape, temperament, etc. seem to be determined by many genes each of which has a rather small effect. Such characters are typically continuous or 'quantitative', and are normally *measured* in terms of inches, grams, degrees centigrade, etc. rather than *counted* as discontinuous traits such as black-spotted or liver-spotted, male or female, haemophilic or not-haemophilic.

When studying continuous characters like height, it is usually impossible to recognise the individual genes that are involved. As a consequence, geneticists cannot identify genotypes, and are compelled to work with phenotypes. This means that each animal is represented by an individual measure – a weight of 21 kg; a height of 14ins; a BVA Hip Score of 16; etc. The most important attribute of a metric trait, after its size, is its variation among a group of individuals such as a litter. In statistics, this variation is termed the variance, and the fundamental equation of quantitative genetics describes this variance as follows:

Observed (Phenotypic) Variance = Genetic Variance + Environmental Variance.

The importance of this is evident by thinking about the situation in agriculture. A farmer wishes to grow cereals. He wants all the plants in a field to be ready for harvest at the same time, to be equal in height, and all the seeds to contain a similar proportion of protein. That way, he can cut all the field on the same day, set the blades at one height, and sell all of his crop to a baker or a brewer. The seedsman will sell him grain that is genetically as uniform as possible, ideally homozygous at every locus. That way leads to a uniformly homogeneous crop – i.e. zero genetic variance. There may be differences across the field in moisture, shading or rabbit grazing, but that is environmental variation, and managing this is a matter of husbandry, not genetics.

Conversely, a gardener who saves seed from last year's sweet-peas and sows them in a lovingly-prepared trench may find that they vary enormously in height, profusion and colour. The genetic uniformity that had been produced by the suppliers, and for which he paid good money last year, has been dissipated by meiosis, recombination and cross-fertilisation at flowering time. His sweet peas now contain a re-assortment of the alleles away from the genetic uniformity of last year. The trench may give him a uniform environment, but the genetic variance is now very high.

Similar examples can be quoted from the canine world. Distemper kills many dogs, but not every individual exposed to the disease becomes ill. There are probably resistance genes, and a few animals may be fortunate enough to be genetically resistant to the virus. However, these genes will be so rare, and finding them will be so difficult, that a better option is to vaccinate stock against the disease. Effectively, the breeder is saying that it is easier to proceed by modifying the environment through killing the virus before it makes the animal ill, rather than by using genetics to create a line of distemper-resistant dogs. Conversely, a disease that has a strong genetic component, such as hereditary cataract, may be controlled more easily by eliminating the gene responsible from a line than by searching for a cure after the condition has taken hold.

These inter-relations of genetic and environmental variation are of crucial importance in a breeding programme. From a practical point of view, if most of the observed variation in a character is environmental, then improvement will come by changing the conditions in which the animals are kept. The fraction of the phenotypic variance that is due to genetic effects is called the 'heritability', and is a key measure in quantitative genetics. Estimating the heritability of a particular character is not easy, but is essential if a scientific approach is to be made to changing the incidence of a continuous character in a population.

If the heritability of a trait is high, this

means that most of the variation in a character is genetic in origin. This tells the breeder that many of the genes controlling the character are 'polymorphic'. In other words, there are two (or more) allelic forms of the genes, giving the breeder the opportunity of selecting the most desirable ones for his stock. For many traits, a breeder has little hope of improving his stock by modifying the conditions under which his animals are reared. To improve the quality of his dogs, it is necessary to change their genetic architecture: to increase the frequency of alleles that are 'advantageous' and give a desirable phenotype, and reduce the frequency of less desirable alleles. In other words, to exert selection by choosing to breed from animals that possess the desired attribute.

SELECTION

Selection is the term used for the improvement of a population, by choosing individuals which show a trait in its most desirable form and using these as breeding stock for the subsequent generation. If the character involved is under genetic control, selecting and breeding from individuals with a desirable phenotype should favour the alleles conferring this optimum at the expense of the others. Gradually, they will spread in the population, increasing the quality of its members. Clearly, the link between the choice of individuals and the improvement in the stock is the genetic control of the character.

For a character under simple genetic control, such as spot colour, this is relatively straightforward. If a breeder decides to produce a line of Dalmatians that is exclusively liver-spotted, all he needs to do is find animals that possess liver spots and breed from these. Since the trait is determined by a recessive allele, all liver-spotted animals will be homozygous for the

desired allele. The term 'fixed' is used to describe an allele that is the sole representative at its locus in a population. Thus, in this case, the liver-spotted allele will be fixed in the line, and that for black-spotting will have been lost.

The converse occurs when a breeder wishes to remove a recessive allele from his stock. There seem to be very few instances of recessive diseases in Dalmatians, but an example that occurs in other breeds is hereditary cataract, a condition leading to blindness which develops at an early age. This is genetically recessive, so that affected individuals are homozygous for the cataract allele. Since it can be diagnosed at an early age, these homozygotes can be recognised and removed from the breeding population. However, there will remain a residuum of heterozygous or 'carrier' individuals. To completely eliminate the condition from a line, it is necessary to identify these carriers and remove them from the breeding programme. If two phenotypically normal parents produce an affected puppy, they must both be carriers of the cataract allele, hidden by its recessive nature. A simple decision would be to remove both adults from the breeding programme. However, these might be otherwise excellent examples of the breed, possessing attributes that the breeder is unwilling to discard. An alternative approach is then to perform a 'test-cross', and this is illustrated in Figure 7 on page 104. The individual in the centre is homozygous for the recessive trait, and can be mated with one of unknown genotype. If this is a homozygous dominant (as on the left), then all of the progeny will be phenotypically normal; if a heterozygote (on the right), then affected progeny will appear in the litter. Thus, mating back to a homozygous recessive adult 'tests' the other adult: affected progeny imply that it

7

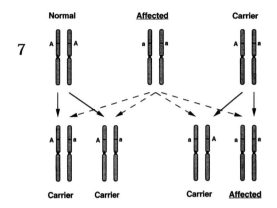

Normal   Affected   Carrier

Carrier   Carrier   Carrier   Affected

The theory behind test-crossing individuals for a recessive allele. The affected individual is mated with the animal to be tested. If this is homozygous for the normal allele, all of the progeny will be of normal phenotype. If it is a heterozygote, half of the progeny will be homozygous for the disease allele, and so affected.

is a carrier. Such test-crossing is an excellent means of recognising carriers. It has even been suggested that, in a breed with a debilitating recessive condition such as cataract, an affected dog or bitch is an essential member of the kennel, but its adoption in a dog breeding programme carries serious moral responsibilities. The affected adults have to be cared for, and hard decisions need to be taken over the fate of any puppies that stem from such test-crosses. This can be more of a problem than is immediately obvious. A dog can easily be shown to be a carrier: a single affected puppy in a test-cross litter shows that it carries a recessive allele. However, the converse is a little more tricky. If the dog is a carrier, then approximately half of its puppies will be carry the affected allele. Thus a litter needs to be sufficiently large to give this allele a chance of being transmitted into the progeny. Clearly, a litter of one or two is not adequate; larger numbers are needed. In practice, this means at least nine or ten unaffected puppies are needed before an animal can be declared not to carry the disease-causing allele. And, of course, whatever the outcome of the test, all of the puppies will be either carriers or affected with the disease, and in neither case will these be of any use in a future

breeding programme. They must be disposed of. Molecular tests are now being developed to reduce the need for test-crosses but, in their absence, this remains the most reliable means of ridding a line of an undesirable recessive allele.

If the character to be selected is quantitative, the problems are greater. We have seen that it is not possible to identify genotypes for most continuous characters, so the breeder has to work with phenotypes. Despite this, great success has been achieved in modifying the appearance of dogs by selecting morphological characters; indeed, most of the difference between breeds of dogs is the result of selection practiced by mankind. The Rothschild Collection in the Natural History Museum at Tring, Hertfordshire, contains stuffed dogs from a variety of breeds. A visit will show how much some breeds have altered over the last half-century and, provided that there is sufficient genetic variation within a breed, selection can still have an effect on changing its phenotype.

An excellent example of this is hip dysplasia (HD) which is discussed at length by Dr Malcolm Willis in his superb book *Genetics of the Dog.* HD is a potentially debilitating condition that occurs in many

8

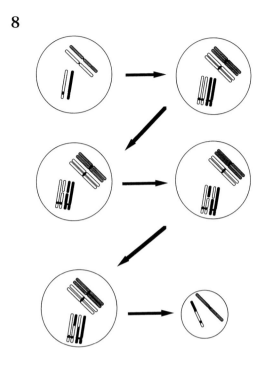

Linkage. The chromosomes replicate in a meiosis, and the doublets come together as in Fig. 2. Breaks appear at adjacent points in one strand of each doublet.

breeds. At its simplest, it is a shallowing of the socket of the hip, leading to a loose fit of the ball joint at the head of the femur. Increasingly bad fit leads to abrasion of the joint, pain and progressive incapacity. There is no doubt that it is a serious condition, and one that breeders should take care to minimise. In the UK, hip dysplasia is monitored through a screening programme under the auspices of the British Veterinary Association. From its data, Willis has shown that the condition has a genetic basis: its heritability is high. For example, between 25-40 per cent of the variation in German Shepherd Dogs is genetic, the remainder being 'environmental'. There is now plenty of evidence showing that selective breeding can reduce the incidence and severity of the condition in a line or a breed. Choosing individuals for breeding that have a low scores results in a progressive decline in the severity of HD among the progeny.

German Shepherd breeders have been in the forefront of this, and the severity of the condition in many lines has been substantially reduced over a period of years. It is very important to realise that selection is rarely rapid in generating a response, and so has to be continued for some or many generations. Changes are slight in any single generation, but gradually the alleles that cause HD can be reduced in frequency, giving subsequent generations a greater chance of being less affected. However, it is a slow process. In each generation, meiosis in the sex cells leads to a redistribution of the alleles that determine the genetic component of dysplasia. The responsible breeder uses his hip scores to identify those animals that are least affected and (hoping that this reflects their genetic composition) selects these as parents for future generations. However, less responsible individuals who either do not score their stock, or ignore the data, can retard the effects of this selection.

A practical problem relating to the examination of a quantitative character is determining a method for its measurement. In the case of HD, the BVA has set up a panel of specialists who undertake the analysis of X-ray plates of the hip joints. These people are regularly checked to ensure that they are all adopting the same criteria; it would be pointless if each was measuring to a different standard. If a new trait is to be examined, then this is an essential pre-requisite. Suppose that a canine society decided that temperament was in decline in its breed. Before the heritability could be determined, it would be necessary to establish a method by which dogs could be assayed. Heritability is most easily determined from the comparison of parents and their progeny, so breeders would have to be available who would be prepared to allow their stock to be assayed, and arrange for the progeny to be tested. The data would need to be collected, and then analysed by a suitable geneticist. Remember that the heritability is that proportion of the variation that is due to genetic effects, and is an estimate of the possibility of a response to a selection regime to improve the character (in this case, temperament) in the selected stock. Monitoring of the selected stock would need to be continued, in parallel with the analysis of non-selected individuals for comparative purposes.

This is not a project to be undertaken lightly, but if a group of breeders believe that it may be necessary to improve or restore the quality of their dogs, it is the only way forward. A final point to remember is that, while a character such as HD may be very distressing, it is not the only attribute of a breed. There is no point in producing superb hips, or temperament or anything else, if other features of the breed are damaged or destroyed. A balance has to be maintained, and the scientific approach leavened with a degree of common sense.

INBREEDING

A consequence of practising selection to improve a line is that the breeder will often wish to mate close relatives together in order to maintain some desirable attribute. The mating of related individuals is called inbreeding and can be detrimental. In many species, it has been shown to have an adverse effect upon the progeny. These problems may be poor growth, lower survival or the appearance of debilitating diseases, and may be sufficiently serious

that entire families die. The reduced survival of inbred progeny is termed 'inbreeding depression' and is something that breeders should be aware of.

It is now believed that much inbreeding depression is due to the existence of rare recessive alleles found at loci scattered through the chromosomes. These have been shown to occur in humans and a variety of other species. In humans, some are rare but well-known traits, such as haemophilia or cystic fibrosis, while others may be much less obvious. Although there are many loci in a population that may carry such recessive alleles, they are all sufficiently rare that individuals who are heterozygous for the same allele rarely marry, and so the chance of producing affected homozygotes is very slight. However, two related individuals may both carry the same recessive allele that they have inherited from a shared ancestor, in which case the risk is much higher. For example, if a male has one of these recessive alleles on one of his chromosomes, the probability that he will transmit it to a child is a half – he either passes on the normal allele or the affected one. The chance that a son and a daughter both receive this allele is thus 25 per cent. We have already seen that one quarter of the offspring of a mating between two heterozygotes will produce a recessive homozygous offspring. Thus, if the son and daughter mate, one quarter of the offspring will show the deleterious phenotype. If the condition is lethal, the mating will show inbreeding depression for a quarter of their offspring who will die.

These recessive alleles do not always kill their homozygous bearers; their effects may be to reduce viability or growth rate, or just lead to a failure to thrive. In any event, the mating of relatives can produce families that include individuals who are subvital, and inbreeding is generally regarded as a bad thing. The mathematical theory of inbreeding is very sophisticated, but there is little data from current breeds. It would be very interesting if breed clubs gathered information from their members relating to litter size, puppy weight and survival, etc., and compared this with the degree of relatedness of the parents. Comparisons between breeds, or between lines within breeds, would be very informative.

LINE-BREEDING

Many dog breeders have a clear preference for a particular combination of characteristics in their own breed, and choose to use only animals that conform to this type. In its extreme form, this leads to 'line-breeding' where there may be relatively small pools of dogs that are mated among themselves with little input from outside. Such practice can lead to a uniformity of type by the accumulation of the desired alleles, and the selective elimination of those that lead to less wanted phenotypes. Over a few generations, clear differences can emerge. However, while selecting for one trait, there is always the risk of unconsciously enhancing the frequency of a less desirable characteristic elsewhere, and a regular objective appraisal of where the line is going, and its relationship to the breed standard is essential. For example, an enthusiastic rush to improve temperament may also lead to less assertive behaviour, or selection to lower hip scores may introduce concomitant changes in skeletal conformation. Such associated changes need not relate to the character under selection. A stud dog that is especially attractive in one character may be weaker in another. Again, objective assessment at regular intervals is very important.

There is also the possibility that line-breeding will lead to inbreeding depression. We have already seen that a limited pool of animals carries with it the inevitability of mating between relatives, and that this may lead to inbreeding depression. However, this need not always be the case. Evidence from other species has shown that in some situations, mating of relatives does not lead to inbreeding depression, perhaps because the initial stock did not contain any disadvantageous alleles, or alternatively because these have been removed by natural mortality early in the breeding programme. However, it should always be borne in mind that there may be risks and problems associated with establishing a new line by selecting and breeding from a limited number of founders.

OUT BREEDING

The converse of inbreeding is outbreeding, where a breeder chooses individuals that are distantly related to his own. This reduces the chances of inbreeding depression, but crossing between lines does have the chance of disrupting the harmonious combinations of alleles that have been produced by the breeders of the two different lines. This is especially likely to occur in second generation crosses, but can occur in the first hybrid generation. There seems to be little data relating to this from dogs, though it has been recorded in other species. It is another area where breed clubs could make investigations.

MOLECULAR MAPPING

Recently, genetics has taken a great leap forward. Molecular techniques have been developed that allow the genes to be examined in very great detail. I mentioned at the start that genes are made from DNA, and this in turn consists of a linear molecule composed of chemical subunits called bases. There are four different bases, and

9   *Outline of the processes involved in genetic testing*

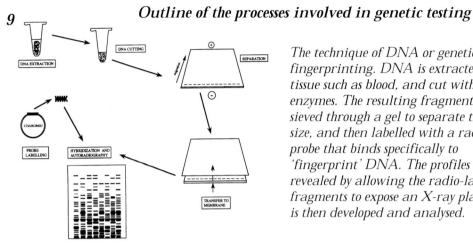

The technique of DNA or genetic fingerprinting. DNA is extracted from tissue such as blood, and cut with enzymes. The resulting fragments are sieved through a gel to separate them by size, and then labelled with a radio-active probe that binds specifically to 'fingerprint' DNA. The profiles are revealed by allowing the radio-labelled fragments to expose an X-ray plate which is then developed and analysed.

the sequence of these determines the structure of the molecule that the gene controls. It is now possible to 'read' this sequence in an individual strand of DNA. A great deal of effort is being expended on this in human research. The 'Human Genome Project' is intended to discover the base sequence of every chromosome in the human nucleus.

One of the uses of this will be in identifying individuals who carry a particular disease-causing gene. The sequence of bases can be determined for the 'normal' and the disease-causing alleles. An individual is screened for this gene; this can be at any age, but may be early in pregnancy. If only the 'normal' sequence is found, the individual will be unaffected; if only the 'affected' sequence is identified, it will be homozygous for that allele; if both sequences are found, the subject will be a heterozygote or carrier. In the case of humans, advice is then offered by the genetic counselling service, and termination may ensue.

In the case of dogs, research lags far behind. However, the principle remains that when the sequence of normal and disease-causing alleles is known for a particular locus, it will be possible to screen

new-born puppies for their genotype. Individuals that will grow into affected adults can be culled, and carriers identified with a view to their use in any future breeding programme. There is no problem with using a carrier individual as a parent in a future mating, provided that the breeder accepts that a proportion of the progeny will similarly be carriers. This way, an individual that carries a disease-causing gene but otherwise has a particularly desirable phenotype, is not lost to future generations. Planned breeding, coupled with early screening of the progeny, will permit puppies lacking the deleterious allele to be identified.

This procedure is now becoming available. The problem is that screening DNA to identify the gene causing the disease, and then determining its base sequence, is very expensive, requiring sophisticated equipment and highly trained personnel. However, a canine genome project is now under way, supported by the Animal Health Trust. It is realistic to expect that within five or ten years, genes will have been identified for several of the commoner diseases, so that screening of litters will become a recognised part of a breeder's options.

10 *BREEDING DALMATIANS*

BREEDING PROGRAMMES

Initial interest in a dog breed is usually superficial. Without knowing how it happens, it is surprisingly easy to find yourself involved and, when that involvement reaches a certain stage, then – almost invariably – you will wish to breed it on.

Breeding is a colossal subject, and you need only study one small part to become aware of just how much there is to learn. Litters can be planned by their breeders years ahead; indeed, the sire and dam themselves may have been bred with this litter in mind. However, do not be carried away or overwhelmed by science. Like learning to drive, take each point separately and in turn.

As the owner of either bitch or dog, take this opportunity to look at the animal totally devoid of rose-tinted spectacles. Yes, your Dalmatian may be a real beauty, who has won well for you in the ring and become a much-loved companion. At the same time, does it carry the genes of an inherited fault? Does the dog exhibit shyness, nervousness or aggression, all of which are allied faults? Is the animal correct

The Phaeland Family: The nine Champions pictured are: Ch. Phaeland Phisherman, Ch. Phaeland Patron, Ch. Konavlje Miss Gorgeous, Ch. Phaeland Phorgetmenot, Ch. Phaeland Phreda, Ch. Delvallie Dark Bronze, Ch. Phaeland Phergus, Ch. Delvallie Blueprint and Ch. Phaeland Phrench Phern.   *Photo: Anne Roslin-Williams.*
The aim of a breeder is to build a family line with its own distinctive type.

LEFT: Ch. Beaumore Night Owl of Olbero: 8CCs, 7RCCs, BIS DCS Ch. Show 1987, BIS BDC Ch. Show 1987, BOB and Group 2 WELKS 1989, sire of four UK and three Int. Champions. RIGHT: Ch. Elaridge Endeavour: 7CCs, 11 RCCs, BIS NOEDC Ch. Show 1985, BIS DCS Ch. Show 1988, BVIS BUBA Ch. Show 1993.
A stud dog must be an outstanding example of the breed ,
sound in temperament and free of all inherited conditions.

structurally, with that all-important flowing movement? The perfect Dalmatian has yet to be born, but do take care not to double up on faults which could be reproduced in your precious puppies.

In-breeding, line breeding and out-breeding are all terms you have heard discussed. In-breeding consists of using animals of the closest possible relationship, father/daughter, mother/son, etc., and by doing so restricting the breeding pattern to what is already present, fixing both good and bad points. This is for very experienced breeders only, who have exceptionally good and fault-free stock which they know intimately, and who are prepared to cull any serious faults from their litters.

Line breeding is a modified version of this, and means just what it says. Breeding takes place between animals from similar lines, though not so closely related as those described above. By this means you hope to double up on good points, and improve on bad, but you will avoid the disasters which can beset the true in-breeder.

To breed out, you are free to choose a dog you really like who is compatible in type and character with your bitch,

irrespective of breeding. Here, the experts say, you will be just as likely as anyone to breed an outstanding winner, but whether or not the good qualities of that dog will be passed on to the progeny is another matter. They have not been duplicated in the mating and may, therefore, by-pass the puppies.

A further aspect to consider is colour. Breed black to black, or black to liver, and the puppies will be either black or liver spotted, with one or both colours in the litter. The only exception is if you breed liver to liver, when the puppies, too, will be liver spotted. If you keep to the same colour generation after generation, then colour and pigmentation can sometimes deteriorate. Many experienced breeders advise that to correct pigmentation or colour, or even to enhance excellence in either, it can on occasion be helpful to use the alternative liver or black as appropriate.

It only remains to say that both animals should be in tip-top condition, possess normal hearing certificates, good X-ray results for hip dysplasia and up-to-date inoculations.

FINDING THE RIGHT STUD DOG

We now come to that most difficult problem, finding the right dog for your bitch. Take advantage of all the information and advice you can get, particularly from those breeders whose blood lines are carried in the sire and dam of your bitch and of any dog you are considering.

Without doubt, their opinions will differ, but do not despair; take a good look at all the dogs which have been mentioned. Ask the owners for copies of the pedigrees and, most important of all, take a look at their progeny and a litter of puppies in the nest, if possible. If the dam is similar in breeding to your bitch, her puppies may well give an indication of what you can expect.

There will be some who urge you to select the dog with a pin, and others who suggest that you choose a dog you 'like the look of'. However, if you want to carry through temperament and type and improve the good points you already have, then the study of pedigree and performance must come into the picture. In-depth study of this description takes years rather than months, and many of us start while the prospective mother is still in the nest, and sometimes before then.

Having listened to all the advice, having read the books, studied the pedigrees, looked at dogs, progeny and puppies, avoid agonising and last-minute changes of mind – make your decision and stay with it.

THE BITCH

As a novice breeder it is as well to know what you are taking on if you are contemplating breeding a litter.

From a purely practical point of view, you need sufficient space. There must be a room where you can have a four feet square whelping box, and space for the puppies to stagger round when they first come out of the nest. As they grow they need space to run and play under cover in case the weather is bad, and an accessible garden area where they can exercise freely in good weather and also learn initial house training.

There is a heavy financial burden which you may, or may not, recover at the end of the day. Sufficient money must be readily available during the eight weeks before the puppies are sold and paid for by their new owners. The cost of day-to-day food and upkeep for the bitch and puppies is exceedingly high, and escalates alarmingly throughout the last five weeks. Rearing a litter, and giving it the best possible start, will take all your time and strength for the full eight weeks. It is quite true that for the first three weeks or so the bitch is mainly responsible for the puppies, but for you this is a time of gradual acclimatisation to an ever-increasing workload.

THE MATING

From the first time your bitch comes into season, note down the date she comes in, the date she seems ready for mating and the date she is finished. This record will help you to establish her cycle. To complete a successful mating, it is important to recognise the first day of your bitch's season. As soon as you sense this may be imminent, press a piece of tissue very gently on her vulva before she goes outside each morning. For a few days it will merely show a certain wetness, but sooner or later there will be touch of pink and that is Day One.

You will know from your previous notes on which day she normally seems to be ready for mating, and it is useless to quote the cycles of other bitches because they can all be different. The 14th day is a good average, but place no reliance on it as a certainty. Keep a close eye on her posterior, and watch carefully for when the blood starts to lose its colour. At the same time,

Ch. Dalregis Cressida: 3CCs, 3RCCs. Top Dalmatian Puppy and winner of BP & Puppy Leeds Ch. Show, BOB Crufts 1990. Her two litters sired by Ch. Konavlje the Wayfarer at Miragua have produced two UK and two overseas Champions.

Ch. Tamaron Tic Tac of Bawhinnan: 12 CCs, 8RCCs, BIS Joint Clubs Ch. Show, BIS NOEDC Ch. Show, RBIS DCS Ch. Show, RBIS Joint Clubs Ch. Show, BIS all breeds Open Show.

the pad of skin under the vulva softens and becomes slightly 'spongy'. That is normally the day she is ready. If you are uncertain, consult your vet and he will explain the various tests which can be carried out.

Let the stud dog owner know as soon as your bitch has come into season and, once you have established when the bitch will be ready, arrange a time and a place to meet. Normally, the bitch travels to the dog, but obviously you make whatever arrangements are most convenient to you both. When the pair come together for the mating, they should be introduced to each other on the lead, and can quickly be let off to play. This foreplay is a most important part of the mating, and should never be omitted.

Providing it is the right day, after a short game the bitch will plant her feet firmly on the ground, swish her tail to one side and the dog will promptly mount her. At this stage, the owner of the bitch can take her collar and gently dissuade her from moving. As soon as the tie has been established, the owner of the dog gently takes one hind leg and lifts it across the back of the bitch so that the two animals can stand comfortably

back to back. Continue to steady them both by the collar and eventually, after 15 to 20 minutes or so, the tie normally comes to an end quite naturally. It can go on a good deal longer, so be warned and have a pair of stools strategically positioned for you to sit on while you wait. Very occasionally, you get a dog and bitch who simply do not like each other and will not mate. This happens extremely rarely but, if it does, then accept that nature knows best and that, if you persist with the mating, it is unlikely to be a success.

As to a second mating, opinions differ. Some hold that one good mating should be sufficient, others believe there should be a second mating 24 hours after the first, while some breeders leave two or even three days between the first and the second mating. One tends to follow one's early teaching, and I have always mated my bitches twice, with 24 hours between. However, if you get precisely the right day, one mating is obviously sufficient.

Once the bitch has been mated, she will not only be intensely interesting to other dogs but will be only too anxious to repeat

112

The Greenmount bitch line (Pictured left to right): Ch. Lazaar's Gay Gipsy of Greenmount, her daughter Ch. Greenmount Greensleeves, her grand-daughter Ch. Greenmount Golden Guinea and her great grand-daughter Ch. Greenmount Grace Darling.

the performance. Take the greatest care for the next ten days or so that there is no opportunity for her to go seeking new friends. Exercise is fine. but strictly on the lead and with a large walking stick on hand to deter any would-be admirers.

Wash down her quarters each morning and evening with a weak solution of antiseptic and warm water. After ten days or so, the season will be over completely and the bitch will snap quite fiercely if a passing dog shows any interest. This is not bad temperament but completely natural, so she should not be scolded.

CARE DURING PREGNANCY

I was first amused, and later helped, by the whelping cycle of Boxer pups shown in Kay White's original book. With some trepidation I asked if I might reproduce this, and felt quite overwhelmed at Kay's immediate response: "Would you not prefer to have it re-drawn for the Dalmatian?" I hope you will enjoy this and find it useful. Her husband, Harold White, was the artist.

There are nine weeks of pregnancy in all, the first five weeks of which are a waiting game. Start a major collection of newspaper (take care not to store it where rats or mice can run over it) and try and get well ahead with all household tasks. Exercise your bitch normally, but try and prevent her from hitting her sides against hard surfaces. If other dogs share the house, then you may care to hold her back so that she escapes the usual mad stampede through the door. Fights of any sort should be avoided at all costs.

Raspberry leaf tablets can be introduced from mating onwards, but otherwise keep the bitch on her normal diet of best-quality high-protein food. Do not be persuaded to give her extra rations until it is quite certain that puppies are on the way. If she has 'missed', she will only build up excess weight and you will have this to deal with in addition to the inevitable false pregnancy. As the fifth week of pregnancy approaches, begin to look for signs of an impending family. Look straight down the bitch's back and you may see a faint smudging in her outline and thickening of her previously trim waist. The bitch will also become very confidential and loving.

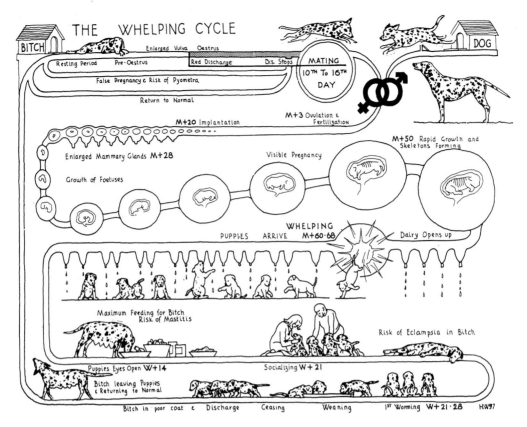

The Whelping cycle

Drawing by Harold White.

You may be happy to let nature take its course, but if you prefer you can ask for a scan, or your vet can suggest various tests. However, in whatever way you establish pregnancy, from then on the programme changes.

FEEDING: MATING TO WEANING
All puppies are sweet, but you will hear some referred to as 'real little beauties'. Without exception these will have strong bones, depth of substance, coats that glow regardless of the spot pattern, and that wonderful smell, like a summer evening you wish you could bottle and keep. None of this comes by magic. The correct feeding and the well-being of the bitch has a direct bearing on the quality of the puppies. First-rate puppies demand first-rate feeding and this is guaranteed from the beginning by the quality of the bitch's milk. To produce

this, she requires good food with a high level of protein and the correct additives throughout.

Although I refer below to fresh food, if you normally use dried complete formula it should not be difficult to translate; the correct quantities are always given on the packet. Feeding the bitch correctly needs great care. Even when the pups have been weaned, her diet should not be reduced until her body substance has been completely replenished, and then only gradually so that she does not lose condition. All bitches have different requirements, but the following suggestions will give you a general idea of how the normal diet increases to meet the needs of the pups.

Normal Diet before Mating
BREAKFAST: 4 oz wholemeal biscuit

(soaked), 4 oz protein (fish/tripe/turkey etc.), 2 garlic and 2 greenleaf pills, 1 teaspoonful sterilised bonemeal, 1 teaspoonful corn oil, followed with small cup milk diluted with hot water. TEA: 1 lb raw meat (beef), 4 mineral tablets (increase through pregnancy as per instructions). BEDTIME: Hard biscuits.

From Mating onwards
Meals as above. Add Raspberry leaf tablets (instructions on packet).

Mating plus four weeks
Meals as above. TEA: Increase meat to 1.25 lbs.

Mating plus five weeks
BREAKFAST: Increase biscuit and protein to 5 oz of each. Add 10cc calcium supplement. Replace cow's milk with evaporated milk and water (one tin milk x one tin hot water). TEA: Add 10cc calcium supplement.

Mating plus six weeks
BREAKFAST: Increase biscuit and protein each to 6 oz. Divide meal into two, half each at breakfast and lunch. TEA: Increase meat to 1.5 lbs. Divide into two, giving 1 lb at teatime and 8 oz at nine o'clock supper.

Meals at Whelping
Unlikely to eat but offer frequent drinks: water with honey or glucose added; evaporated milk if she prefers (well-diluted with water or it will make her loose), plus honey or glucose.

Meal after Whelping
Milk pudding or possibly a light meal of boiled chicken; if she has eaten all the placentas she may simply prefer evaporated milk with water plus glucose or honey.

Meals post-whelping
BREAKFAST: 5 oz wholemeal biscuit (soaked), 1 lb protein, 3 garlic and 3 greenleaf tablets, 4 mineral tablets, 2 teaspoonfuls sterilised bonemeal, 2 teaspoonsfuls corn oil, 10cc calcium supplement. Follow with evaporated milk/water. LUNCH: 3 eggs scrambled, cereal made with broth, 4 mineral tablets, 10 cc calcium supplement. (This meal about one lb in weight in all). TEA: 2 lbs beef, 3 garlic and three greenleaf tablets, 4 mineral tablets, 10cc calcium substitute. (This can be divided into 1.25 lbs tea and .75 lb early supper). LATE SUPPER: Rice pudding. BEDTIME: Hard biscuits.

Keep to this diet until the puppies are about seven weeks old and then decrease gradually. By the time the puppies are three months old, the bitch will have reverted to her normal diet.

PREPARATIONS IN PREGNANCY
Discuss with your vet the various problems that might arise. Enquire if he is prepared to make house visits; you may not wish to take the bitch and puppies to the surgery. If you have an over-large litter, as Dalmatians are prone to produce, ensure the vet will cull this to the number you consider your bitch can deal with happily. Check also that your vet will remove the dew claws at the age of three days in your own home. Remember to let the vet know as soon as the bitch starts whelping, so if there are problems he will not be surprised to get a call. Equally, do tell him when the whelping is safely over and, at the same time, arrange a convenient time for him to call and check your bitch.

You will need a whelping box, 4ft square with sides 18ins high. It looks enormous, but I can assure you it will end up being exactly right for a Dalmatian litter. Plastic-coated chipboard is ideal, but equally it can be made from wood. The front should be removable in two sections of equal size. The bottom half keeps the puppies safe while they are tiny; add the second section when they are becoming bigger and more adventurous. Once they can hook their elbows over the top and hurl themselves to the floor, remove both sections and give them permanent free access.

A removable bar, fixed around three sides of the box at a level which fits nicely into the centre of the bitch's back, ensures she is comfortable when she leans against it. This provides an escape area for the puppies while they are tiny and can usually be dispensed with three or four days after whelping, when the bitch has become fully-accustomed to her new family.

As far as bedding is concerned, Vetbed is the miracle of the age. I put two, one on top of the other, across the end of the whelping box. The 54 x 36 inch size leaves plenty of room for a good covering of newspaper in the remaining half of the box. Place the whelping box somewhere quiet and private where she will feel secure and undisturbed. Pull thick curtains across the window, keep the lights down as far as possible, and hang a heat lamp about five feet above one corner of the whelping box. The bitch and puppies can then move away and back as they wish.

Assemble the whelping box a week or two before the litter is expected, but be prepared for the bitch to ignore it completely. My other dogs always make a detailed inspection but I have never caught any of the expectant bitches putting so much as a paw inside at an early stage, although I have little trouble in persuading them there when the puppies are imminent.

On the basis that you should not buy the pram before the baby is born, you may like to leave the actual preparations until shortly before the birth. However, do not get caught out or you will panic, so make a list of the things you will need and make sure they are in the whelping room in good time:

Two sacks to hold soiled newspaper, etc, surgical scissors, antiseptic liquid, soft fine towels, packet gauze swabs, notebook and biro, weighing scales, glucose, clear honey, evaporated milk, fresh water, thermometer, clock, kitchen paper, bottle of brandy and teaspoon, cardboard box lined with bedding, hot-water bottle, puppy feeding bottle with teats, packet of commercial bitch replacement milk, bucket with lid in case of dead puppy, etc., mattress or cushions, plus book for you, electric kettle, coffee and milk, telephone numbers of vet and experienced breeder.

If you have not been accustomed to taking your bitch's temperature, do so once or twice at this stage to get you both used to it. Make sure you have the necessary paperwork for registering the puppies from your national Kennel Club.

WHELPING

For the last week of her pregnancy keep a close eye on the bitch and for your own peace of mind take her temperature each morning. The normal reading is 101.5 degrees F (38.5 degrees C) and when you are within 24 hours of whelping it almost always drops a degree or two. That is the moment to alert the vet, have an experienced friend on standby if you can, check the puppy room, and then maintain, as far as you can, a reasonably normal life.

The bitch should continue to take short walks around the garden, though not off your own premises at this stage. She may well refuse to eat, but ensure there is always plenty of water available for her to drink. I never owned a bitch who did not find an inaccessible spot which she assured me would be ideal for her puppies. So far, we have always ended up in the whelping room, but it takes tact and eyes in the back of your head. Keep a strong torch handy if the bitch goes out in the garden at night, in

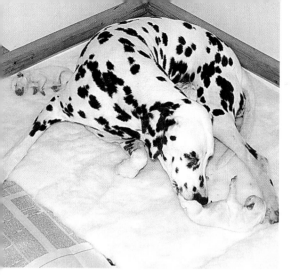

The Dalmatian mother with her newborn puppies. Dalmatian puppies are born white.

Nine days old, and the spots are just beginning to show.

case the first puppy arrives unexpectedly on the lawn.

Try to be matter-of-fact as well as comforting; if your bitch senses your anxiety this will communicate itself to her and she may well hold up her own whelping to the danger of the puppies. If you watch carefully, you may see her get up, hunch over slightly and give a little push as though she is starting to empty her bowels. It is a very slight involuntary movement, easy to miss, but it is the first sign of birth. From then, it is usually no more than half an hour before the first puppy arrives.

Persuade her into the puppy room, if you can, though do not distress her by insisting. She will pant heavily, possibly circle round and crouch, and you will see her body contracting. Record the time of these contractions for future use. The bitch should produce a puppy within an hour of this first contraction at most; a lot longer, and it is possible that you have a problem. A gush of fluid will come from the vulva and the bitch may find it comforting if you stroke her sides gently. A shiny, greyish-black water bag arrives with the puppy inside and the bitch will break this open

with her teeth to allow the dark-green fluid to escape. At the same time the placenta, a piece of liver-like matter, arrives. The bitch will eat it, and this is quite natural. In the wild, the pack provides food for the bitch so that she does not have to leave the puppies too soon to go hunting. The placentas should do no harm, will possibly help the let-down of milk, and may also stimulate subsequent stages of whelping.

If the bitch is very full of puppies, she may find it difficult to reach round to her rear to see to the water bag and free the puppy. If this happens, break open the bag around the puppy's nose with your nail, or cut it with the scissors and, with a gauze swab, wipe away the mucus from the puppy's mouth. The bitch will then normally bite the cord free while you hold the puppy and at this stage the puppy should start to cry. Delivery head-first is more usual, but do not be alarmed if the puppy arrives bottom-first. This rarely causes a problem. If you hear the newborn puppy gurgle, it means that fluid is going down into the lungs. Hold the puppy head down and shake it gently, as you would a thermometer, until the gurgling stops and you hear a clear cry.

117

If the bitch does not bite away the cord herself, you may have to cut it. Run your fingers back up the cord away from the bitch to get as much blood as possible back to the puppy, and then cut the cord as far from the puppy as you can. Do not worry about the cord, the bitch will deal with this and it will drop off within a day or so. There is no need to clamp or stitch it in any way. The bitch will lick and clean the puppy herself, but you may then like to pick it up in one of the towels and rub it briskly, holding it right down near the bitch's head so that she can see what you are doing. This will warm the puppy up and get its circulation going. As soon as you have finished, put it down alongside the bitch. Offer your bitch a drink of well-diluted evaporated milk with a little honey or glucose, and wait for puppy number two. At this stage they are, of course, white but, if there is any colour on the nose, this will help to distinguish black from liver. Weigh the puppy when you can do so without worrying the bitch.

Once several puppies have arrived, it can be useful to put the cardboard box under the heat lamp and place the puppies in it while the next is being born. Sometimes the bitch is happy for you to do this, and it does avoid the puppies being drenched with birth fluids, but, if she becomes agitated, leave the puppies where they are. Note the time of birth and sex. One of your most difficult decisions is to estimate how long a period between each puppy is reasonable. After the first puppy, you may well get three or four at anything from 20- to 30-minute intervals. Then could follow a long period of anything up to two hours before the next puppy is born. Unfortunately, this could also mean a puppy is held up coming through the cervix, which puts not only that puppy's life at risk, but also the lives of the remaining puppies behind it. If more than two hours elapse, you should consider a telephone call to the vet.

Another cause for delay is inertia which is difficult to recognise if you have not met it before. I first experienced it in my last litter, and by the time I called the vet it was too late. A shot of Peturitin brought the puppy down immediately, but two days later she faded and died. I blamed myself for not having called the vet in more quickly, but, as I said, this problem is difficult to recognise if you have not met it before. Most newborn puppies are warm and strong but occasionally, if there has been a delay, they arrive looking blue and limp and may need to be revived. Rub the puppy vigorously in a warm towel, and then apply artificial respiration by very gently using the finger and thumb to compress the ribs at a speed of about 20 times per minute. You can also apply mouth-to-mouth resuscitation, but take great care to breathe very gently or you may injure the puppy's lungs. Once breathing has started, the blue colour will disappear and the pup reverts to a nice pink. Return the puppy to the bitch, as soon as possible, to be licked and suckled.

Count the placentas carefully, in case one of them is retained inside the bitch. This causes a bad infection but, if you know it is there, the vet can give the bitch an injection which will expel it. Although nature is never wrong, the feast of placentas from a large Dalmatian litter can encourage loose bowels in the bitch, which are bad for mother and puppies. Thus, if you take a few away without her noticing, so much the better.

How will you know whether all the puppies have arrived? When you think she has finished, run your hands gently down her sides and, if there is still a bump or two, you will know there are more to come.

Once she feels smooth, has stopped panting, and is lying in a completely relaxed fashion with the puppies, assume cautiously that she has finished. You can then put a lead on the bitch and suggest firmly that she comes outside to be clean. Sometimes she will and sometimes she will not, but do not upset her by dragging her if she refuses. However, this is the only opportunity you will get to ensure the bitch's comfort and to put clean bedding in the whelping box, so it is worth making a real effort. If you are single-handed and take the bitch out on the lead, you must leave her outside the door for a few seconds while you change the bedding. The bitch will be extremely agitated, so bring her in on the lead and encourage her to return to the box slowly to prevent damaging the puppies.

At this stage the bitch may like a small meal, and you could try her with an egg custard or milk pudding. She may even welcome some boiled chicken with breadcrumbs, but do not worry if all she wants is a drink. If necessary, wash the bitch down later with antiseptic and warm water, a little baby shampoo added if she is badly-stained, but avoid upsetting her at all costs.

Take time now to examine the puppies carefully. Watch that each one is sucking well and check that none has a cleft palate. Try to see each one both urinate and defecate, and note and report to the vet if any puppy looks blue. Once the bitch has settled, put a low bulb in a reading lamp and switch off the main lights, leaving the heat lamp on. The room should be at 75 degrees F (23 degrees C) during whelping, and this can be reduced gradually over the next few days to 60 degrees F. If you keep the room temperature at this level, the puppies will use their energy to grow and not waste it keeping themselves warm.

I usually sleep in the same room as the bitch for the first couple of nights and, after that, retire with great thankfulness to my own bed. However tired you may be the next day, find time to telephone the stud dog owner with the result. Puppy owners come later. During the next working day, ask your vet to come in and check the bitch and puppies. He may suggest an injection in case a small piece of debris has been left behind which will cause a later infection; at the same time you can point out any problems that you have seen. If there are obvious faults, or the litter is too big for the bitch to deal with happily, some puppies can be removed tactfully when the bitch is not looking and the vet will euthanase them during his visit.

WHELPING TO THREE WEEKS
You will feel like a zombie long after the bitch has recovered. She will become less reluctant to go outside and, once a day, harden your heart and shut the door on her, talking reassuringly when she demands to come in. This will give you a few minutes to wash out the whelping box and arrange clean newspaper and bedding. When she returns, keep a restraining hand on her collar until she is safely back among her family.

For some time, all food and drinks must be offered to the bitch in the whelping box. Keep an old towel to put over the puppies or they will become splattered in dog food and milk. Hopefully, your bitch is regaining her appetite but it is particularly important to see that she gets constant drinks. Eventually life will return to normal and she will eat her meals away from her puppies.

Within a day the puppies will be dragging themselves off the bedding to the newspaper and then back again to their mother. It is an amazing undertaking for them, tiny as they are, but it is the first lesson in house training. The puppies are

At 18 days old, the spot pattern is begining to emerge.

constantly washed by their mother and she will also clean up anything off the newspaper. This is perfectly natural and will continue until weaning begins. Remove and replace any marked newspaper immediately. The puppies will return to the paper only when it is clean, and for house training purposes it is vital not to interrupt the process.

It is wise to book your Hearing Test in advance, so complete the registration form once you are certain of the colour of your puppies, and it will be returned in time for your test. Dew claws should be attended to on the third day and the tips of the toenails can be trimmed at the same time. They will have already grown spiky points and these must be kept cut or they will make the bitch sore.

Check her teats every day for any signs of soreness. The puppies knead the bitch with their feet in order to stimulate milk and, if you have not removed the little sharp hook, it can make an agonising sore on the bitch in no time at all. Puppies can also miss the nipple and suck hard on a small adjacent piece of skin. That too can cause a sore.

Check every evening and apply a soothing antiseptic cream on any area, including the nipples, which looks red or angry. If you neglect this and the bitch is in pain, she may well refuse to feed the puppies. The puppies' toe nails should be checked every day.

WORMING
Plan to worm your puppies at three, five and seven weeks. The vet will send you the correct doses, which will be determined by the weight of each puppy, and will be in either tablet or liquid form.

WEANING
I mentioned earlier the three traumatic events in the first eight weeks of a puppy's life; being born, being weaned, and departing for the new home. All three require tact and care, but correct weaning, I believe, has an ongoing effect, both physically and temperamentally. With a normal litter, weaning can begin at about three-and-a-half weeks and should be made as trouble-free as possible for the mother. The bitch's instinct is to feed her puppies

Weaning can start at about three-and-a-half weeks of age.

Nails need to be trimmed on a regular basis, roughly every two to three days.

immediately after she has eaten her own meal. You have to act quickly and feed the puppies before she does, only then allowing her back in to top them up. The pups will thus take a little less from her and she in turn will produce a little less milk.

So nature takes its course and, over the space of the next four weeks, the puppies will gradually come to take all their food from you, and the bitch will cease to make milk for them. If you can complete this process without anxiety on either side, then your puppies will be well adjusted and healthy, and the bitch will soon be her old self, both in mind and figure.

At this stage do not decrease the bitch's food. She has a great deal of body substance to make up, as well as still providing vast quantities of milk. Reduce her rations by all means when the puppies are about eight weeks or so, but do it slowly.

In the wild, the bitch regurgitates food for her puppies at the weaning stage. You will find that she still does this, actively encouraged by the puppies. However, this holds up the weaning process, and the bitch will lose condition, so it must be discouraged. From the beginning, feed each puppy individually for the main meals, though the rice pudding at supper time can go down on the floor in big dishes so that they may experience eating together. All food should be lukewarm, including the milk, but cold water should be available at all times. You have about four weeks to achieve complete weaning, so, if possible, establish the four main meals during the first week. After that, add new foods and increase the amounts each day as the puppies grow.

FEEDING – FIRST WEEK
Day One: Teatime: Half-teaspoonful

121

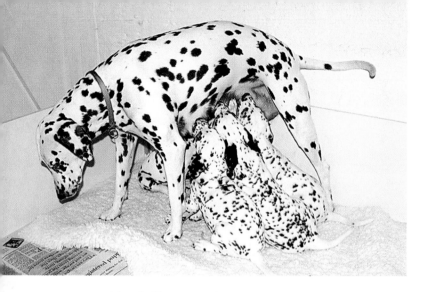

Even when weaned, puppies are still keen to take advantage of what is on offer. These eight-week-old pups left for their new homes the following day!

scraped beef. (Scrape surface of rump or good braising steak with sharp blade until you obtain a pulp.) Initially, feed from your finger.

Day Two: Breakfast: Small saucer of diluted evaporated milk (one tin to one tin hot water).Tea: As for Day One.

Day Three: Breakfast: As for Day Two; Tea: As for Day Two; Bedtime: Quarter of a baby's rusk.

Day Four: Breakfast: Add pulped boiled fish to milk; Lunch: Evaporated milk; Tea: Best butcher's mince put twice through mincer; Supper: Evaporated milk; Bedtime: Quarter rusk.

Day Five

Breakfast: As Day Four.
Lunch: Add egg yolk (one per two pups) to milk.
Tea: As Day Four.
Supper: As Day Four.
Bedtime: Quarter rusk and small-size biscuit.

Day Six: Breakfast: As Day Five; Lunch: As Day Five; Tea: As Day Five; Supper: Add rice pudding to milk (1 teaspoonful per puppy); Bedtime: As Day Five.

Day Seven: Breakfast: As Day Five; Lunch: Add baby rice to thicken; Tea: As Day Six; Supper: As Day Six; Bedtime: As Day Six.

You have now established the four main meals. During the second week, replace the egg yolks at lunchtime with scrambled egg; finely-minced raw tripe or boiled turkey breasts can also be added to breakfast. Increase the quantities daily. At six weeks add half a teaspoonful of soaked puppy meal to each breakfast, plus sterilised bonemeal and corn oil (a quarter teaspoonful per puppy). At teatime, add half a mineral tablet per puppy and put a bowl of evaporated milk mixture down after each meal before allowing the bitch back in to top up.

As to quantity, it is difficult to estimate correctly. As a general guide, I would suggest that a puppy of eight weeks should be having six to eight oz for both breakfast and tea, with rather less for lunch and supper. If you feel they are still hungry after any meal, put a dish of soaked puppy meal down to fill up the corners. Continue to feed the puppies individually for all the main meals, holding the bowl up at a comfortable height so that they do not go over at the shoulder. This also creates a good relationship with the puppy, and prevents him from becoming over-protective about his plate.

By the time the puppies are seven-and-a-half weeks old they will be weaned, though from the comfort point of view they delight in taking advantage of anything their mother may offer. If the bitch is willing, never prevent her from feeding them, either lying down or standing up. The bitch

As the puppies grow, time is divided between sleeping and frantic bouts of activity.

knows best, and, though her undercarriage may seem terribly swollen, you will be surprised how quickly it disappears if nature is permitted to take its course.

THE LEARNING PROCESS

From the squeak of agitation when they first leave the whelping box, life is a continual learning process for the puppies. The more people, smells and situations they encounter, the less trauma there will be when they finally join their new families. The more they can learn, the less difficult that transition will be. Try to extend their experience every day with something new. Once they have staggered round the puppy room, a large cardboard box gives them endless joy, both as a play house and as a toy box. As they grow, so do the number of toys, and the box gets filled with old tennis balls, a small-sized ragger, a couple of old slippers, and one or two tea towels, knotted in the middle. As soon as one area of the house or garden becomes familiar, introduce another, and when this is indoors have a pile of newspaper ready for house training. Once the garden is available the litter's communal sense of adventure really takes over, though you will find the bitch keeps a close eye on them. If there is general agitation for any reason she will quickly offer an extra feed there and then for comfort. The various rooms and different parts of the garden where they play will help the puppies with the change in geography when they go to their new homes. It is much easier for them to be clean in new surroundings if they have had to learn already that doors are to be found in different places.

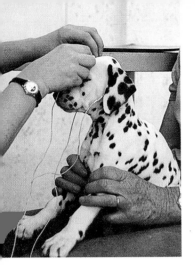  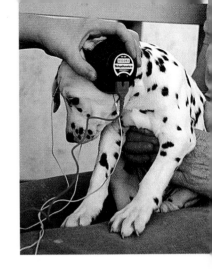

THE HEARING TEST
LEFT: Tiny acupuncture-type needles are inserted into the puppy's head.
CENTRE: The needles are now in place.
RIGHT: A cover is placed over one ear and an amplifier
is placed over the other ear ready for testing.

HEARING TEST

The Hearing Test will have been booked to take place when the puppies are about six weeks old. The puppies' registration numbers and names will be with you by then and should be taken to the test with you. Alternatively, if you have your puppies tattooed, this number can be entered on your Hearing Certificate.

The preparations are somewhat similar to going to a dog show. Take spare newspaper, a sack for soiled paper, fresh bedding for the return journey, a warm drink for everyone and a meal for the puppies. You will need a cage for the puppies to travel in and, if you are bringing the bitch, she can lie alongside to reassure her family. Start in good time, drive slowly and go round corners as though on glass. With luck, the puppies will settle down and go to sleep. Try to arrive early and feed the puppies before they are tested. Playpens are usually provided; these are cleaned and disinfected between litters and are moved between litters to a different section of the floor. Put newspaper down in the playpen and bring the puppies in, though the bitch

must be left in the car because of the proximity of the other dogs. The puppies can stay in their playpen and be fed and, by the time your turn is called, they will be feeling both comfortable and sleepy.

Carry each puppy into the testing area separately and sit it on your knee. The nurse will show you how to support it by the shoulders while she inserts tiny acupuncture-type needles into the puppy's head. Staff are very expert and the puppy feels no pain. The nurse then places a cover over one ear and an amplifier over the other, while the vet monitors the reading. The results are shown on a graph and, when it is all over, you receive a certificate giving the hearing status of your puppy and a copy of the graph. The next chapter deals with this subject in depth, and various aspects of the hearing problem in Dalmatians are discussed.

THE LAST TWO WEEKS

You are now reaching the stage where you are able to confirm the puppies' destinations to their prospective owners. You will need to detail worming to date,

124

Ready to go: After eight weeks of hard work, the puppies are now ready to take their place in the world.

and make out a diet sheet which not only sets out food for the present, but explains how it should increase and continue into adulthood. It is also helpful if you set out quite simply the routine of one day in the puppy's life. First-time owners find this particularly useful, and it helps the puppy if it is dealt with in a familiar way for the first few days. Telephone calls, letters, photographs and Christmas cards will keep you up-to-date with the next generation, but when they are around six months old, try and see each puppy you have bred. You may then judge for yourself the success or otherwise of the breeding line you chose.

11 *THE HEARING PROBLEM*

One of the most disturbing subjects to be tackled in connection with hereditary disease in Dalmatians has been the hearing problem. We are in debt to the USA, whose concern over this subject led experts to carry out extensive testing programmes, followed by the initiation of the BAER testing system that the breed uses today.

A report, published in America in 1992, brought the matter to a head when it stated that 30 per cent of Dalmatians were deaf. The Animal Health Trust made a BAER machine available, and 15 owners volunteered their dogs for testing. Experienced breeders can detect bilateral deafness (deaf in both ears), but much concern was felt when four animals were found to be unilaterally deaf (deaf in one ear).

Unilateral deafness can be diagnosed almost solely with the help of this machine. You may ask, is it important to know whether a dog can only hear with one ear? Perhaps not in the case of a pet, but when it comes to breeding it is imperative. Research has now established that a unilaterally deaf animal, used for breeding, will pass on deafness genes and this will recur in later generations. No-one who has faced discovering deaf puppies in a litter can doubt the anguish of the breeder; nor that of a new owner who has taken a puppy from an untested litter, only to find it is deaf.

The problems of keeping a bilaterally deaf Dalmatian are legion. They are large and powerful animals. Some people maintain they can be trained to obey hand signals. I do not doubt it, but the question inevitably arises: how do you control a deaf dog who is not looking at you? The dog may not be looking at you when, unaware of traffic, he causes an horrendous accident; he may not be looking at you before chasing after farm animals, which later must be destroyed. If a child comes upon the dog unexpectedly and he whips round in alarm, canine teeth are on a level with a youngster's face and the consequences may be serious.

There are some owners who devote their lives to such dogs and I say at once they have my entire admiration. Unfortunately, in the busy modern world, few have the opportunity or inclination. It is a responsibility which will increase with time and, as the Dalmatian grows, he faces the prospect of a free-running life curtailed on the end of a lead. Security is not helped by a careless tradesman, an unexpected guest,

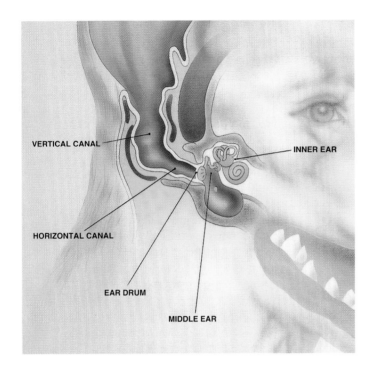

VERTICAL CANAL

INNER EAR

HORIZONTAL CANAL

EAR DRUM

MIDDLE EAR

Inside the dog's ear.

a forgetful child, or even a hurried exit of your own. A gate or door can be left open so easily, and there is no way to call the dog back.

All these reasons, and more, were taken into consideration when the BDC and NOEDC reached the decision that, when their advice was sought, they would advise that bilaterally deaf puppies should be humanely put to sleep. This advice is not given lightly, and is a heartache to all concerned. The BDC, in conjunction with the Animal Health Trust and later the Hearing Assessment Clinic, put together a scheme offering hearing tests to all Dalmatians and litters of puppies at a specially agreed price. Mary Greening agreed to undertake the organisation, and the effort and dedication she has put into this have resulted in hearing testing sessions becoming a normal and on-going occurrence. She could have no greater

reward. Nobody pretends this is anything but the start of a long and arduous journey for the breed, but research has already advanced the subject as far as animals are concerned, and has contributed to tests being carried out on deafness in children. We work towards the time when a DNA blood test will be available to all. In the meantime, we can only act with common sense, breeding from tested stock with bilateral hearing.

To obtain the information vital to research, it is particularly important that the whole litter is tested, not just the one or two puppies whose future owners have requested it. When the price of a puppy is quoted, the new owner should be made aware that the cost of the hearing test has been added to this.

Some advice on taking Dalmatian puppies to a hearing test has already been given. The various testing centres differ slightly in their methods, but this will give you a good overall picture. In all cases, take with you a copy of the pedigree, which the centre will retain for its records, together with your KC registration papers. It is very important, in these days of easy litigation, that you know precisely what you are selling to the public. If you are passing on a puppy, complete with its Hearing Certificate and graph showing the hearing status, there can be no argument. Equally, if the puppy has unilateral hearing, this must be explained to the prospective buyer. Such a dog will make an admirable pet, provided it is not required for showing or breeding, and preferably where there are no young children in the family.

The reports which follow should bring you up to date with work currently being carried out in the UK on this critical problem, and I am very grateful to Julia Freeman (nee Washbourne), her colleagues at the Centre for Small Animal Studies, and Celia Cox, of the Hearing Assessment Clinic, for their contributions.

HOW HEARING WORKS
Sound waves enter the external ear canal and strike the ear drum, which begins to vibrate. This, in turn, causes vibration of the tiny bones in the middle ear (the ear ossicles). These vibrations set up waves in the fluid of the cochlea, the spiral-shaped structure in the inner ear. The change in pressure ultimately causes vibration of the hair cells inside the cochlea, which are connected to the auditory nerve. This triggers a nerve impulse via the auditory pathway to the brain. (See Fig. 1)

Any interruption in the delivery of sound to the brain results in one of several types of deafness, defined below.

TYPES OF DEAFNESS
Deafness can be defined as 1) conductive, 2) sensori-neural, 3) congenital or late onset, 4) inherited or acquired.

1.) **Conductive deafness** is due to interference in the transmission of sound waves to the inner ear, for example caused by a foreign body or wax in the ear canal, rupture of the ear drum or infection in the middle ear.

2.) **Sensori-neural deafness** results from damage or defect in any part of the auditory pathway; from the cochlea in the inner ear, via the auditory nerve to the auditory cortex of the brain.

3.) **Congenital deafness** is present at birth, while **late onset deafness**, as its name suggests, occurs later in life, such as hearing loss associated with old age.

4.) **Inherited deafness** is passed down through one or both parents, whereas **acquired deafness** is due to external factors such as injury or disease.

It has been recognised that the Dalmatian breed is affected by inherited, congenital, sensori-neural deafness since the last century (Rawitz, 1896).

DEAFNESS AND PIGMENTATION
The association between coat colour and deafness has been described for several species, including mice, cats, mink and dogs. As long ago as 1859, Darwin noted the relationship between the white, blue-eyed cat and deafness. In dogs, deafness is often associated with the gene that causes merled coat colour, for example in the Border Collie or Old English Sheepdog. Absence of pigment in one or both irises, resulting in blue eye coloration

(heterochromia iridis, HI), may also be present. Predominantly white coat coloration is also thought to predispose certain breeds to deafness, for example, the Boxer or the English Bull Terrier.

The relationship between deafness and pigmentation is thought to be due to the fact that all pigment cells, except those of the retina, develop from the same embryonic source as the cells of the cochlea, the neural crest. It has been suggested that inherited deafness, linked with white coat coloration, could be due to some abnormality in the migration of these cells, or their interaction with other structures in the inner ear during development of the embryo (Holliday et al. 1992).

The genes governing coat colour in the Dalmatian are the extreme piebald gene, expressed as solid white coat colour, combined with the dominant ticking gene to give the spotting on the white background (Strain et al. 1992). The spots are either black or liver in colour, with black being dominant to liver. Very occasionally, spots may be lemon (very dilute liver) or tricolour. Dalmatian puppies are born with a completely white coat, and the spots begin to develop at about ten to 14 days old. Areas of pigmented coat may sometimes be present at birth. These are larger than the spots, which develop later, and also differ in hair texture. Such patches occur anywhere on the body, legs or tail, but are most often found on the head. It is thought these blocks of colour are due to partial failure of the extreme piebald gene to suppress the underlying black or liver coloration (Greibrokk, 1994).

The merling gene is not reported to be present in the Dalmatian, but blue eyes do occur in the breed. Because of the relationship between blue eyes, white coat and deafness in cats, an association between blue eyes and deafness in the Dalmatian was suggested. One study (Holliday et al. 1992) reported a link between HI and deafness in Dalmatians, but this was not conclusive.

The lower incidence of deafness in the UK population (21.5 per cent affected, or one in five Dalmatians), where blue-eyed dogs are not bred from, when compared to the US population (29.7 per cent affected), where blue-eyed dogs are used as breeding stock, seems to imply that removing blue-eyed individuals from the breeding population reduces the incidence of affected offspring. This hypothesis is supported by recent information from the US, now that data is available from many more dogs, which shows a statistically significant relationship between deafness and blue eyes (Strain, 1994).

DEAFNESS IN THE DALMATIAN
As mentioned before, the type of deafness suffered by Dalmatians is a congenital, hereditary, sensori-neural deafness. The mode of inheritance of this particular type of deafness is unknown. Hereditary conditions may be due to dominant or recessive genes or may be sex-linked.

Deafness in the Dalmatian does not seem to be caused by a dominant gene, as deaf offspring result from hearing parents. Neither does it appear to be a recessive disorder, as normal hearing puppies were obtained when two bilaterally deaf animals were mated. These findings could possibly be explained if there was more than one gene involved, or if it was necessary for a combination of two different recessive genes to be present before the disorder is expressed. Another possible explanation could be that deafness was due to a syndrome with incomplete penetrance, so that individuals inheriting the problem may not exhibit all the signs of the disorder, which means they may not be deaf, although they are affected.

Whether or not there is a link between deafness and gender is as yet unclear. One study (Holliday et al. 1992) found that females had a significantly higher incidence of deafness than males, another reported that slightly more males than females were affected (Marshall, 1986). However, Strain et al. (1992) found there was no difference in incidence between the sexes. Figures from one Testing Centre in the UK (Animal Health Trust, Newmarket) show that significantly (statistically: $p<0.05$) more females (22.7 per cent) are affected in either one or both ears compared with males (17.6 per cent).

One further factor which may govern hearing status is whether the dog is patched. Since the patch is evidence of a weakness in the expression of the piebald gene (one of the genes thought to be responsible for deafness), dogs with a patch are less likely to be deaf (statistically: $p<0.0001$) (Strain, 1994). No conclusive proof has been found to support any one theory as to how the defect is passed down, so further study needs to be carried out.

PATHOLOGICAL FINDINGS

The anatomical changes that take place in the inner ear due to this disorder have been extensively studied. Microscopic examination has shown that the deafness which affects Dalmatians is caused by degeneration of the blood supply to the cochlea in the first few weeks of life. This is followed by destruction of the hair cells and, ultimately, further deterioration of components of the inner ear and nerve degeneration. The loss of the hair cells is permanent and irreversible. The passage of sound to the auditory nerve is interrupted, resulting in the dog becoming deaf. Affected puppies can be detected by four

weeks of age, and one study showed no evidence of progressive hearing impairment beyond this age (Shelton et al. 1993). Deafness may occur in both ears (bilateral deafness) or in one ear only (unilateral deafness).

DETECTING THE PROBLEM

It is not possible to assess hearing in puppies before the ear canals open at 12 to 14 days, as sound waves cannot enter. After this age, bilateral deafness can often be identified by the skilled observer, as totally deaf animals often show very characteristic behaviour patterns. Deaf puppies are often difficult to arouse from sleep other than by touching, and may be slower to respond at feeding time unless following their siblings. They are often more aggressive, because they do not hear the cries of pain from their littermates, and may be highly vocal, with a characteristic high-pitched cry. Separation from their siblings may cause distress as they become highly dependent on their physical presence.

It is sometimes difficult to recognise a deaf puppy in the nest, as it may take its cues from the littermates and seem perfectly normal in behaviour. The puppy may be in a new home for several weeks, or even longer, before the owner begins to suspect there is a hearing problem.

Suspicion that an animal cannot hear may be confirmed by observing the response to an auditory stimulus such as banging on a saucepan, a handclap or jingling keys. It is important that the stimulus occurs outside the animal's field of vision and that the stimuli used do not produce vibrations detectable by the animal. Any such reaction may be mistakenly interpreted as hearing when, in fact, it is a response to a visual cue or sensitivity to the vibration.

However, this subjective method of testing hearing ability is very open to misinterpretation. Some hearing animals are unreactive, others adapt quickly and stop responding, and highly-stressed animals may also not respond. Deaf animals may sense the presence of an unseen examiner, or respond to other cues (vibration, air current, body smell) which are undetectable to the person conducting the test.

A dog who is unilaterally deaf is difficult to identify, as it hears perfectly in the non-affected ear and so usually behaves normally. A unilaterally deaf animal may have difficulty in localising the source of a sound as it lacks normal binaural cues (information from both ears), and occasionally may be difficult to waken if lying on its hearing ear. However, such an animal adapts well to hearing in one ear only, so these abnormal responses may not be observed.

Even if it is suspected that a dog is unilaterally deaf, the condition is almost impossible to confirm without performing a more objective test. A test first used to assess hearing in dogs in the US has been available since 1992 in the UK. It is known as the Brainstem Auditory Evoked Response or BAER test, and offers a quick, non-invasive and, above all, unequivocal assessment of an individual's hearing status.

THE BRAINSTEM AUDITORY EVOKED RESPONSE (BAER)

When a sound enters the ear, tiny electrical impulses are generated by components of the auditory pathway in the inner ear and brain. These signals can be picked up by recording electrodes positioned on the head, and are in turn passed into a specialised electrodiagnostic machine. A series of approximately 500 stimuli, usually clicks, are passed into the ear through a headphone. These are signal-averaged by the machine's integral computer, to

eliminate electrical activity generated by other parts of the brain. In a normal-hearing dog a series of peaks and troughs is produced (see Fig. 2), which is displayed on a small TV-type screen. Thus, the BAER can be defined as the electrical response of the brain to a series of auditory stimuli.

Presence of a normal BAER is not synonymous with hearing in every case, as it assesses the auditory pathway only as far as the auditory cortex of the brain. In the Dalmatian, deafness occurs due to degeneration of structures in the cochlea. Thus a normal BAER trace confirms these structures are intact, and is a valid screening technique for this type of deafness. Deafness from cochlear damage eliminates all peaks in the BAER waveform, so a straightforward yes-or-no assessment of hearing is possible. Inability to obtain a BAER waveform can be likened to running a train on a track with a piece missing – the train gets as far as the point where the track is broken and stops. When the BAER cannot be obtained in a deaf dog the auditory signal travels only as far as the degenerated cochlea, so no electrical signal is generated further up the auditory pathway, and no BAER trace is produced.

Dogs with bilaterally absent BAER traces do not respond behaviourally to auditory stimuli; conversely no dogs with a normal BAER trace in each ear have been clinically deaf. This confirms that the test is a reliable method of assessing hearing in the Dalmatian.

The BAER test does not require patient co-operation, and is performed without sedation in puppies of five-to-seven weeks of age. They tolerate the test extremely well, often remaining asleep throughout. Older dogs may require a light sedative to relax them and enable a good trace to be obtained, although some dogs are calm enough to be tested without sedation. Each ear is assessed in turn and, if the expected waveform is generated, that ear is deemed to be normal. Some dogs produce a waveform from one ear only, and the other ear generates a trace where the required peaks and troughs are absent. There may be some activity recorded in the early part of the trace from the deaf ear, but this is due to the response of the other ear to the stimulus. If the hearing ear is blocked using a headphone, producing random 'white noise' (a hissing sound), this activity is eliminated and a flat line is obtained. Dogs who produce this result are identified as having unilateral hearing (see Fig. 3).

It is worth emphasising at this point that the hearing ability of the unaffected ear is, in fact, better than in humans. Many unilaterally deaf dogs will have gone through life unrecognised as such because their behaviour is completely normal.

When it is impossible to elicit a waveform in either ear and only flat traces are obtained, even with increased loudness of the stimulus, the dog is unfortunately bilaterally deaf (see Fig. 4). The deafness is complete. There is no partial hearing in this case, and any perceived 'hearing' by the owner is probably due to the dog's reaction to cues picked up by other senses, such as vibrations or scent.

IMPLICATIONS OF THE BAER TEST RESULT

Unilaterally deaf dogs are usually completely normal in behaviour and make excellent pets, but they carry the genetic material for deafness. As the condition is hereditary, it is recommended not to use affected individuals for breeding. In unilateral to normal matings, the incidence of affected offspring is approximately double that obtained from matings where both parents have bilaterally normal hearing (Strain et al. 1992). It is hoped that a blood test will eventually be available to identify carriers of the disorder but, until then, the only way to know with certainty the hearing status of each individual, and go some way towards reducing the percentage of affected dogs, is to evaluate every animal using the BAER test.

LATEST DEVELOPMENTS IN THE USA

In 1994 an excellent update on deafness research was published by Dr George M Strain, Professor of Neuroscience at the Louisiana State University. One paragraph stands out:

"Finally, there are significant relationships between a dog's hearing status and that of its parents, which should not be surprising for an inherited disorder. There is a significant correlation between deafness in a dog and unilateral deafness in either parent. In fact, unilateral deafness in just one parent doubles the likelihood that a dog will be unilaterally or bilaterally deaf. Therefore, knowingly breeding unilaterally deaf dogs means increasing the incidence of deafness".

Eva Berg's forthcoming article *Dalmatian Hearing – Where are we Going?* sets out how Brainstem Auditory Evoked Response (BAER) Testing has evolved over the past twelve years. In dealing with breeding stock, apart from the prospective sire and dam, the article suggests that the hearing status of littermates and results of previous matings should be made known, and an open registry established which would eventually expand to include Dysplasia and other genetically transmitted diseases.

An open registry is described as a data bank from which the genetic history of any animal can be traced. To control these diseases, it would be essential to know how prevalent they are in any particular line, and for this reason each owner would have to agree to the release of all data obtained. The DCA has formed a separate sub-committee to explore the establishment of an open hearing registry and has appointed the Institute for Genetic Disease Control in Animals (GDC) to take this forward.

When testing has been standardised, it should be followed by the registration of previously-tested dogs, which would provide a means of 'grandfathering' (and grandmothering) tested Dalmatians into the register. To register the tested Dalmatian, the owner must present all relevant papers, plus a copy of the BAER hearing graph. Grandfathered dogs would have separate identification from those accepted through normal means. To be accepted into the registry, a young puppy, together with the whole litter, would have to be tested at an approved centre and show permanent identification; in addition the owners must agree to submit results to the GDC. Registration of older puppies

and adults would also be possible.

Permanent identification can be provided by tattooing, though some difficulty has been experienced in applying this to young puppies. Microchipping, although acceptable, cannot be used at present on puppies under 14 weeks of age. The committee suggests DNA identification in the form of a saliva swab, stating that it is non-invasive, simple, fast and may prove cost-effective.

The AKC is working with the DCA in developing both the DNA testing and open hearing registry, and co-operating fully with the GDC. As the Dalmatian is being used, not only as the pilot breed for the open hearing registry but also to test the feasibility of saliva DNA testing as a form of permanent identification, the DCA is hoping that the AKC will provide substantial financial support. The aim is to limit the cost so that all breeders can participate.

12 THE GREAT DALMATIAN TRADITION

Dalmatian clubs the world over produce handbooks and books of champions. Enthusiasts have contributed to pictorial records of outstanding Dalmatians from all eras, but now there are fewer to remember the outstanding champions of yesterday. Newcomers to the breed are naturally more interested in their own stock and their immediate forbears.

For the purposes of this book, I have tried to bridge the gap. With the unstinting help of their breeders, I have taken nine lines of world-wide reputation and shown how they have come down over the years, proving their worth in breeding programmes and, with one exception, appearing still in the show ring today. In each case, I have asked the breeders to pinpoint the dog which in their opinion was the starting point, and I have then pictured the progeny they feel have carried forward the type and excellence of that dog.

For various reasons, not all good dogs become champions, and no attempt has been made to limit these dogs to those with championship status. Excellence in the eye of the breeder has been the criterion. Obviously, each of these breed names

carries many other lines of champions; for the purposes of this exercise I have merely taken the line directly back from the dog in the ring.

It has been a fascinating exercise and one which I would recommend to you. If you research back along the lines of your own dog, you may well be able to form a judgement on what direction to take with your own breeding programmes. The pedigree is obviously all-important, but photographs of the dogs in question certainly concentrate the mind.

HORSEMAN'S
Joan Agate-Hilton came into the breed in 1932 as a trainee in Mrs Eggo's kennel (Mesra). She introduced both Kath Heard and Pat McClellan into Dalmatians. Joan has always been a strong advocate of out-crossing, although she points out that, due to two World Wars, finding a real outcross is most unlikely. She considers sound temperament to be of paramount importance, and at no time would include a nervous or bad-tempered animal in her breeding programme.

Choice of stud dog is undertaken with particular care. The dog must be examined from every viewpoint to ensure his virtues

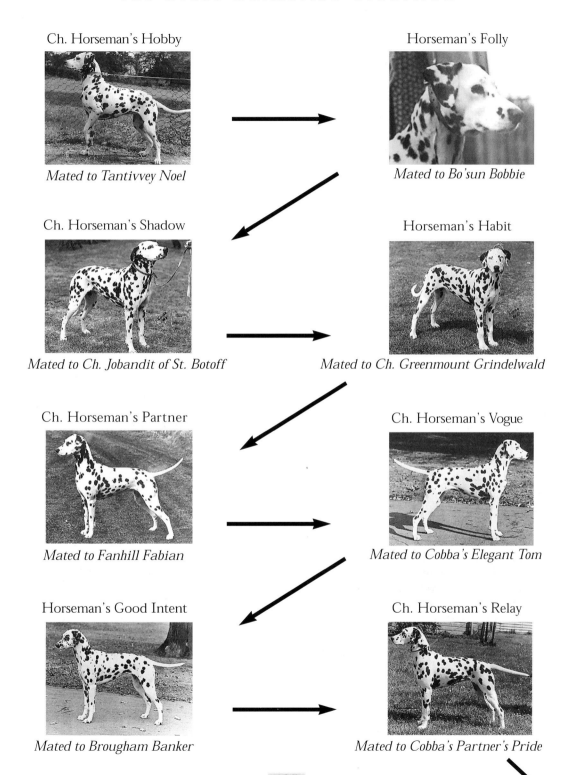

Ch. Horseman's Hobby

Mated to Tantivvey Noel

Horseman's Folly

Mated to Bo'sun Bobbie

Ch. Horseman's Shadow

Mated to Ch. Jobandit of St. Botoff

Horseman's Habit

Mated to Ch. Greenmount Grindelwald

Ch. Horseman's Partner

Mated to Fanhill Fabian

Ch. Horseman's Vogue

Mated to Cobba's Elegant Tom

Horseman's Good Intent

Mated to Brougham Banker

Ch. Horseman's Relay

Mated to Cobba's Partner's Pride

Horseman's Bygone

Mated to Ch. Brythennek Basil Fawlty

Horseman's Hallmark

Mated to Ch. Elaridge Endeavour

Ch. Horseman's Heritage

Mated to Olbero Ongoing Situation

Horseman's Harmony

complement those of the bitch and do not double up on a fault. Careful study is given to pedigrees with this in view, and Joan suggests enlisting help from a knowledgeable friend if necessary to check on the various hereditary factors. Breeding a standard-size dog to a standard-size bitch is essential, and Horseman's have been bred type to type through the years, aiming always to achieve the correct structure.

Following this thinking, Ch. Bo'sun Bobbie was chosen as mate for Horseman's Folly, producing Ch. Horseman's Shadow, Kath Heard's Ch. Horseman's Bobsworth and S. African Ch. Horseman's Outrider. Folly's 7 x great grand-daughter Horseman's Bygone, bred to Mr and Mrs Watson's Ch. Brythennek Basil Fawlty, produced Horseman's Hallmark and Can. and Am. Ch. Horseman's Topper Too. Ch. Horseman's Heritage, Hallmark's daughter by Ch. Elaridge Endeavour, was bred to Olbero Ongoing Situation, and from this came Horseman's Harmony, currently with two CCs (both with BOB) and five RCCs. The Horseman's kennel has produced an unbroken direct line of bitches spanning 57 years, which must stand as a unique record world-wide.

DUXFORDHAM
(Taken from *Some Personal Thoughts on Breeding* by the late Mrs Catherine Gore)

"You have to have heart and lots of it when you go in for breeding. A heart that can take being broken over and over again by failure, and yet carry to success if you can stay the course. There are no short cuts, but you can make success less difficult by observing certain 'rules'. The late owner of the famous Colonsay prefix (Miss Macfie)

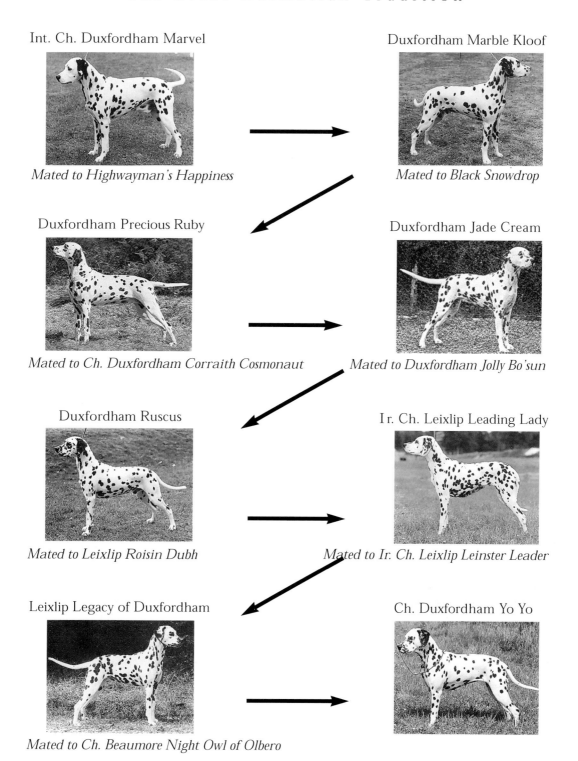

Int. Ch. Duxfordham Marvel

Mated to Highwayman's Happiness

Duxfordham Marble Kloof

Mated to Black Snowdrop

Duxfordham Precious Ruby

Mated to Ch. Duxfordham Corraith Cosmonaut

Duxfordham Jade Cream

Mated to Duxfordham Jolly Bo'sun

Duxfordham Ruscus

Mated to Leixlip Roisin Dubh

Ir. Ch. Leixlip Leading Lady

Mated to Ir. Ch. Leixlip Leinster Leader

Leixlip Legacy of Duxfordham

Mated to Ch. Beaumore Night Owl of Olbero

Ch. Duxfordham Yo Yo

was, I have always understood, breeding for 29 years before she bred a Champion!

"Spotting, although not the be-all-and-end-all, is the main characteristic of the breed, so you aim for good spotting. If you start with an indifferently-marked bitch, choose a mate with bold clear spotting, even one which is sparsely spotted as long as there are no flecks (tick marks). Keep a bitch from the litter that has no flecks at eight months, though be prepared for them to appear up to one year of age. If the coat is clear at that stage, then later she can be mated to a dog of similar markings to her father; if you intend to keep a dog for stud work, then continue on with this breeding pattern for yet another generation, by which time you should be starting to 'fix' these clear spots.

"The same breeding pattern can be used to eliminate other problems, poor tail carriage and structural faults, etc. Never breed from deafness, nervous and/or bad-tempered stock or from faulty mouths, all of which are highly hereditary. Regarding size, dogs just do not breed to height. Our Marvel (Int. Ch. Duxfordham Marvel) always bred sons (and grandsons) much bigger than himself. Miss Byrd, breeder of winning stock not only in dogs, always maintained it was a great mistake to put a small bitch to a large dog if one was hoping to improve size in bitches. This sort of mating only produced still larger dogs and still smaller bitches and she advocated medium dogs being mated to small bitches.

"How can genetics help? In some animals, where only a few factors are involved, no doubt genetics are a feasible proposition. However, with the numerous items to be bred for in Dalmatians, there are many who feel genetics are of little help. Our forefathers bred stock of all kinds, which was the envy of the world, on the basis of 'like to like' and 'the best to the best' but, although I personally agree with this and believe firmly in line breeding, please do not let me put anyone off genetics."

When Air Commodore Gore and his wife were married in 1930 they chose a Dalmatian puppy rather than a tea service as a family gift. 'Pat' arrived, was later mated to Mrs Hackney's Ch. Snow Leopard, and produced three prize winners including Duxford Ambition (Amy). All present-day Duxfordhams are descended from Amy, Int.Ch. Duxfordham Marvel being her great-great-great-great-grandson. Air Commodore Gore died in 1975, and Mrs Gore in 1981, but the Duxfordham line lives on under the careful eye of their daughter, Oonagh.

PHAELAND
Colonel and Mrs Gatheral met originally at Manchester Championship Show, he exhibiting Sealyhams and the then Miss Macpherson (daughter of Hugh Macpherson of Bulldog fame) with her first Dalmatian, Serena, daughter of Ch. Aristocrat. The prefix Phaeland was registered in 1932, and Phaeland Felicity was Miss Macpherson's first Champion. Made up in 1937, her tickets were awarded in the same year at Glasgow (Mr J.H. Alexander), Ayrshire (Mr J. Garrow) and the SKC (Miss R. Monkhouse), all names to bring back many memories.

'Phaeland' was a corruption of 'Phaeton' and 'Landau', both of which were submitted but turned down by the Kennel Club, but the renowned 'Ph' names were instigated by Susan Gatheral. Susan had her own prefix 'Conyers' but handled the Phaelands in the ring from the early 1950s. When Mrs Gatheral died in 1968, Susan took over the Phaeland prefix and Conyers is now used for Susan's Miniature

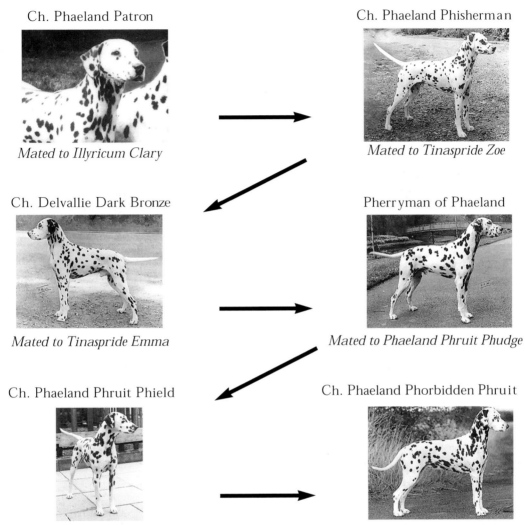

Ch. Phaeland Patron

Mated to Illyricum Clary

Ch. Phaeland Phisherman

Mated to Tinaspride Zoe

Ch. Delvallie Dark Bronze

Mated to Tinaspride Emma

Pherryman of Phaeland

Mated to Phaeland Phruit Phudge

Ch. Phaeland Phruit Phield

Ch. Phaeland Phorbidden Phruit

Mated to Dalmark the Rambling Rose

Dachshunds. The Phaelands are based on line breeding, with only a handful of outcross dogs used in sixty years. Knowing that 95 per cent of the dogs will be going to pet homes, has meant that temperament has always been paramount, with conformation coming a close second. Susan herself feels that the latter is not helped by the present-day tendency to over-exercise young puppies, and suggests feeding a balanced fresh food diet and leaving them to develop at their own rate.

A noted handler herself, she came to admire both Miss Clay (Tantivvey) and Miss V. Smithers (Aldham), who both had a very relaxed manner in the ring. There has been a long line of Phaeland Champions, but the Gatherals have found particular pleasure in breeding dogs who were then sold on and made up by their new owners.

Seeing Ch. Phaeland Phrench Phern take

BIS at both the BUBA Ch. Show and the Joint Dalmatian Clubs' Ch. Show in 1977 was a great thrill but, taken all in all, one of Susan's best memories lies with Ch. Phaeland Phishpie, who was never beaten in a puppy class. The latest Phaeland Champion, Phorbidden Phruit, featured on the pictorial family tree, came from a litter which contained Phaeland Phruitman and Phruitful and, in a repeat mating, has produced Passion Phruit, Phruit Pudding and Phruit Phlan, all winners at championship shows, with Passion Phruit emulating her great-grand-aunt in being unbeaten in puppy classes.

WASHAKIE
The prefix 'Washakie' will always be indelibly linked with Mrs Pat McClellan, who died in 1994. She owned her first Dalmatian in 1935, under the prefix 'Merrycroft'. Having spent the war years in America, she returned to find that Merrycroft had been assigned to another breeder, and she was granted 'Washakie' in its place. The prefix originates in Wyoming, USA, where Pat and her husband lived, and was the name of the Native Indian Chief of the Shoshones, who co-operated with the white man against other Indian tribes. Chief Washakie died in 1900 and was the first Indian to receive a full military funeral.

Pat was a firm believer in line breeding. She considered it the quickest way to breed out faults and standardise good qualities, but was insistent that the quality of the basic stock must be totally true to the standard and type desired. Pat maintained that, if the best of each generation was bred and those animals were closely related, then the resultant quality would be not less than that of the grandparents. She pointed to breeding success in racehorses and cattle as proof of her argument.

Most well-known dogs carrying this prefix have closely-related parents and, with many generations of related breeding behind them, go back to Colonsay and Towpath sources. Ch. Washakie Heirloom was considered a major force, and he lies behind most of the great champions, not least Ch. Washakie Othello, who in turn sired Ch. Washakie Spotlight. It would have been the greatest pleasure for Pat McClellan to know that, through her god-daughter Karen Goff, the Washakie line continues. As a child, Karen spent much time with her godmother and, at the age of nine years, was already handling for her in the ring.

Pat and Karen were joint breeders of the litter from Washakie Taboo to Pat Kindersley's Ch. Review at Knightstone, producing Karen's winning pair, Ch. and Am. Ch. Washakie Dancing Brave (22 CCs, six RCCs, Top Winning Dalmatian 1994), and Ch. Washakie Indian Summer (18 CCs, 18 RCCs, Dalmatian of the Year 1995). These two have won prolifically in the UK at every level, with Dancing Brave winning BIS All Breeds WELKS 1991 and later obtaining his title in the USA. Both dogs have won top honours at Cruft's, with Indian Summer winning BOB in 1994 and Dancing Brave in 1995. At Cruft's 1996 they each took the CC, with BOB awarded to Indian Summer, who then went on to Reserve in Group, all at seven-and-a-half years of age. As a final touch to a wonderful day, Dancing Brave's son, the McCarthys' Truthful Tango at Kilndandy, won the BDC cup for Best Puppy. Tango has since gone on to win one CC and one RCC, both from Junior. Karen now has two grandchildren of Dancing Brave in the ring, Washakie Indian Brave and Indian Sunset, the latter having already won a RCC from Puppy.

Ch. Washakie Othello

Mated to Ch. Tirriemore Twilight

Ch. Washakie Spotlight

Mated to Ch. Washakie Wishing Well

Washakie Tanya

Mated to Ch. Buffrey Jobee

Ch. Washakie Debonaire

Mated to Ch. & Ir. Ch. Washakie Psychedelic

Washakie Taboo

Mated to Ch. Review at Knightstone

Ch. & Am. Ch. Washakie Dancing Brave

Mated to Am. Ch. Hideaway's Agatha Christie

Hideaway's Washakie Fandango

Mated to Ch. Tommy Brock

Washakie Indian Brave

Ch. Lazaars Gay Gipsy of Greenmount

Mated to Ch. Tompkins of the Towpath

Ch. Greenmount Greensleeves

Mated to Ch. Howbeck Admiral

Ch. Greenmount Golden Guinea

Mated to Ch. Tompkins of the Towpath

Ch. Greenmount Grace Darling

Mated to Brougham Banker

Greenmount Grand Marnier

(retired due to injury)

Mated to Ch. Greenmount Gemini

Ch. Dallyvista Drummer Boy

GREENMOUNT

For the first fifteen years of the Pipers' married life, Dalmatians held court in their household, starting with Mikey, a young patched dog who won their hearts when they were searching the pound for a Fox Terrier. It was not until 1955 that Mr and Mrs Parker (Towpath) subsequently presented them with Lazaars Gay Gipsy and persuaded them to start exhibiting. Ch. Lazaars Gay Gipsy of Greenmount went on to win seven CCs and nine RCCs, including the 1957 Cruft's BCC under Mrs Gatheral.

Gipsy was mated three times to the Parkers' Ch. Tompkins of the Towpath, on each occasion producing an excellent litter, but in particular Ch. Greenmount Greensleeves (Twinkle) winner of 17 CCs, 11 RCCs and holder of a record four-times BOB at the LKA during four consecutive years (and this while producing two litters).

Twinkle's daughter by Ch. Howbeck Admiral, Ch. Greenmount Golden Guinea, continued in the family tradition, winning 13 CCs and ten RCCs and, mated back to her grandfather, Ch. Tompkins of the Towpath, produced Ch. Greenmount Grace Darling, who won 12 CCs and 11 RCCs. Gracie, mated to Ch. Washakie Othello, in turn whelped Ch. Greenmount Grebe (four CCs). A later mating to Brougham Banker resulted in a fine b/s dog, Greenmount Grand Marnier who, after winning one CC and the RCC at Cruft's, was retired due to a severe injury. However, he proved his worth at stud, siring several champions.

Mrs Piper later wrote: "Little did my husband and I imagine, when we mated our Gipsy to the Parkers' Tompkins, that 57 Champions would be born, either whelped from a Greenmount bitch or sired by a Greenmount dog. Perhaps new exhibitors may be encouraged by this, as we knew very little when we started out."

Dr John Piper died in 1972, shortly after judging bitches at the BDC Championship Show, and Mrs Piper retired from exhibiting, though she has continued to judge, officiating at Cruft's in 1978. President of the BDC from 1989-1992, she is now a vice-president, and concentrates her energies on running the Dalmatian Rescue Service.

In addition to sending top-quality stock overseas, the Greenmounts produced an unbroken line of outstanding bitches at home and, although there are no dogs carrying this prefix in the ring today, they provided the foundation for a number of well-known prefixes including Brougham, Clydevale, Dallyvista, Delvallie, Konavlje, and Starmead, and their presence is valued in many pedigrees.

KONAVLJE

Over 30 years ago, Monica Davidson and her husband watched Dalmatians at Otley Show, fell into conversation with Mrs MacDonald-Smith, and Monica was 'hooked'. Their first bitch, Greenmount Golden Glow, was mated to Ch. Colonsay April Jest, producing Konavlje Golden Jester and Susan Gatheral's Ch. Konavlje Miss Gorgeous. The prefix came from the name of a valley running inland from Dubrovnik on the Dalmatian Coast – ignore the 'j', and the rest is easy to pronounce.

Jester won two CCs and some RCCs and sired healthy, well-boned stock. However, Monica was looking for the clear, good spotting she so much admired, and eventually found a puppy (Carmargue Charisma of Highstables x Ch. Delvallie Dark Bronze), and Ch. Highstables Countess of Konavlje became her foundation bitch.

Countess's daughter by Mrs Beale's Ch. Charioteer Daniel, Ch. Konavlje Miss Fabulous, bred to the Watsons' Ch. Brythennek Basil Fawlty, produced Ch. Konavlje Creme de la Creme and Diane Dinsdale's Ch. Konavlje Donna at Dalesbred, later the dam of Ch. Dalesbred Donna Bianca (x Ch. Miragua St. Valentine). Creme herself had a wonderful show career, starting with winning the overall Windsor Ch. Show Puppy Stakes over four days in 1985, and becoming Best Dalmatian Puppy for the year, and in 1986 Monica was named Top Breeder of the Year. Apart from Creme's contribution to the Miragua line (Fiona Hartley's Ch. Konavlje The Wayfarer at Miragua), mated to Konavlje Mr Wonderful she produced Mrs Haywood and Mrs Ridgeway's Ch. Konavlje Rather Special at Luccombe.

Creme's grand-daughter, Ch. Konavlje Bella Figlia, was killed in a tragic accident at

Ch. Highstables Countess of Konavlje

Mated to Ch. Charioteer Daniel

Ch. Konavlje Miss Fabulous

Mated to Ch. Brythennek Basil Fawlty

Ch. Konavlje Creme de la Creme

Mated to Ch. Miragua St Valentine

Ch. Konavlje the Wayfarer at Miragua

Mated to Konavlje Nessun Dorma

Ch. Konavlje Bella Figlia

Mated to Courbette Connexion at Cragvallie

Konavlje Ill Mio Tesaro

Mated to Ch. Fincham Fast Talking Tinker

Konavlje Viva la Diva

the age of six years, but she left her daughter, John and Lesley Suggett's Ch. Konavlje Caro Nome of Kintegus (x Courbette Connexion at Cragvallie) and her grand-daughter, Konavlje Viva la Diva, to begin a promising show career.

The Konavljes follow a policy of line breeding without in-breeding. A dog is chosen to correct any faults in the bitch, and enhance her good points, and Monica takes great note of the pedigree, preferring strong definite lines with a good proportion of champions. She has listened carefully to other experienced breeders, though no one person has influenced her. She says: "The person I admired most for her ability to breed the most beautiful bitches from a very small kennel, and for her downright common sense, was Mrs Phil Piper. In my opinion this lady has been one of our very best breeders and her dogs have had such a marvellous influence on the breed."

Monica feels the quality and temperament of today's dogs is in good order, but insists that excellent spotting must play an important part in any breeding programme. Her strong advice is to avoid keeping too many dogs at one time, lest they end up in kennels rather than in their rightful place as loving companions.

WEAPONNESS
Ch. Weaponness Sweetalk Sophie (Geronimo Bell Bird x Ch. Phaeland Patron), had the greatest influence on Mrs Pilgrim's present line. She was chosen as pick of litter, being the great grand-daughter of her first Dalmatian, Kurnool Estelle, litter sister of Diana MacDonald-Smith's Ch. Kurnool Echelon.

Sophie was a clearly-spotted black with great bone and substance. A lovely head, with beautiful large eyes and regal expression, she had a calm, friendly temperament and sound movement, which she has passed on to her progeny. She won seven CCs, one with BOB at Cruft's from Miss S. Gatheral in 1975; the Utility Group at Birmingham under Joe Braddon; and went on to win the Pedigree Chum Veteran Stakes at the age of ten.

Sophie was first mated to Midnight Runaway of Pentwyn (who went back to Miss McFie's Colonsay line), which produced Ch. Weaponness Statesman of Pentwyn, Weaponness Pineapple Poll and Weaponness Beach Boy. Her second litter, by Ch. Delvallie Dark Bronze, produced Weaponness What Katy Did (also Ilex Whiting's Ch. Weaponness Cragvallie Curry who won 12 CCs and the UG at WKS). Katy, bred to Ch. Weaponness Statesman of Pentwyn, brought the line together, and from this came Weaponness Topsy Turvy (also Brenda Rance's Weaponness Eliza of Hollycombe). Eliza was the dam of Shirley Aldenhoven's Ch. Hollycombe Polaire of Courbette (x Knightstone Much Ado).

Topsy Turvy, mated to Kurnool the Tetrach at Cragvallie, resulted in Ch. Weaponness Andromeda, who in turn was bred to an outcross, Teisanlap Shifting Gold and produced Ch. Weaponness Firebird. She has been a joy to own, winning ten CCs, Reserve UG, Driffield 1991, and the Bitch CCs at Cruft's under Ferelith Somerfield in 1992, and again in 1994 under Oonagh Gore.

Firebird, mated to Courbette Connexion at Cragvallie, produced Weaponness Tarquin of Kurnool, whom sadly Mrs MacDonald-Smith did not live to see become a Champion, (also Weaponness Vincent, siring good stock and CC winners in Denmark for Lisa and Bjorn Hageskov).

Ch. Weaponness Sweetalk Sophie

Mated to Ch. Delvallie Dark Bronze

Weaponness What Katy Did

Mated to Ch. Weaponness Statesman of Pentwyn

Weaponness Topsy Turvy

Mated to Kurnool the Tetrach at Cragvallie

Ch. Weaponness Andromeda

Mated to Teisanlap Shifting Gold

Ch. Weaponness Firebird

Mated to Courbette Connexion at Cragvallie

Ch. Weaponness Tarquin of Kurnool

OLBERO

Peter and the late Mrs Jean Rance decided that a Dalmatian would be an ideal dog to run behind the horses and, in early 1959, Tessa of the Chaise (by Ch. Tompkins of the Towpath) had arrived. She gained a 2nd at her first open show and the die was cast, so, with much encouragement from the late Mrs Freda Hayman (Widdington), 'Olbero' came into being.

From Tessa's first litter came Odette of Olbero; her second, to Les Clarke's Fanhill Fillip, produced Ch. Olbero O'Keefe. Odette was then also mated to Fanhill Fillip, resulting in the Curtis' Ch. Olbero O'Rourke. O'Keefe's daughter, Ch. Olbero Orabella, in one particular litter, whelped three outstanding Champions, OverTheRainbow (winner of 18 CCs), OverTheMoon (sire of Mrs Aldrich-Blake's

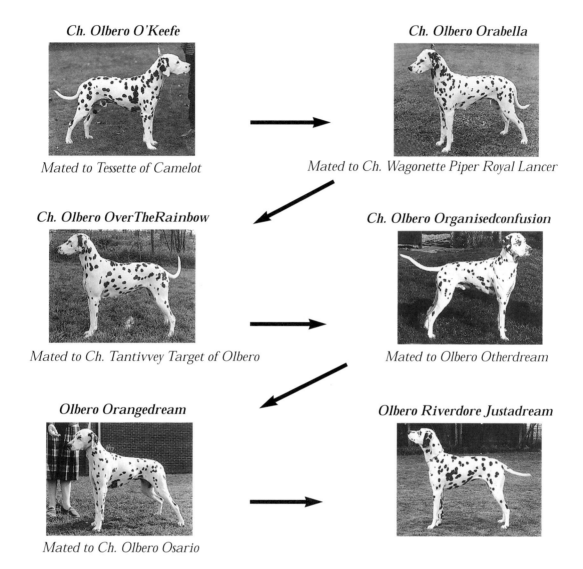

Ch. Olbero O'Keefe

Mated to Tessette of Camelot

Ch. Olbero Orabella

Mated to Ch. Wagonette Piper Royal Lancer

Ch. Olbero OverTheRainbow

Mated to Ch. Tantivvey Target of Olbero

Ch. Olbero Organisedconfusion

Mated to Olbero Otherdream

Olbero Orangedream

Mated to Ch. Olbero Osario

Olbero Riverdore Justadream

Illyricum Targe), and Sh. Ch.
OverTheSeas, by Brenda Budge's Ch.
Wagonette Piper Royal Lancer, then still
young and unknown.

From OverTheRainbow, bred to Sh. Ch.
Ilbertas Kij of Olbero, came Mrs Taylor's
Ch. Hartspring Hillbilly, sire of Ch.
Tantivvey Tawny Owl of Olbero, who in
turn lies behind many top winners in the
ring today. These include the Atkinsons'

Ch. Beaumore Night Owl of Olbero, Mrs
Stanton's two-times Cruft's winner, Ch.
Olympic Star of Olbero, and the Bulls'
Chs. Cocheperro Brown Owl and
Buttermint.

OverTheRainbow, mated this time to Ch.
Tantivvey Target of Olbero (Fanhill
Fred/Olbero Old Gold of Tantivvey),
produced Ch. Olbero Organised
Confusion, who in turn bred Nor. and Sw.

Ch. Golden Boy of Trumpeters, Nor. Sw. and Scand. Ch. Olbero Onsdag Poijke, Int. Ch. Olbero Orange Prince and Nl. and Belg. Ch. Audhumlas Allerfineste Strik.

Organdie of Olbero (unshown), mated to Ch. Wardell Watsizname, produced Ch. Olbero Organdie Collar, considered by Peter Rance to be the best Olbero bitch. From Organdie Collar, mated to Ch. Elaridge Endeavour, came Anne Bliss's Ch. Olbero Osario and litter brother Int. Belg. and Dutch Ch. Olbero Ozonelayer. Osario is the sire of Nl. Ch. Cocheperro Oreblo of Olbero and Olbero Riverdore Justadream who are currently being shown in the UK by Peter.

As has been shown, the Olberos have come down from a Towpath foundation bitch, combined with Fanhill and Tantivvey breeding, and a few outcross matings. They have also been used in such kennels as Cocheperro, Theakstone, Spotnik, Van Huis Dalmatho, Elabri, Riverdore, Sydon, Jazdal, Salsusa and Boval.

KNIGHTSTONE

Pat Kindersley had her first Dalmatian in 1968, and a year later persuaded Mrs McClellan to sell her an Othello daughter, Washakie Starturn. However, Pat had set her heart on a daughter of Washakie Clausentum Lucy, and in 1971 Washakie Margaret (x Ch. Washakie Moonraker) arrived to become her foundation bitch (winning nine CCs and becoming top Dalmatian in 1973), going back on her dam's side to Ch. Washakie Heirloom, a double grandson of Washakie Corduroy. Dennis Cudd, an authority and writer on genetics, considered Illyricum Washakie Witchcraft (now in Pat's ownership and full sister to Margaret and Othello) to be an important factor, and Pat has since based her line firmly on Washakie breeding.

Margaret, bred to Witchcraft's son,

Washakie Illyricum Blue Magic, produced not only Ch. Knightstone Augustus but also Lynda Lewis's Ch. Knightstone Matilda. Washakie Tanya, bred to Ch. Knightstone Augustus, produced Ch. Knightstone Native Dancer and Knightstone Tzigane in the same litter, and Knightstone Dilys in a repeat mating. Tzigane was, of course, the dam of Ch. Review at Knightstone, (13 CCs, 13 RCCs, BOB Cruft's 1991, Top Sire 1990, and Top Stud Dog 1993/94/95). Review has sired many fine Champions, including Marie Rickwood's Ch. Knightstone Ned Kelly (ex Knightstone Spring Fever) and Karen Goff's Ch. Am.Ch. Washakie Dancing Brave and Ch. Washakie Indian Summer (ex Washakie Taboo); also Marion Carter's Buffrey Barnum at Marcata ex Knightstone Party Piece.

Knightstone Dilys, mated to Avril Bale-Stock's Ch. Spring Classic by Appaloosa, produced Knightstone Spring Fever and Val Black's Knightstone Classique at Boval, dam of her Ch. Boval Beginning and, in a repeat mating, Boval Boomerang. Mated subsequently to Ch. Brythennek Basil Fawlty, Tanya bred Knightstone Kris and Edith Gladstone's Am. Ch. Knightstone Huntsman. Huntsman has proved his worth in the ring and at stud, siring many Champions, including Am. Ch. Belle Aire's Summer Night and Am. Ch. Belle Aire's Star E Night among his progeny.

Having followed a policy of line breeding, Pat admits the American and European lines have contradicted her theories. Huntsman has been bred to entirely unrelated bitches and produced many champions, and the same has happened in Europe, where Next at Knightstone's litter brother, Dutch and Belg. Ch. Super Trooper at Knightstone, has produced equally good stock, again to unrelated bitches.

Ch. Washakie Margaret

Mated to Washakie Illyricum Blue Magic

Ch. Knightstone Augustus

Mated to Washakie Tanya

Knightstone Tzigane

Mated to Dalinda Dandino Dancer

Ch. Review at Knightstone

Mated to Knightstone Spring Fever

Knightstone Benetton

Mated to Buffrey Birthday Girl

Next at Knightstone

13 THE DALMATIAN IN NORTH AMERICA

Did George Washington own several Dalmatians in the latter half of the 18th century? It is said that he did, but I have not been able to trace a picture to prove it. In the meantime, no-one claims to know precisely when the breed arrived in America, or by what means.

Certainly, few Dalmatian bitches of uncertain parentage can have been so well documented as 'Bessie'. Entered in the American Kennel Club Stud Book as No. 10519, Volume 5, Part III, we read only that she was owned by Mrs N.L. Havey of San Francisco, was whelped in October 1886, colour black, white and tan, pedigree and breeder unknown, and that she appeared at a benched show in San Francisco in 1888. So few facts are known, yet Bessie is a name familiar to all as the first-ever Dalmatian to be registered in the USA.

'Good Times', owned by Joseph Thomas of New York, was the only Dalmatian registered in 1889 but, from then on, slow but steady growth continued until, in 1905, the stud book showed an entry of nine dogs and six bitches, the majority coming from the Rockcliffe and Windy Valley Kennels.

In 1905, a group of 26 enthusiasts who had been meeting regularly for a year or more, decided to form the Dalmatian Club of America, and a set of rules was drawn up, including a clause limiting the membership to 50. However, by 1937, the growing popularity of the Dalmatian had produced long waiting lists for the club, which forced the abandonment of this rule. In 1996, the membership currently stands at approximately 1,000, including more than 50 Canadian and 20 overseas members.

Two World Wars had their inevitable effect on the dog scene at large, but the DCA has never looked back. Today it is firmly established as the parent club, responsible to the AKC on behalf of all subsidiary breed clubs in the USA. Many Dalmatian clubs have grown up, both in North and South America. These include over 20 regional clubs in the US, among which such names as Delaware Valley, Greater New York, Pittsburg, Chicagoland, Northern and Southern California represent only a few. These regional clubs operate as separate entities, but all come under the umbrella of the DCA.

One name stands out in the early history of the breed. Flora MacDonald, as a very young woman, joined the DCA in 1913, and was appointed secretary and treasurer, an office she held until her death in January, 1967. Miss MacDonald later married, and became Mrs Leonard Bonney (Tally-ho kennels). Her Am. Ch. Tally-ho of Sunstar won the first DCA Specialist Show in 1926, another in 1927 and again in 1931. The 44 years which this lady devoted to the breed made her an invaluable asset to the DCA, helping it to establish the Dalmatian in the premier position the breed occupies in the American dog scene today.

THE AKC STANDARD
Initially, the DCA adopted the British KC Standard, but in 1960 it was decided that this should be amended and the AKC Standard was issued. The latest version, approved in July 1989, has already been set out. This Standard is now used universally in the United States; the South American countries have chosen to adopt the FCI Standard.

BREEDING PRACTICES
Those who have researched their pedigrees back to the years immediately prior to or following World War II, will be familiar with names such as: Quaker's Acre (Mrs O.J. Smith); Reigate (Mr and Mrs Leigh and Mrs Close); Gladstone (Mr F.J. Willock); Head of the River (Mrs Sanger); Four in Hand – originally Le Mel (Mr L. Meeker) who imported among other dogs Eng. Am. Ch. Queen of Trumps, bred by Mr Wardell. Other prominent names were: Tattoo (Mrs P. Hohmiller-Orr); Rabbit Run (Mrs Reeves); Sarum (Mrs M. Firuski); Walls (Mrs Evelyn Wall); Stock Dale (Mr S.C. Stockdale); Whitlee (J.W. Verre); Whiteside Sious (Mrs W. Dewell) and Regal. Another influential kennel at this time was Williamsdale in Cincinnati. Their Am. Can. Ch. Elmcroft Coacher came originally from Canada, and was sent to the US, having completed his Canadian championship. Among notable imports were Eng. Am. Ch. Penny Parade of Williamsdale (Kim of Welfield x Cabaret Commandant) and Am. Ch. Colonsay Tantivvey Claudia, together with Eng. Am. Ch. Beau of Hollyroyde (Welfield Tracer x Dazzling Marjorie).

Am. Ch. Coachman's Chuck-A-Luck.

A famous sire-line (pictured left to right): Am. Ch. Coachman's Chuck-A-Luck, Am. Ch. Lord Jim, Am. Ch. Coachman's Canicula and Am. Ch. Count Miguel of Tuckaway.

Booth Photography.

Mrs Bonney's Tally-ho kennels were a major force in the breed, concentrating on line breeding but using an outcross every few generations to bring in new blood. Several good dogs from the UK were imported, among them Eng. and Am. Ch. Midstone Ebony (bred by Miss Walford) who gained her Am. title in 1933, and latterly Am. Ch. Duxfordham Yessam Marquis (Ch. Tantivvey Brill x Duxfordham Gina).

At this time several important kennels were founded, including the late Mrs Barrett's Roadcoach kennels, who imported Eng. and Am. Ch. Tantivvey Godetia. Roadcoach breeding was based mainly on Tally-ho, Tattoo, Hollow Hill and Reigate lines, and is known particularly for the famous Am. Ch. Roadcoach Roadster, who won 176 BOB, 17 BIS and 79 Groups. Roadster was later bought by Mrs Ratner-Allman (in the Valley) and it was her extensive campaigning of the dog, a new venture at the time in America, that set the style for the show scene as it is today.

Dr and Mrs Doane's Green-Starr is another familiar name, seen as far back as 1950 when a litter from Am. Ch. Beloved Scotch of the Walls x Shad's Dottee of Whitlee produced no less than four champions. They appear more recently as the breeder/owners of the famous Am. Ch. Green-Starr's Colonel Joe (another to be found in Spotlight Spectacular's extended pedigree on her dam's side). Colonel Joe is still listed today among the top 50 dogs All Breeds and number of dogs defeated. (For those unfamiliar with this phrase, it indicates the number of dogs, All Breeds, defeated in the Non-Sporting Group or BIS.)

Other names one cannot miss are: Korcula (Dr and Mrs J. Garvin) with the current great winner, Am. Ch. Korcula Midnight Hour; Paisley (Sue MacMillan); Dalwood (Georgiann [Peggy] Rudder and Carol Haywood); Melody (Dr and Mrs John White); Watseka (Mr and Mrs D. Schubert); Proctor (Mr and Mrs K. Berg); Blackpool (Mr and Mrs N. Peters) who imported Am. Ch. Colonsay Olaf The Red; of Croatia (Mr and Mrs Forrest Johnson); and Tuckaway (Dr Sidney Remmele).

All these names, and many more, can be seen in today's successful pedigrees. However, one studline of outstanding sires cannot be overlooked. Am. Can. Ch. Coachman's Chuck-A-Luck, was grandsire of Am. Ch. Tuckaway Dinah and sire of Am. Ch. Lord Jim, the respective parents of Am. Ch. Count Miguel of Tuckaway, himself a prolific sire. Miguel, mated to Diamond D's Dot to Dot, produced the

Am. Ch. Fireman's Freckled Friend.
Photo: Tatham.

Am Ch. Knightstone Huntsman.
Photo: Graham.

Am. Ch. Proctor's Dappled Duchess.
Photo: Callea.

Am. Ch. Proctor's Hi-Flyer.
Photo: Callea.

multiple winner Am. Ch. Fireman's Freckled Friend, and Freckled Friend bred to Am. Ch. Bottom's Up Sentimental Journey resulted in Am. Ch. Tuckaway Augusta. Augusta's progeny are too numerous to mention, but suffice to say they number among them Ch. Spotlight's Spectacular (x Am. Ch. Spotlight's Rising Star) of whom more later in this chapter, and Am. Ch. Tuckaway Winged Foot (x Am. Ch. Tuckaway Havanip), currently rated the US No. 2 Dalmatian 1996, second only to his half sister.

With careful study of the pedigrees set out in *The Spotter* and elsewhere, this pedigree line leaps to the eye over and over again, either entirely or in part, and has obviously played a significant role in the foundation of the general excellence of the breed today in North America.

Some of the great names of English breeding can be found far back in the US pedigrees – among them Colonsay, Cabaret, Welfield, Mesra, of the Wells and Widdington and, more recently, Tantivvey, Washakie, Phaeland and Duxfordham. Far fewer dogs are now imported, but mention should perhaps be made of two, who have proved themselves both in the ring and at stud.

Edith Gladstone's Am. Ch. Knightstone Huntsman (bred by Pat Kindersley), apart from winning well in the ring, has also produced many champions to unrelated bitches. Eng. Am. Ch. Buffrey Jobee (bred by Mr and Mrs Neath and owned by Benito Vila) has also produced many champions, and was American Top Stud Dog, All Breeds, in 1989. In 1994, the South African 'Dog of the Year' was SA Ch. Dallmalli Eclipse, whose mother, SA Zim. Ch. Dallmalli Shoothemoon, was a Jobee daughter, her dam having been sent from South Africa to be mated and then returned to her homeland to whelp.

THE SHOW SCENE
The American show scene is known for its professionalism, with possibly 25 per cent of the top dogs exhibited by professional handlers. Most Dalmatian people show in their local area but will travel great distances for Specialty shows. It is also quite common for a winning dog to be flown with a handler all over the country. However, as in most countries, owners/handlers predominate, and the dog fancy remains mainly in the hands of deeply committed enthusiasts, who regard it as an absorbing hobby.

To most Dalmatian breeders it is essential that their dogs are exhibited at the major Specialty shows, for which there is no restriction. The two notable shows in the USA which require qualification are Westminster (known as The Garden), where only champions are eligible, and the Top Twenty Show at the DCA Specialty.

To achieve champion status, the dog must win a total of 15 points, including at least two Majors (three points or more) under different judges. The points on offer at each show are commensurate with the number of dogs entered in the region the previous year, with a maximum of five points to be won at any one show. Every recognised Dalmatian club has one or more Specialty Shows and these must have the approval, firstly, of the DCA and, subsequently, of the AKC. All Breed shows require approval only from the AKC; all judging panels and show dates are approved by the AKC.

One interesting innovation is the list, made up by the DCA, of every person entitled to judge Dalmatians, which is issued to all clubs every five years. Exhibitors are required to mark each judge to whom they would give an entry, the papers then being returned to the DCA. A central list is then assembled of the top 25 most popular names, and from this the

LEFT: Am. Ch. Tuckaway Augusta.
Photo: Bill Meyer.

FACING PAGE: Am. Ch. Green Starr's Colonel Joe.
Booth Photography.

main judging appointments are made. This is an idea which might well attract the attention of countries other than the USA.

I have asked a variety of exhibitors whether specialist judges or all-rounders are preferred; the answer, without exception, has been in favour of breed judges. A trend would now appear to be emerging, however, where the majority of new judges with large group assignments are ex-handlers, as opposed to breed specialists. It is felt that, although handlers have a working knowledge of most breeds they handle, they may be focused on conditioning, presentation and showmanship, while the breed judge is more concerned with breed type and improving the dog as a whole. Anxiety is felt that the handler judge, expert at covering faults and emphasising good points, will tend to reward the qualities he knows. The breed judge, on the other hand, will be impressed with a dog that exhibits type, overcomes breed faults and would be a valuable breeding animal. A difficult problem and one which, no doubt, gives rise to much discussion.

A friend who returned from America recently reported seeing one of the loveliest liver-spotted bitches she could remember, these days known to all as Am. Ch. Spotlight's Spectacular – Penny to her friends. Penny, now four years old and bred by Connie and Stephen Wagner (Am. Ch. Tuckaway Augusta x Am. Ch. Spotlight's Rising Star), was purchased from the Wagners by Isabel Robson some three years ago. The first Dalmatian to be handled by Dennis McCoy, Penny is now the top winning Dalmatian in US history. She has 57 All-Breed BIS awards and is the top winning Dalmatian bitch of all time, as well as the top winning liver. In 1995, Penny was the No. 1 Non-Sporting Dog in the US, and in 1996 is the current leading Non-Sporting Dog and in addition No. 4 All-Breeds. In August 1996 she achieved BIS at the DCA National Show for the third time. However, Penny's greatest triumph to date took place in February 1996, when, watched by a television audience of 15 million, she won the Group at the Westminster KC Show, only the fourth Dalmatian and second bitch to do so. This was a wonderful win for a bitch who, according to Mrs Robson, has an equally delightful disposition. It is endearing to hear, nevertheless, that Penny is full of mischief and even one of the finest American handlers has his work cut out to ensure she keeps all four feet on the ground at the important moments.

Am. Ch. Spotlight's Spectacular.
Photo: Taham.

Am. Ch. Tuckaway Winged Foot.
Photo: Baines.

Am. Ch. Belle Aire's Summer Knight.

RESEARCH

The DCA has a record to be envied in the support they give to all forms of research. Their official research committee consists of a number of sub-committees which address the most prevalent issues. Excellent papers are published from time to time, which currently include those on: urinary stone forming, with an additional note on purine-yielding foods; Hip Dysplasia; preliminary results on a seizure study; report on allergies, etc.

Detailed reports, such as those mentioned above, compiled by each of the sub-committee chairmen, are published in *The Spotter* about every two years, covering each particular subject, and Eva Berg, current chairman of the research committee, was kind enough to send me several, which were of the greatest interest.

THE DCA FOUNDATION INC.

Georgiann (Peggy) Rudder, president of the DCA, has sent details of the newly-formed DCA Foundation. This is a non-profit-making charitable corporation, formed to provide financial and other support for individuals and organisations focusing their charitable, educational and research efforts on dogs in general and the Dalmatian in particular. In its mission statement the purposes of the Foundation are set out as follows:

1. To foster and promote the public's knowledge and appreciation of dogs in general and Dalmatians in particular.
2. To promote further understanding of the diseases, genetic anomalies and injuries which affect dogs in general and the Dalmatian in particular.
3. To support and promote study of and research on the character, history, genetics, diseases, breeding and related characteristics which establish the Dalmatian as a distinct breed of dog and, as a consequence, establish a database of educational and resource materials on the Dalmatian.
4. To develop and make available to the

general public and Dalmatian fanciers in particular, information about the proper care, treatment, breeding, health, development and training of Dalmatians.

To advance these purposes the Foundation will grant projects in the following areas:

1. Education.
2. Veterinary Research.
3. Library and Communications.
4. General Research.
5. Dalmatian-related research.

Grants will be made only to organisations that commit to providing evaluation reports. This Foundation, to which DCA members are invited to contribute, is a most interesting development and one which will be watched with the closest attention by all those concerned with this breed.

HEALTH PROBLEMS

The various problems that beset Dalmatians are virtually the same the world over, and are generally covered in Chapter Five. In addition, Dr Remmele reports that there is an increased incidence of Staphylococcal Dermatitis in Dalmatians, but that, at present, people do not understand the condition or how to treat it properly. He adds that another problem which is slowly creeping into certain lines is Epilepsy, but that the cause is currently unknown.

PET DOG SCENE

By whatever name they are known – puppy mills, puppy farms, backyard breeders – the result is the same in every country in the world. Large numbers of poorly-reared puppies, of nondescript parentage, are sold to indiscriminate homes. Concern is expressed that few breeders of pet animals have their puppies tested for deafness, and deaf animals are therefore not infrequently sold through these channels.

I am told by Dr Doane that in Tennessee the lack of licensing laws exacerbates the problem. Unwanted puppies and stray dogs are abandoned along the roadside, something which, sadly, can also be seen in many countries worldwide. Dr Doane maintains that a proper licensing system, used to finance neutering and welfare, would reduce the large numbers of dogs concerned.

SECOND WORLD CONGRESS, 1984

From an historical viewpoint it should be

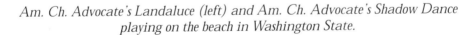

Am. Ch. Advocate's Landaluce (left) and Am. Ch. Advocate's Shadow Dance playing on the beach in Washington State.

recorded that, on November 12th to 14th 1984, the DCA hosted the immensely successful Second World Congress on Dalmatians, using a subtly-altered slogan 'Dalmatians of the World United'. Fortunately, this coincided with the 100th anniversary of the American Kennel Club, and as part of its celebrations the AKC Centennial All-Breed Dog Show and Obedience Trial was held on November 17th and 18th. This was preceded on November 16th by the DCA Centennial Specialty Show, and on Monday November 19th the Kennel Club of Philadelphia held its All-Breed Dog Show. All these events took place at the Philadelphia Civic Centre and created four days of unique interest for a worldwide audience of the showing fraternity.

The Congress was hosted by the Delaware Valley Dalmatian Club (chairman, Alfred Treen). Representatives of 59 Dalmatian clubs attended a reception which included an exhibition of *Dalmatians at Play,* the winning photographs from a recent contest held by *The Spotter.* The Congress was warmly welcomed by Forrest G. Johnson, president of the DCA, who then introduced the AKC president, William F. Stifel.

In his address, Mr Stifel included a quotation from the British All-Rounder, Leo C. Wilson, known internationally both as a judge and writer on dogs, who died in the late 1960s. Keeping in mind that this was said some 40 years ago, I think it bears repeating now:

"I can see a big switch-over to the breeds which have so few requirements for perfection, once it is realised what a big advantage they have over those with tedious Standards, which call for specific proportions and virtues which are difficult to breed. When you consider that, for instance, a Dalmatian must be either black

and white, or liver and white, and both colours solid – no black hairs in the white or white hairs in the black – and that there should be no liver spots on a black-marked one or black spots on a liver-marked one, or tan spots on either, and that these spots should not be smaller than a sixpence or bigger than a florin, that they should be evenly distributed all over the dog and that each spot should be round and well defined and not intermingling with each other; when you consider all these requirements for colour and markings alone, plus all the anatomical points laid down, you marvel at the fact that any Dalmatian could possibly go Best In Show All-Breeds at a Championship Show when there are breeds in the ring for which the requirements are so few.

"That is, of course, if judging is to the Breed Standard. If not, then what is to be the criterion? If you must breed dogs, why make life difficult for yourself? Why not go in for a breed with a sketchy Standard which fits almost any dog, and let your dog's showmanship, eye appeal and personality, plus your own show presentation, be the deciding factors? In an age where expertise and attention to detail are growing unfashionable, why be handicapped?"

Mr Stifel also took the opportunity of outlining the position with regard to the AKC Standards, explaining that under their bye-laws the parent club for each breed has the authority and responsibility for writing the Standard. For the next two days, the Congress worked extremely hard with papers presented by Gwen Eady for the UK, Gordon Morris for Australia and New Zealand, together with a paper by the late Dr Margaret Topping entitled *Hearing in the Dalmatian.* An assessment on congenital deafness in Dalmatian dogs was given by Sheldon A. Steinberg and George

C. Farnbach. The all-rounder's impression was described by Harold R. Spira, and Ann-Marie Hammarlund spoke on Dalmatian colours and the inheritance factor; her paper on deafness presented at the London Congress was included, plus some thoughts on skin problems and their cure. Mary Young (Australia) presented a paper on *Selecting a Stud Dog.* One of her finishing comments will surely strike a chord in us all: "There is a strange obsession in every true breeder, an obsession that keeps the breeder thinking that the next litter will be the answer to his breeding hopes."

One Breed – One Standard by Sam Andrew Hart was followed by an account of *Dalmatians in Brazil* by Jane Hayes. Uric acid problems, still such a problem today, were dealt with at some length by Messrs Richard M. Heriot, C.D. Fetner and J.C. Lowrey, Kenneth C. Bovee and Robert H. Schaible. *The Domestication of the Dog* by Dr I. Lehr Brisbin was accompanied by some delightful photographs, and the set papers were concluded by *Reproduction in the Dog* by Dr S.W.J. Seager. These papers, reprinted and bound, form an invaluable record.

Thursday was a chance for slight relaxation, with time for sightseeing in the beautiful city of Philadelphia, while some toured the School of Veterinary Medicine at the University of Pennsylvania. The following four days, spent at the civic centre, gave the opportunity of watching the best American Dalmatians take part in three great shows. The immense trouble taken by everyone connected with the Congress, in particular the Delaware Valley Dalmatian Club, was more than appreciated. Their professionalism was matched only by the splendid hospitality and warmth of their welcome.

CANADA
SHOWING
While the number of entries in various areas fluctuates, interest in showing is currently at an all-time high. More novice owners are becoming involved and more Champions made up each year than ever before. To gain a Canadian Championship, a dog must win a minimum of ten Championship points from at least three different judges. The points awarded for going 'Winners' are determined by the number of dogs defeated at Breed and/or Group level.

The Dalmatian Club of Canada sponsors a yearly National Specialty show for Dalmatians, as well as regional promotions called 'Boosters' at All-Breed shows, in which special prizes are donated for the major wins. These provide an excellent opportunity for enthusiasts to meet, exchange ideas and see a larger variety of exhibits in one location. Each year, 'Top Dalmatian in Canada' is awarded to the dog gaining the highest number of points

A BIS brace: Can Ch. Colonsay's Jester's Bell and Can. Ch. Camosun's Christmas Carol.

Can. Am. Ch. Camosun's Fiona Macleod.
Photo: Don Hodges.

Can. Ch. Camosun's Briony.

at Breed, Group/BIS level. Because the country is large, there tend to be regional differences in 'type', and dogs being campaigned for 'Top Dog' awards may never actually compete directly in the ring. In recent years, a different dog has achieved the 'Top Dalmatian' award each year, indicating that more individual Dalmatians are being campaigned at this level of competition. More kennels are also currently active in this area, making competition keen.

BREEDING

Can. Am. Ch. Camosun's Fiona MacLeod, owned by Catherine Blinko (BOB at the First Canadian National Dalmatian Specialty in 1978) and the never-shown Camosun's Rory Mor, owned by William Murdoch, were two outstanding l/s littermates bred by Mrs Blink from Am. Ch. Doubletrees Break-in-the-Rein out of Can. Ch. Camosun's Christmas Carol – a daughter of two English imports, Can. Am. Ch. Colonsay Jester's Bell out of Can. Ch. Belisima of Maidun.

Alison Merritt's home-bred Ch. Amodal's Blackberry (son of Rory Mor and Can. Ch. Camosun's Sesame Can. CD) and his daughter, Can. Ch. Amodal's Leading

Lady Can. CD (BOS at the Canadian National Dalmatian Specialty in 1984), have also won well.

Canadian-bred Dalmatians are often placed highly in Group competition at All-Breed shows, doing well in American Specialty and All-Breed shows. Each country tends to put a slightly different emphasis on various areas of the Standard. The use of top-quality stock imported from countries such as Britain and the USA helps to keep the quality high by combining the strengths of assorted strains.

PET DOG SCENE

Dalmatians are the ultimate companion dog, and pets are integrated into all aspects of family life. Always ready for adventure, the Dalmatian makes an excellent hiking, jogging or cycling companion, a comforting watchdog, even a children's playmate/baby-sitter. Pet owners support many activities including Obedience, Agility and charity fundraising. Pet Dalmatians in Canada tend to be treasured and prominent members of the family.

With the increased popularity of Dalmatians and resultant puppy sales in pet stores, many more inexperienced and often uneducated breeders are advertising litters.

161

ABOVE: Can. Ch. Amodal's Blackberry.

RIGHT: Can. Ch. Amodal's Leading Lady Can. CD.

This has resulted in deaf puppies being sold to unsuspecting buyers and some deterioration in the stable, happy temperament usually associated with this breed. Reputable breeders do their best to educate the public, and remain available to help new owners with questions or problems they may encounter.

DEAFNESS TESTING
No unified BAER testing scheme is currently available in Canada. Few testing facilities exist other than those at the four Veterinary Medical Colleges: Saskatchewan, Ontario, Quebec and Prince Edward Island, plus a few clinics with private equipment and expertise. BAER testing is inaccessible in many areas of the country, but increased awareness and demand will eventually lead to an improvement. Occasionally, special BAER testing clinics are arranged, with visiting veterinarians performing the tests. Sadly, universal BAER testing is not yet available, and breeders must still rely on home testing in some cases.

It is encouraging to note that, because of the increased profile of deafness in this and other breeds, many veterinarians are now aware of this problem and so can provide educational information for breeders. A uniform testing standard and All-Breed

Hearing Registry would be welcome. It appears that the Dalmatian Club of America is working toward this and, when in place, it is hoped that Canadian breeders will support it, as they currently do with the OFA (Orthopedic Foundation for Animals) for Hip Dysplasia certification.

ACTIVITIES
For many years, apart from showing, Obedience and tracking were the only recognized activities leading to the addition of officially recognized titles to the dog's name. However, more recently new and exciting events have been developed, including: Agility, Flyball, Road Trials, and the Canine Good Citizen Test.

WELFARE
PALS: Dalmatians have been accepted into the Pet Access League Society. Dogs and their handlers make regular visits to patients in nursing homes, psychiatric and other hospital wards, and with their great sensitivity Dalmatians are well suited to this work.
Fire Safety: Dalmatians are used by some Fire Departments to teach children fire safety techniques such as the 'stop, drop and roll' for clothing on fire.
Charity Fundraising: Many Fire Departments produce annual 'beefcake'-

type calendars, often graced by photos of Dalmatians along with the fire fighters, to raise money in support of hospital burns units. Dalmatians and their owners regularly participate in fundraising activities to provide seeing-eye dogs for those in need, and to raise funds for the SPCA. Rescue: No formal Rescue scheme exists, but some interested fanciers assist in local re-homing. Reputable breeders deal with their own stock, and most Rescue Dalmatians come from pet stores or inexperienced breeders. Some breeders keep lists of people looking for older or abandoned Dalmatians, and some also list any such animals available. However, care must be taken that only temperamentally and physically sound animals are placed.

CURRENT HEALTH PROBLEMS
Health problems are typical of those found in the breed worldwide, and the actual incidence is unknown as there is no central registry.

Deafness: The incidence of unilateral and bilateral deafness is likely to be somewhere between that found in the US and the UK, as Canadian breeding is based on American and British stock. However, blue eyes are listed as a 'fault' in the Canadian Standard, and the resultant selection away from blue eyes may result in slightly lower numbers of offspring affected by deafness.

Hip Dysplasia: A hip-scoring scheme is available at the Ontario Veterinary College (OVC) in Guelph, Ontario, where one veterinarian assesses the X-rays. A dog must be at least one year old to be certified under this scheme. Recently a new scheme for hip evaluation has been introduced. Called the Penn-Hip system, it involves stress radiography to determine joint laxity. It is too early to determine whether this scheme will be of value, and/or whether

breeders will switch from the traditional OFA system, use a combination, or stay with OFA evaluations. It is likely to take some time to evaluate the potential benefit of Penn-Hip scoring.

Skin Problems/Allergies: Some Dalmatians show evidence of a rash, typically found along the spine and/or on the topskull. The hair may be somewhat coarse, short or like stubble, and standing away from the skin, which may be pinker than normal. It appears that while this tends to follow family lines, diet may sometimes aggravate the problem. This may indicate food or inhalant allergies as an underlying cause. The Dalmatian Club of America research committee is currently studying this problem, and information is available on the Internet.

Urate Crystals/Stones: These problems and/or stone formation can tend to be familial, but the actual incidence in the population is unknown. The DCA is also studying this, and information is available on the Internet as well as in the DCA booklet *The Stone Primer.*

Epilepsy: Cases of epilepsy have been reported, but the incidence is unknown. Again, the DCA research committee is currently studying this problem.

Demodectic Mange: Both localized and generalized forms of Demodex have been reported. Individuals with generalized Demodex should not be bred from. The localized form should be closely monitored, as this indicates some disturbance of the immune system. If bred this will be passed on and, if doubled up, may result in the tragic generalized form; it is far preferable to eliminate affected and 'carrier' animals from a breeding population at the onset.

14

THE DALMATIAN WORLDWIDE

Interest in these uniquely-spotted dogs has continued to grow over the years, and Dalmatians have now been made welcome in almost every country in the world. Despite variations in the Standards, the dogs remain unmistakable, and we all chuckle when stories are told which mirror so closely our own experiences. Whatever the circumstance, a Dalmatian remains a Dalmatian.

Representatives from many countries have been good enough to send the following accounts of the Dalmatian in their particular part of the world, and the time and trouble they have taken over this is greatly appreciated. As you read, you will find we share not only the same love of the breed, but also the same problems and difficulties. It is rewarding to know that this common interest has established a bond which survives irrespective of nationality, distance and even the quarantine laws.

AUSTRALIA
THE SHOW SCENE
Distance is the keynote to dog showing in Australia, and entries reflect this. The National Specialty Show, held every four years, took place in Brisbane in June 1996 with an entry of 156, under US judge Forrest Johnson. He awarded BIS to Ch. Dizzidot Bobby Brown and complimented exhibitors on the quality of the dogs. However, to illustrate the distances involved, Mary Young drove for 14 hours to reach Brisbane from New South Wales and then 14 hours back again. The local Sydney, Melbourne and Brisbane All-Breed shows usually draw an entry of between 20 to 50 Dalmatians, with fewer in other states.

R.M. and P. Young's Aus. Ch. Brackleigh Aquarius (Aus. Ch. Kayell Bunting x Lady Lollipop of Exhurst – UK import) holds the record as Australia's greatest sire to date, with 37 Champions to his credit. Two of his line are currently being shown, Aus. Ch. Dumbledeer Tivoli Tess (Aus. Ch. Bravissimo of Washakie x Aus. Ch. Dumbledeer Ukon Blaze) and Aus. Ch. Dumbledeer Xtreme Dlite (Aus. Ch. Dumbledeer Zippity Dooda x Aus. Ch. Dumbledeer La Bomba).

The Marshall family arrived in Australia from the UK, bringing with them Eng. Ch. Pickledwalnut from Pampard who holds the record to date for a Dalmatian bitch in Britain of 27 CCs. Her grand-daughter

Aust. Ch. Dumbledeer Tivoli Tess, owned and bred by R.M. and P. Young.

Robleeare Pandora, mated to Eng. and Aus. Ch. Pyschic Power at Pampard (imp. UK) produced Aus. Ch. Daltonico Pandora, who holds the record in Australia for a Dalmatian bitch, winning the highest number of challenge points (3,000).

Apart from 17 BIS and 35 BIG awards at All-Breed Championship shows, Pandora took BOB at both Melbourne Royal and Canberra Royal and was top Dalmatian in 1994 for the Oz Dog/Pal Competition. She was a Supreme Dog finalist in 1993 and 1994, and between 1992 and 1995 was top Dalmatian for the Dalmatian Club of Victoria and also the Non-Sporting Group Club. Pandora has whelped two litters and her progeny include: her l/s son, Aus. Ch. Pampard Pickled Phorever, the present 1996 leader in the Dalmatian Club and Non-Sporting Group point scores; Aus. Ch. Pampard Pistol Night, top Dalmatian dog 1995 DCOV; Aus. Ch. Pampard Phancy Nancy, BIS Dalmatian National Ch. Show 1995 (UK judge Mrs Jull); and Aus. Ch. Pampard Pistol Packer, who won his title from Junior.

Aus. Ch. Kirindal King's Gift (Kirindal Edwardian Era x Kirindal Silver Spangles), owned and bred by Jan and Ivan Kirin, was Australasia's No. 1 Dalmatian from 1993 to 1995 in the Friskies/National Dog Australasian Top Dalmatian of the Year competition, finishing ninth in Australasia's Top 10 Show Dogs for 1995 in the same competition. 'King' was born six days before Christmas 1988, hence his name

Aust. Ch. Daltonico Pandora: Bitch record holder with a grand tally of 3,000 Challenge points.

'King's Gift', and began his show career by winning Baby Puppy in Show at his first outing at three months of age. Since then, he has amassed an amazing 4,000 CC points, a breed record. His wins include 122 Best Exhibit in Group All Breeds, 27 BIS, Specialty and All Breeds; 31 RBIS, Specialty and All Breeds; BOB and RBIG, Melbourne Royal Show 1993 (judge Jacqui Quiros – Argentina) from an entry of approximately 1,000 Non-Sporting Exhibits.

In 1995, King took the Dalmatian Club of NSW Dalmatian of the Year Club cup and sash, together with the prize for best country Dalmatian. His trophies include the Australian Capital Territories Top Dog All Breeds, the Friskies/National Dog Point Score 1995, BIS at the Canberra Kennel Associates Golden Anniversary Show 1994, and he also achieved the distinction of winning the ABKC's 'Peter Pan' Memorial Trophy for Best Non-Sporting Exhibit in Group for five consecutive years. King has sired three BIS winners, and Jan and Ivan Kirin are pleased to acknowledge his English bloodlines, coming down from Leagarth, Clydevale, Colonsay, Phaeland, Randan and Chasecourt.

NEW ZEALAND

The history of the Dalmatian in New Zealand is not well-documented, although they were known to be in existence from about the 1840s. With the growing numbers of local and imported dogs and registered breeders, it was recognised by Dr Margaret Topping that a breed club would be beneficial and the Dalmatian Club of New Zealand was formed in 1970.

Predominantly Australian bloodlines were prevalent from the 1960s and the introduction of British lines, namely a litter brother and sister by Ch. Howbeck Admiral, boded well for the future of the breed. Pat Turney's litter brother and sister NZ Ch. Colts Admiral Ben Boy and NZ Ch. Colts Bronze Gay Venture complemented the existing Australian bloodlines, producing a more elegant type of Dalmatian with better movement. Most of today's prominent kennels have these names behind their pedigrees.

Over the years further imports have left their mark, these being Ch. Fanhill Fowey, Tantivvey Tamar, Mariscat Maricaibo, Ch. Olbero Organdiebonet, Ch. Stallions Dido, Clydevale Ursula, Clydevale Highlander, Ch. Tip Top Torchbearer of Theakston and Bowdally Fatal Attraction. Frozen semen has also been imported from Eng. Ch. Northern Granada of Leagarth, Eng. Ch. Hartspring Hillbilly, and the father and son combination of Eng. Ch. Beaumore Night Owl of Olbero and Eng Ch. Theakston Tamerlan.

Dalmatians have always been prominent in the show ring. One of the earliest notable show dogs was Ch. Korrundulla Twist N Time, bred and owned by Lloyd and Glenis Hatton. Several dogs have achieved All-Breeds BIS status, the first being Dr Topping's Ch. Britzka Tressilian, followed by Ch. Daniel of Dalmanor, Ch. Korrundulla Sundances, Ch. Stedfast Gruesome Goose, Ch. Ben Hur Quizmaster, Gr Ch. Tantara Ragtime Ryan, the Australian import Aust/NZ Ch. Paceaway Blue Moon, Ch. Kornwalharry of Kalesha and, the only bitch to win a BIS, Kornwalharry's daughter, Ch. Kevel of Kalesha.

The club has an annual Championship show, very often judged by an English specialist. The first show was judged by Mrs Phyllis Piper (UK) who also started the Rescue Service with a generous donation and has continued to support it over the years.

Regarding health generally, skin disorders, deafness and the uric acid problem need to be watched.

ARGENTINA

The Dalmatian is popular in Argentina and at present approximately 200 dogs are registered each year. The first Dalmatians imported for breeding purposes arrived in the 1960s, from Uraguay and Germany. In the early 1970s, Mr Sanllorenti imported Lodgehill Alexander and Olbero Old Chelsea, and Mr Maxera purchased Kurnool Utopia, all from the UK. The main breeders and exhibitors at that time were Mr Sanllorenti, Mr Lloveras and Mr Castro. Around 1975, a number of breeders joined together to found the Club Argentino del Dalmata, which remained active for about ten years. Specialties were organised with more than 40 entries, and great interest was taken in improving the breed. In the mid-1980s, Mrs Alvarez imported Ch. Dorwendis Points of View from the UK, and a number of dogs were purchased from the USA and Brazil. The most active breeders were Mr Coudis (Silviyul) who imported many Brazilian dogs, 50 per cent UK (Oudenarde) and 50 per cent USA (Tosland), Mr Ferrari (Del Maiten), Ines Noguera (Tamure Maitai), who imported several Dalmatians from the USA, and Andrea Paccagnella (Zagreb).

Andrea Paccagnella established the Zagreb line in 1976 and has over 30 home-bred Champions, including the 1993 World Winner, Ch. Zagreb Hallmark. The Zagreb kennel is based on the American lines Melody, Paisley and Watseka and has recently imported two US Dalmatians, one from the Pill Peddler/Montjuic kennels and one from the Spotlight kennel, with Buffrey and Washakie bloodlines. Over 23 Champions have been sired by Zagreb Dalmatians in different countries, and others have been exported to the USA, France, Chile, Italy and Uraguay. The Dalmatians sent to the USA have been BAER hearing-tested, and all had bilateral hearing.

The title 'World Winner' is awarded annually at the World Dog Show, organised by the FCI and held each year in a different FCI country. The World Winner title is awarded to the Best Dog and Bitch of each breed (CACIB winners), and exhibitors attend from all over the world. The World Dog Show took place in Argentina in 1993, the second time it has been held in South America. In 1996, it was held in Hungary and, in 1997, will take place in Puerto Rico.

Outstanding show dogs include Lucas Castro's Int. Ch. Domino Uxmal, the first Dalmatian to obtain this title, and the All-Breed BIS winners, Int. Ch. Von Achen Ali of Almeida and Int. Ch. Final Act de Nutwoot, both owned by Juan Coudis. Apart from his own show career, Int. Ch. Caravan Zagreb The Challenger, owned and bred by Andrea Paccagnella, is the sire of two American Champions, a BIS winner and the No. 1 Dalmatian in France, an unparalleled accomplishment for an Argentine dog of any breed. Int. Ch. Alma del Maiten (owner/breeder Oscar Ferrari) was the only bitch to become No. 1 Dalmatian and to win several BIS awards.

FINLAND

It is a particular pleasure to be writing about Finland as, during 1996, the Finnish Dalmatian Club celebrated its 25th anniversary. In 1970, the Finnish Dalmatian Club held its first Special Show, which took place at Käpylä, where an entry of 60 Dalmatians was judged by Mrs Phyllis Piper. In 1972, Mrs Piper returned, together with Gwen Eady, and they judged a total entry of 112 Dalmatians. Since that

ABOVE: Sato and Timo Makipaa's Fin. Dk. MVA MV-94 V-94 Zabavan Bolji Pas.

LEFT: Mrs Traja Meskanen's Int. Fin. Swe. Est. Ch. Kisanne Apicorico.

time, dog showing has become an extremely popular hobby and the number of Dalmatians registered compares well with other breeds in the Group. I had the great pleasure of judging Dalmatians at the Turku Championship Show in January 1995, and can vouch for the wonderful hospitality and organisation which lies behind the scenes. On that occasion, I chose a splendid b/s dog for BOB, Satu and Timo Makipaa's Zabavan Bolji Pas, who went on to win Group 6 under Hans Lehtinen.

BREEDING

In 1991, the 'First Breeder's Prizes' were awarded for the five most successful breeders. In addition, the first Championship of the DALS Competition was held, between all winners of BOB and BOS prizes during the year.

Many Finnish Dalmatians have English breeding behind them and, for the last seven years, the top Dalmatian of the Year has been Ann-Sofi Sandbacka's Int. Fin. Swe. Est. Ch. Elaridge Prince Rufus ('Bobby' at home), who was Youth World Winner 1989, Wien Sieger 1990, European

Winner 1991, Estonian Winner 1993, Saarland Sieger 1994 and Finnish Winner 1995. Bobby has sired over 20 Champions, been a Group Winner on several occasions, and has been awarded BIS at five All-Breed Championship Shows, on the last occasion from Veteran. One of his most successful daughters, Tarja Meskanen's Int. Fin. Swed. Est. Ch. Kisanne Apicorico, is pictured here.

Nord. Ch. Bosville Colbost Curlew, who died recently at the age of 12, was another very successful English import, both in the show ring and at stud. In 1981, 38 breeders were registered with the Finnish KC and, of those, names such as Caesands, Dalimattas, Eevariitan, Luonnonpuiston and O'Soul are still to the fore today.

NORWAY

The Dalmatian is not a numerically strong breed in Norway. The number of registered puppies is currently around 100-150 annually, and the relatively few active breeders are fortunately very conscious of the responsibility incurred by the difficult task of breeding. Current breeders include Anne K. Lund (Timanka), Helle and Ole

Christian Hoie (Spotnik), Randi and
Orving Bjornli (Liberline), Hans Olav
Hansen (Kolo-Line) and later Trine
Ssenderud (Dalming), Kari Ditlefsen
(Perdita), Gerd and Ulf Eriksen (Busby),
Kirsti and Tyge Greibrokk (Dalmo), Aase
Jakobsen (Toots), Erling Sch. Nilsen
(Svolvaergeita) and a few other smaller
breeders not mentioned here. Strengthened
by high-quality English, Swedish and
Finnish imports, the Norwegian
Dalmatians of today can be characterised as
a melting pot of dogs from different
countries, resulting in good types, strongly-
built, with good movement and
temperament.

Mrs Greibrokk's Int. NS Ch. Dalmo's
Educated Edgar is by Int. Nord. Ch.
Knight of Gold at Theakston x Int. Nord.
Ch. Spotnik's British Breeze, and his
grandfather was Int. Nord. Ch. Olbero
Onsdag Pojke, the top winning Dalmatian
in Scandinavia. The quality of the
Dalmatians in Norway today is considered
high by most judges but, as in the UK,
every effort is being made to improve on
this. Since the breed is numerically small,
some breeders occasionally import dogs,
particularly from the UK, and use stud
dogs from neighbouring countries to
maintain a healthy breeding base.

Int. NS Ch. Dalmo's Educated Edgar.

Nord. Ch. Ridotto Zoe.

SWEDEN
THE SHOW WORLD
Although numbers remained small in the
early 1960s, the breed continued to make a
good entry at shows. The SDS began to
organise Special Club Shows, and Dr
Eleanor Frankling was the first overseas
specialist to judge the breed at Stockholm
in 1964. The following year, the SDS held
its first Club Show, and invited Miss I.B.
Clay to judge a record entry of 75 dogs.
The Club Shows grew in popularity, entries
sometimes exceeding 100 dogs and, since
1980, the SDS has organised four
Championship Club Shows annually.
Swedish dogs continue to hold their own
and, at the 1996 European Show in
Luxembourg, Barbara Kacens awarded
Annika Lellep and Carl-Magnus
Gustafsson's l/s bitch Int. and Nordic Ch.
Skartoftas Clothilde BOB, and she was then
placed 2nd in the Group.

The Bobby print: This print is sold to raise money for the BAER Hearing Project.

BREEDING

At present (1996) there are about 40 really committed breeders. Club policy encourages the use of as many different male dogs as possible in breeding programmes, to enlarge the gene pool. For instance, 454 puppies were registered in 1994, coming from 73 litters sired by 53 males. Apart from two males siring four litters each, five with three litters and four with two litters, 42 dogs sired one each of the remainder.

THE 'BOBBY' FUND (BOBBY-FONDEN)

Early in 1992, two members offered the SDS a limited and signed edition of prints of an original watercolour, in memory of their first Dalmatian 'Bobby'. The print shows the oldest Seriefigur of Sweden, Kronblom, his wife Malin and mother-in-law, together with four Dalmatians. By the end of that year, sale of the prints had realised about £10,000 which in turn became the 'Bobby Fund', to be used to promote the BAER Hearing Project. The SDS sponsored the purchase of an EMG Machine, and BAER testing began.

AUSTRIA

In 1923, the first Dalmatian to be registered in the Austrian stud book was a bitch named Flora. The Osterreichischer Dalmatinerclub (Austrian Club for Dalmatian Dogs) was founded in 1971. The best-known member of the foundation committee was Annie Handel, who held the position of president until the end of 1990. The most famous dog of her breeding was Austrian and Int. Ch. Danko von Krekelborn (ÖCh CIB). Mrs Handel died in 1993. The Austrian Kennel Club is affiliated to the FCI. Twice a year, normally in the spring and at the beginning of autumn, the club organises a testing session for dogs intended for use in breeding. To pass this they must have good overall structure and excellent temperaments. The Austrian Club now has nearly 300 members. Most dogs are kept as family pets, but some also distinguish themselves in other fields. In particular, mention should be made of Jurgen Grabmayer's bitch Laura-Angela von Freizeithof, who won the Austrian Championship in 1991 for Agility, and Prath Claudia's bitch Austrian Ch. Mogli von der Villa Justi FH3 (ÖCh) who passed at Austria's highest level for tracking.

BELGIUM

The Club Belge du Dalmatien was founded in 1962 and has a membership of approximately 400, some of whom are from overseas. A newsletter, *Spotted News,* edited by Liliane De Ridder-Onghena, is published four times a year (very creditably, in four languages: Dutch, French, German and English). Two special days are organised each year, usually a dog walk and a barbecue, which are regarded as occasions to get members more interested in working with their dogs.

SHOWING

A Championship Show is held annually, normally at the beginning of November, and a foreign specialist judge is invited to officiate. Entries are now received from Denmark, Germany, Luxembourg, Holland, France, Italy, Spain and Croatia, so a visit to this show gives a good overall view of what is happening on the European Dalmatian scene. At the World Show, held in Brussels in 1995, there was an excellent entry of 120 Dalmatians with Liliane De Ridder-Onghena judging. Some members have been successful with Obedience and Agility, and Mr and Mrs Brison's Jacky's Smiling French Farandole is quite a star in this field.

EIRE

As is normal procedure, all pedigree Dalmatians are registered with the Irish Kennel Club and breeders are becoming concerned that, with the advent of puppy farms, many litters are not now registered. The puppies are sold on at unrealistic prices and reputable breeders are fielding the inevitable questions regarding lifestyle, health, feeding, etc. This is a problem which exists in almost every country and education is really the only answer. Awareness of the breed, however, is on the increase and great interest is shown in the dogs on family outings. As far as shows are concerned, the entries are not large and most exhibitors are UK visitors.

FRANCE

France has a unique system whereby all dogs are presented at a certain age (12 months for Dalmatians), when a judge/confirmateur decides whether it is of a sufficient standard to be granted a pedigree; this means that the 'Certificat de Naissance' is confirmed. If a puppy is not confirmed, a pedigree cannot be issued to any ensuing offspring. However, any dog or bitch can be presented for confirmation and be issued with a pedigree 'Au Titre Initial' if the animal reaches the required standard, and the pedigree will start at that

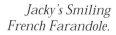

Jacky's Smiling French Farandole.

*Ir. Ch. Leixlip
Leinster Leader.*

point. For this reason there are many more non-pedigree than pedigree Dalmatians in France. The authorities permit only one club per breed in France and the Dalmatian Club Français was founded by the current president, Mme Garaix, shortly after the Second World War.

SHOWING
Dalmatian entries in shows are not large on the whole and, at Longchamps (the equivalent of Cruft's) this year, there was an entry of 34 dogs. The annual Club Show (Nationale Elevage) attracts more, and an entry of about 70 Dalmatians was made at the show last year.

In France a CAC cannot be awarded until the dog is confirmed, and a year and a day must elapse between the first and last CAC. One of these tickets must come either from Longchamps or the Club Show, so only a maximum of two dogs of each sex can be made up each year. Of the other two necessary tickets, one must come from a National and one from an International show in France, under three different judges and within a two-year period. In 1995 the Dalmatian was moved from the FCI Group 9 (companion dogs) to Group 6 (Scent hounds) in all FCI countries in Europe with the exception of France. Mme Garaix feels strongly that Dalmatians belong in Group 9 and, as far as France is concerned, the FCI have deferred to her wishes.

GERMANY
Paintings show Dalmatians in Germany as far back as the 17th century. It is a popular breed today, and breeders have worked hard to establish a high standard. Despite

Tollcross Celtic Ayre.

the troubled times at the beginning of the 20th century, some Dalmatian breeders met together at Ettingen, near Karlsruhe, and founded the Deutscher Dalmatiner Club. A well-known breeder at that time, Ferdinand Kamps from Cuxhaven-Westerwich with the affix 'von der Nordseewacht', used imported dogs as a foundation for his breeding. Following the problems created by the Second World War, Dalmatians were in serious difficulty, but a group of breeders came together to re-establish the Dalmatian Club of 1920. A new set of rules governing breeding and judging was issued and the Dalmatian Club became associated to the VDH (Verband für das Deutsche Hundewesen), which necessitated the registration of all puppies into the newly created stud book. One of the best known post-war breeders, Edith Huch (vom Braunschweiger Okerstrand), was followed by Irmgard Brosius-Heusmer (von Waldhagen) who imported several dogs from Britain, including Cobbin-End Choirboy, Berricot Christopher Columbus and Duxfordham Jolly Gladiator, who form the basis for many lines in Germany and Europe to-day.

For many years the Deutscher Dalmatiner Club von 1920 e.V. remained in isolation but, in 1980, they integrated with the Allgemeiner Dalmatiner-Club e.V. Hamburg. After the fall of the Berlin wall, the club of the DDR became amalgamated in 1990. In 1987 a second Dalmatian Club was formed, the Club fur Dalmatiner-Freunde e.V., and some years afterwards a third club called the Dalmatiner-Verein Deutschland e.V. was added. All three clubs were accepted by the VDH and are therefore affiliated to the FCI.

The three clubs work together in general co-operation and an annual Breeders' Day is organised, covering breeding and raising puppies. In addition, training days and weekend seminars take place on a wide variety of subjects.

HOLLAND
The first Club show was organised in Utrecht in August 1948, and an entry of 49 dogs was judged by Eleanor Frankling from England. Dr Frankling later exported some excellent stock from her Winnall kennel and these dogs are considered to be the foundation of the breed in the Netherlands. Later, in the 1960s, more imports of importance came from the Illyricum and Dalati Kennels and later the Jarvey's, Ascotheath, Washakie, Duxfordham, Clydevale and Greenmount kennels. At the end of the 1970s, a few dogs from the Olbero kennel arrived and today Holland's most important lines are based on Olbero breeding.

To become a Dutch Champion, a dog must obtain four CACs under at least two different judges, with the last CAC obtained after the age of 27 months. A dog with three CACs and four Reserve CACs can also qualify for the title. The CACs which are to be won during the Club Championship show and at the Winners show in Amsterdam, count as double CACs. There are, on average, 15

Enrica von den Beverstedter-Huhlen, based in Germany.

Gayfield Charles Brown: Belg. Winner 95,
Lux. Winner 96. Bred by M.and J.
Bruton, owned by R. and A. Morgans.

Int. Dutch Belg. Ch. Idris V Huis
Dalmatho JW Lux 91, BIS Belg. Ch. Club
Show 92.

championship dog shows held in Holland
each year. It is not easy to become a Dutch
Champion, and few foreign dogs have
managed to win this title as yet.

LUXEMBOURG
The first pure-bred Dalmatian litter to be
bred in Luxembourg was born on October
24th 1970. The sire was a son of Int. Ch.
Albert King of the Green Beret (a Dutch-
bred son of Ch. Winnall Lancer). Until that
time, a few Dalmatians had been brought
into the Grand Duchy from neighbouring
countries, but the breed was practically
unknown. Most puppies from this litter
remained in the country and certainly did
not go unnoticed. Dalmatian puppies are
always endearing; these youngsters
moreover had very good temperaments. By
the time the second litter was born in
1971, the Dalmatian was part of the
Luxembourg scene.

In 1973, after a successful show career in
England, Ascotheath Aquarius (bred by
Joan and Dennis Cudd) joined the
Del'Amena Contrada Dalmatians in
Luxembourg. Within one year, he gained

his International Champion title. He was
very successful in the show ring in various
European countries, and sired several
excellent litters. His best progeny came out
of the combination with another high-
quality import from England, Coachbarn
Crystal (a grand-daughter of Brougham
Banker and Ch. Greenmount Grindelwald),
bred by Marion Chapman. Crystal was also
very successful in the show ring, gaining
the titles of International, Dutch, and
Luxembourg Champion. A bitch out of this
combination, mated to a Dutch-bred dog
of English parentage, is at the base of the
successful 'Plum Pudding' line in Slovakia,
which appears in many Dutch, Belgian, and
other pedigrees.

In 1973, during a social gathering of
Dalmatian enthusiasts from several
countries, it was decided to form a novel
association to serve the Dalmatian world,
promoting the breed by means of
collaboration and information on an
international basis. Since the idea
originated in the Grand Duchy – the cradle
and domicile of the European Union – it
was decided to give it the name of the

Luxembourg Dalmatian Club. It must be remembered that the Grand Duchy is a very small country (2,600 sq km and 365,000 inhabitants), and hence has a small canine population. Consequently, the number of Dalmatian owners and dogs is minimal.

Today, two breeders are each producing one or two litters annually. The oldest of these, 'van de Gevlekte Egel', started with a foundation bitch from 'Del'Amena Contrada', who was then mated to top-quality sires in Belgium and Holland. This kennel has produced some worthy champions and continues breeding beautiful Dalmatians with very good temperaments. One of their lines, a very successful show dog residing in Belgium, has in turn sired several good puppies in different European countries. The other breeder (with a foundation bitch from the 'Gevlekte Egel'), imported a Swiss-bred dog going back to Coachbarn Chevrolet who has been used several times in Germany. His kennel name is 'vun der Lankert'. The latest arrival in Luxembourg is 'Desiree' (Dallas Devonia Gardens), bred by Mrs Hammarlund in Sweden. She lives

with the Del'Amena Contrada Dalmatians.

SPAIN

It would seem that in Spain very large or very small dogs are preferred, with Dalmatians unfortunately qualifying as neither. Nowadays, there are only a relatively few dedicated breeders and, of necessity, they have to travel long distances to show their Dalmatians at the various specialist shows taking place in Switzerland, Germany, Belgium, etc. There is no organised Dalmatian club as such but, sadly, even in Spain, puppy farms are not unknown. This means that many litters are not registered and puppies without papers are sold not only in Spain but also to various Eastern countries.

Dalmatians are used from time to time in advertising but unfortunately there is as yet no move to use Dalmatians in connection with Obedience, Agility or work with the disabled. There is no deafness testing programme or rescue service. On a happier note, Mr Belles describes his own ideal Dalmatian home, where his dogs follow the same indulgent lifestyle that ours take for granted. Mr Belles' Int. Fr. Sp. Ch.

Tyrodal Cibrith Blues Singer, based in Switzerland.

Humble-Bee v. Haslenriet, based in Switzerland.

Gayfield Asteria, a UK import (bred by Mike and Jaquie Bruton), has won at all levels, including Best of Group and Reserve Groups, and has also been awarded Reserve BIS All-Breeds, in France and Spain.

SWITZERLAND
BREEDING

From the age of 12 months, all Dalmatians are subjected to a special test by a breeding committee before they can be used for breeding. This test is in accordance with the FCI Standard, and states that the dog must have a perfect regular scissor bite with a maximum of two missing teeth only. A special character test is included, and dogs are eliminated from any breeding programme if they appear nervous or aggressive. No bitch may be bred from under the age of 20 months, nor a stud dog used under the age of 18 months, and neither may be bred from over the age of eight years. No bitch may be bred from more than once a year. Permanent identification of all puppies by tattooing or microchip is compulsory.

THE SHOW WORLD

Apart from foreign shows, in Switzerland itself there are three or four International dog shows each year and one National club show. In recent years, ten to 20 Dalmatians have been exhibited in the International dog shows, and there has been an entry of about 40-60 Dalmatians at the special Club shows.